Dakota Stories II

Dakota Dusk
Dakota December
Dakota Destiny

Books by Lauraine Snelling

One Perfect Day
Breaking Free
Saturday Morning
The Healing Quilt
The Way of Women
The Brushstroke Legacy
Washington
Once Upon A Christmas
Yuletide Treasure

A Secret Refuge
Daughter of Twin Oaks
Sisters of the Confederacy
The Long Way Home

Dakotah Treasures
Ruby Opal
Pearl Amethyst

Daughters of Blessing
A Promise for Ellie
Sophie's Dilemma
A Touch of Grace
Rebecca's Reward

Red River of the North
An Untamed Land The Reaper's Song
A New Day Rising Tender Mercies
A Land to Call Home Blessing in Disguise

Return to Red River
A Dream to Follow
Believing the Dream
More Than a Dream

Youth Fiction
What About Cimmaron?

Available at www.dakotabooknet.com

LAURAINE SNELLING

Dakota Stories II

Dakota Dusk
Dakota December
Dakota Destiny

Bismarck, North Dakota

Dakota Stories II
2008

Cover design by Sydney Bren, Clearwater Communications, Bismarck, North Dakota.
Cover photograph Main Street, Almont, North Dakota 1910.

Scripture quotations are from the King James Version of the Bible.

Published by Smoky Water Press
Post Office Box 2322
Bismarck, ND 58502-2322

Smoky Water Press is a division of Capital Communications, Inc.
Bismarck, North Dakota

Printed in the United States of America

ISBN: 978-0-9820752-1-0

DEDICATION

TO TODAY'S SONS AND DAUGHTERS OF THE PIONEERS.
May we always remember those who came before us.

LAURAINE SNELLING is the award winning author of numerous novels, including the beloved Red River of the North and Daughters of Blessing series. She and her husband Wayne live in the Tehachapi Mountains of California with their basset hound, Chewy. Visit her at her website, www.LauraineSnelling.com.

Dakota Dusk

Chapter 1

Ma, how would you like it if I moved back home?" Jude Weinlander dropped a kiss on his mother's cheek. "I know things ain't been goin' good for you. I…you…ah…the farm needs some work done, bad."

"You would do that?" Tall, iron-stiff Augusta turned from the black iron cookstove and waved a wooden spoon in the air. Shock and heat painted her face bright red.

"Well…uh…I'm kinda between jobs right now, so's Melissa, and I could stay around for a time, until you get someone to help you again, that is." Jude stuttered over the words while raking a hand through the dark blond curls that fell over his forehead in a charming tangle. He leaned his six-foot frame against the kitchen counter. The smile that had broken half of the female hearts west of the Mississippi and north of the Missouri erased the unaccustomed worry lines from his forehead and relit the flame in his clear, sky blue eyes.

Augusta left off stirring her pot of stew on the stove and sank into a chair at the square oak table, scarred and scuffed by years of hard use. She stared across the room at her son, a gleam of moisture evident in her faded blue eyes, eyes that had once matched those of the young man before her. "Have you spoken with Dag?" She pushed a strand of steel gray hair back into the bun at the base of her neck.

"Nah, why should I?" Jude pulled his rear away from the counter, snagged a chair out with his foot, and joined her at the table.

"He has been helping me out some with beans and flour and coffee and such," she said.

Don't you keep the hens and cow no more?"

"Ja, sure, but the 'hoppers took the garden and I had no one to do the hay, so they got that, too." Augusta stared out the window. "Not been easy the last couple of years. My hired man quit this spring, you know. Sometime after you left town." She pushed herself to her feet as if the cares of the world were pounding her into the sod. "You want another cup of coffee?"

Jude nodded. "Things'll be easier now, Ma. You'll see." He accepted the chipped mug she offered him.

"Why?" Her tone sharpened. "You got some new scheme up your sleeve?"

"Not yet. Come on, Ma, I left off the cards and such. I aim to help you put this place back together. Dag ain't the only one in this family can take care of his ma." He patted her work-worn hand where it lay on the table. "You'll see."

"It'll be mighty fine having you home again." She sipped from her cup. "Where'd you leave Melissa?"

"She's at her ma's. Said I'd come first and make sure us coming here was all right."

"Son, this is your home. You're always welcome here."

"Not like some other places, huh?"

"You in some kind of trouble?" Augusta peered at him, as if delving behind the smile in his eyes to see if he was fooling her. When Jude employed this smile, the very angels would hand over their halos; its candlepower wasn't wasted on his mother. "Nah, Ma, come on. I just want to help you, that's all."

"I thank you, Son. I most surely do." Augusta straightened her shoulders. "Well, I'd best be gettin' at the chores. You want to milk old Betsy while I feed the hens? Then you can dig those spuds that made it through the 'hoppers."

"I. . .ah ... I thought maybe I'd go for Melissa this morning.

She don't take too well to staying with her ma. They don't get along much."

"Oh?" Augusta caught herself before her shoulders slumped, but barely.

"Don't get me wrong, Ma. I'll milk first." Jude held up a placating hand. He rose to his feet as if anxious to be at his work. "You still keep the bucket out in the well house?"

After the chores were finished, Jude hitched up the old horse to the ancient wagon and, leaving his saddle horse in the pasture, drove out of the yard. He watched the dust spurt up from beneath the horse's hooves and caught the caw of a crow, but otherwise the fall day stretched empty before him.

I've got to get some money, get some money. The thoughts kept time with the jangle of the harness and the *clumph, clumph* of the hooves in the dust. "Ya suppose there's a game going tonight in Soldahl?" he asked the world at large.

The crow circled overhead and cawed an answer.

"If only I didn't have to get Mellie. Sometimes women are more trouble than they're worth." He shook his head. *And this one ain't been worth much for some time.*

If only the baby had lived. Then he'd been one up on Dag. The first grandson, now that would have made his ma proud. But now that Dag was married, he'd probably have a whole houseful of kids.

Jude groaned and shook his hand at the persistent crow. Another trick on his brother gone sour. What a shock it had been to see the new Dag Weinlander—clean-shaven, neady trimmed hair, decent clothes. Jude looked down at the new hole in the knee of his trousers. The cloth was so weak, it split when he knelt down to milk the cow this morning.

"It ain't fair. My brother, the dolt himself, has a thriving business, a beautiful wife, and that grand house of his. It just ain't fair, I tell ya." The old bay horse flicked its ears and kept up a nodding trot.

By the time Jude had driven onto the lane to his mother-in-law's farm, he had worked himself into a temper. The prosperous look of the farm did nothing to improve his mood. The look she gave him when she let him in the house could have curdled milk.

"Get your stuff. We gotta get back so's I can help Ma."

"I…I'm ready." Melissa dragged a scruffy carpetbag from another room. The effort made her catch her breath on a sob as she pushed a limp strand of dingy hair back from her face. "You hungry?"

"You got it ready?"

"No, but it'd just take a minute. I could slice you some bread and—"

"All right, just quit jawing and do it." Jude kept his gaze from wandering to his mother-in-law, but he could feel her glare stabbing him in the back.

Melissa scuttled over to the cupboard and, after slicing the bread and meat, put them together with butter. Then she poured coffee into a canning jar and, after a quick nod in her mother's direction, went to pick up her satchel. Bread and coffee in her hands, she looked from the carpetbag to her husband and back again.

Jude started for the door. At his mother-in-law's "Harumph," he snorted in disgust and whirled back to pick up the carpetbag. The glare he shot at Melissa made her sob again.

The trip home passed without a word. When Jude cast withering glances at Melissa, she studied her hands or the goldenrod nodding in the evening breeze along the side of the dusty road.

That night in bed, Melissa whimpered in her sleep. When she began to cough, Jude jerked the sheet over him and rolled over in bed. "Can't ya do something about that?" he snarled. "I need my sleep."

When Melissa returned to the bed, the smell of camphor floated around her like a mist. Jude sat up, glared at her in the moonlight, and, after punching his pillow, flopped on his other side. What he wouldn't do for a drink.

In the morning, Jude drove his mother and wife into town for church. After dropping them off, he aimed the horse toward the saloon at the other end of town.

He tied the animal to the hitching rack in front of the flat-fronted building and, after checking the locked door, walked around the back.

"Smitty, hey, Smitty. Open up," Jude called softly as he rapped on the door. The saloon wouldn't open until noon, but by then he should be back at the church to pick up the womenfolk.

"What now?" A rough voice called down from the flung-open window above.

"Hey, Smitty. How ya doin'?" Jude pushed the hat back on his head and grinned up at his friend.

"Well, well. If it ain't Jude come back to town. 'How ya doing' is right. Where you been?" The bartender leaned his elbows on the windowsill.

"Here and there. How about a bottle? I gotta get back and pick up the womenfolk after church or I'd stay for a game or two. How things been, anyhow?"

"Good, good. But not the same without you around. Sure you can't stay for a time or so?" A grin split the man's leathery face. He polished the top of his shiny pate with a cupped hand.

"Not this time, but I ain't gone for good. I'm helpin' my ma out some, you know how it is when they gets older. So I'll be around now and then." Jude shifted from one foot to the other. "What about that bottle or you gonna jaw all day?"

Smitty pulled his head back so fast he banged his head on the window.

Jude laughed and slapped his knee. "Better be more careful with my bottle. I got a thirst 'bout as wide as the Red in full flood." He grinned as he realized it was good to be back in Soldahl. Now, if he could just figure a way to get rid of the womenfolk. His fingers itched for the cards the way his throat did for that first swallow of good, solid whiskey.

The door of the saloon swung open in front of him. "Come on in then, you old buzzard." Smitty scratched himself and headed for the front of the saloon. "You heard about your brother?" He continued without waiting for an answer. "After he married that pretty little thing you brought over for him, they moved into the house with Mrs. Norgaard. In fact, as I heard it, the old lady deeded them two the house. Jude, you wouldn't recognize—you seen Dag yet?"

"Now, why would I want to see him? You think I been pining away for the sight of my brother or something?" Jude clapped his hat down on the counter and hung his rear over a bar stool.

"Nah. I just thought I should bring you up to date, so's you're not too surprised or something." Smitty slapped a bottle down on the bar. "That'll be four bits."

"Ah…I…uh…how about I pay for this later? I'm kinda short of cash right now."

Smitty paused for a moment. "You know, I—" He paused. "All right. Just this once. For old-time's sake."

Jude swung off the stool. "Thanks. If nothing else, I'll pay first hand I win." He raised a hand in farewell and headed out the door.

Once seated in the wagon, he broke the seal of the bottle and, lifting the bottle high, poured a generous slug down his gullet. He sighed and wiped his mouth with the back of his hand. It had been much too long between drinks.

He recapped the bottle and set it down in the back in between the burlap bags on the wagon bed. Now, after a stop at the mercantile for a store of tobacco, he'd head back for the church.

"Jude," the store owner said, slapping his hands on the counter before him and leaning across it. "If'n you ain't a sight for sore eyes. Gunna join us for a game tonight? I still gotta get that hunnert dollars back from the last round."

"Soon, soon. Anything new been happening whilst I been gone?

"You seen Dag? Man, we sure done him a favor, bringing that pretty little gal over from Norway for him."

Jude felt a rage begin a slow burn down about his gut. If he heard about his wonderful brother one more time, he'd smash someone for sure. "Cut the jawing. You got any tobacco? And a couple of cigars. Better add some cheese, coffee, and some of those cinnamon twists. My ma always had a hankering for cinnamon twists." He stared around the well-stocked store as he waited for his order. Cracker and pickle barrels fronted the wooden counter. Boxes of the new dry cereal called cornflakes lined the shelves above the tins of spices. Rakes, hoes, and pitchforks hung from hooks above the boxes of boots and shoes. Kitchenwares filled one aisle and farm implements another.

One of these days, when his ship came in, Jude knew he would come in here and just buy whatever he needed. No more of this putting it on the slip and heming and hawing back and forth over what he could buy. Why, he needed new boots and—he stared down at the split leather on his ancient boots. All he really needed was one good night at the card table. One good night and he'd be back up on top again.

"Here ya go." Adam set the sack up on the counter. "Need anything else?"

"Not for now. Put that on my mothers tab for now. I'll settle up with you later."

"I don't know, Jude. Dag, he's mighty particular what goes on the bill, now that he's payin' it." He glanced up in time to catch the thundercloud racing across Jude's face. "But I'm sure this time'll be okay."

If I hear the name Dag one more time, I'll ... I'll... Jude clamped a lid on his thoughts. He could put up with anything for a time. And what were the chances he'd be seeing his brother anyway? Dag surely didn't bring that highfalutin' wife of his out to the farm, and he sure didn't show up at the saloon to deal a hand or two.

He paused as he swung up into the wagon. Unless Dag had changed in those ways, too. Jude shook his head. Nah, no chance. He dug in the sack for the tobacco and, after stretching open the pouch, dug out a pinch and placed it between his lip and gum. Now that, that was mighty fine. A swallow of good whiskey and a chaw of tobacco. Now, if only he could add a card game to that, the day would be perfect.

He spat a brown gob of tobacco juice into the dirt as he drove the horse and wagon past the Norgaard house. So this is where his brother lived now. He's come up some since the soddie out on the plain. He spat again. Surely, there must be some way to bother his brother again. Some way that wouldn't backfire this time.

When he got to the church he ignored his mother's comments after handing her and Melissa up into the wagon. How could he get even? He jumped when he heard his mother mention Dag and Clara.

"They're what?" The question popped out before he had time to organize his thoughts.

"Dag and Clara are coming out to visit this afternoon. I told them I'd bake a cake, but she insisted they'd bring supper. Sure will be nice to have a treat again."

Jude dug down in the sack at his feet. "I got you a treat, something you always liked." He pulled out the cinnamon twists. "See, I think of you plenty."

"Why, thank you, you thoughtful boy," Augusta simpered in a totally uncharacteristic manner. She took a candy stick from the sack and passed the packet back to Melissa, who huddled on the wagon bed.

"No, thank you," she mumbled.

No, thank you, Jude mimicked in his mind. *Why can't I say no, thank you to Dag coming out? Why does he have to show up? All I heard about today was how great Dag is doing. Him and that wonderful wife of his.* Jude could feel the anger stirring again in his gut. The fire flickered and flamed as if doused by kerosene. He snapped the horse's reins and stamped his foot against the footrest.

All his life, Dag this and Dag that. And now his brother had a wife that all the town praised while his wife mewled from the back of the wagon. The flames flared higher.

The horse broke into a trot. Augusta clutched the side of the wooden bench. Jude heard a whimper from behind him. Even his mother had gone against him. Here she was, glad they were coming because they brought a good supper. He sucked the juice out of his chaw and spat it off the side of the wagon. It'd be a long time before he sat down to eat with his brother.

When they reached the farm, Jude leaped from the wagon, helped the womenfolk down, and trotted the horse down to the barn. He secreted his bottle down into the grain bin. Now he could take a swig when he needed one and no one would be the wiser.

As soon as the dog barked a welcome for Dag and Clara, Jude slipped out the back door, telling his mother he was off to do the chores.

"You be ready for supper in about an hour?" she asked as the door slammed behind Jude's hurrying form. He lurked behind the corner until he heard the visitors go inside the house.

The internal muttering continued while he threw grain to the chickens and walked out in the pasture to round up the milk cow. Usually she waited patiently beside the barn. But today everything was going wrong, even the cow. When he finally found her, laying down in a slight dip in the sparsely grassed field, chewing her cud, he hurried her up to the barn. Udder swinging, she trotted to the barn door and stopped. The look she shot him from over one shoulder would have rebuked a more tenderhearted man.

As Jude swung open the door, he slapped her on the rump. When he slammed the wooden stanchion bar in place, it pinched her neck. She lowed in protest.

Jude stomped off to the well house for the milk bucket. A slight smile lifted the corners of his mouth when he dug the grain out of the bin. His bottle lay snug in the bin, covered by the golden oats. His mouth watered at the thought. He brushed the grain away and lifted the bottle, sloshing the liquid inside. Did he dare? He shoved it back into its nest. Not now…not with Dag on the prowl.

As he milked the cow, its milk streamed into the bucket, the *swish, swish* a music all its own. The milking song covered the sound of the door opening.

"Hello."

At the sound of his brother's voice, Jude jerked on the cow's teats. Before he could recover, the cow planted her foot squarely in the bucket and her tail whipped him across the eyes.

Jude leaped to his feet, milk running down his pant legs. "Did ya have to scare a body to death, creeping up thata way? Look what you made me do." He turned on his brother, fury transforming his handsome face to a mask of hatred.

"I'm sorry I startled you." Dag, his white shirt glistening in the dimness of the barn, crossed his arms over his chest. "But you and I need to talk and this is the only way I could see how to do so without the women around."

"I don't need to talk with you." Jude dumped the milk in a pan for the cats and, after rinsing the bucket out, returned to his stool.

" 'Sides, I gotta finish here."

"I'll make this short and sweet. Ma says you have come home to help her out. We both know she needs help here since the last hired man quit. She can't manage all alone."

"I know. That's why I'm here." Jude returned to the squeeze and pull of milking.

"But the truth of the matter is that I've been bringing her supplies and paying her bills at the stores in town."

"So, you want a medal or somethin'?" Jude pushed his head harder against the cow's flank.

"No, I just don't want to see your tobacco on the tab. And I don't want to hear you're in town gambling and drinking. That would break Ma's heart, she's so glad to have you home again. So the rules are: no drinking, no gambling, and you buy your own tobacco and cigars."

"Who do you think you are, coming here and trying to tell me what to do with my life?" Jude stripped the last drops of milk from the cow's udder and shoved himself to his feet.

"I'm your brother, your older brother, and right now you need to join us for supper. Clara and Ma have it on the table. I'd like you to meet my wife since you had such a hand in bringing her to me. I never had a chance to thank you for that, you know." He offered his hand in gratitude.

Jude pushed aside the extended hand and, after releasing the cow, stalked off to the well house.

While the meal was indeed tasty, as Augusta had promised, Jude squirmed whenever he looked across the table to the woman who smiled so lovingly at his brother. Her laugh, her intense blue eyes, the golden hair waving down her back, the way she charmed his mother—they all irritated him. Especially when he glanced at the washed-out woman sitting beside him.

And the look of Dag himself. Had that man really been hiding under the dirt and stench of the blacksmith? And the way he talked. Why, one would think Dag had been to school for years. And Jude knew for sure that that hadn't been the case.

The apple pie Jude was eating was turning into prairie straw in his mouth. Jude shoved away from the table, mumbling that he had something he had to do. He didn't return to the house until everyone else had gone to bed.

The next few days did nothing to alleviate the anger festering in Jude's heart. A coyote raided the chicken house and killed three of their best laying hens. Every time Jude tried to fix something, he needed a new part or another piece of lumber or fencing wire. Only his secret friend buried in the grain bin consoled him.

One day the sun scorched the earth, ignoring the fact that fall was supposedly on the way. The sun burned down on Jude's head as he dug the few remaining potatoes and dumped them in the cellar. The cow came into estrus and broke through the fence to go visit the neighbor's bull, so he not only had to bring her back but had to repair the fence. All day his temper broiled along with the haat devils whirling away over the prairie.

Supper that day was a silent affair. Even Augusta relaxed her steel spine to sit down on the rear porch and fan herself with her apron.

"You'd think this was July rather than September," she said as she wiped the beads of moisture from her upper Up.

Jude merely grunted. The thought of his bottle down in the barn made his mouth prickle.

"Think I'll go on up to bed." Melissa stood in the doorway wiping her hands on her apron.

"Think I'll go on into town." Jude spit a gob of tobacco juice off the porch onto the hard-packed earth.

"What for?" Augusta jerked awake from her slight doze.

"Just to talk to the fellas at the mercantile. Find out where we can get some cheap grain. Not much left out in the barn."

"You won't go near the sa—" Melissa cut off her question at the fierce look Jude fired at her.

"You can go to the store tomorrow." Augusta drew herself up in the rocking chair. "It will be closed before you get there. The only place open in Soldahl at this hour is the saloon." Her voice brooked no argument.

"If I say I go now, I'll go—"

This time it was the mother's look that stopped the son.

Jude jerked open the screen door, shoved past his wife, knocking her against the counter, and stormed into the sitting room. He dug a cigar out of the humidor and stomped back into the kitchen to light it in the embers of the stove.

But instead of leaving by the back door, he returned to the sitting room. After kicking the hassock into place in front of the brown velvet chair, he flung himself into the chair and propped his boots on the hassock. The puffs on his cigar sent spirals of smoke drifting to the high ceiling.

Who does she think she is to tell me what to do like that? His thought kept time with the billows of smoke. *A man should be able to do what he wants in his own house.* He shifted his dusty boots on the hassock, deliberately ignoring the tiny voice that reminded him of the household rules. No smoking in the house and no feet on the furniture. The only time the room was ever used was when company came.

Tonight Jude considered himself company. He ignored Melissa's quiet "Good night" and refused to respond when his mother started to say something. As the smoke cloud darkened around him, she snorted and made her way upstairs. A lesser woman might have marked her displeasure with heavy feet but not Augusta. Her feelings seemed to float back and freeze the room.

Jude called his mother every name he could think of and then created a few new ones, all in the regions of his mind, of course. When he finished with her, he started on Melissa. Why was he, of all men, so abused?

Sounds ceased from above except for the rhythmic snoring that indicated that his mother had fallen sound asleep. Jude listened carefully. Only the song of his bottle could be heard in the stillness of his mind.

Jude set his cigar on the edge of the small table beside the chair. If he hurried out, he could be back before anyone were the wiser.

The evening breeze that had felt so refreshing on the porch had increased to a wind, raising dust and dancing devils across the empty fields. The harvest moon shone down, lighting the path to the barn like midday.

Jude swung open the barn door and followed his nose to the grain bin. Practice made finding the bottle easy in spite of the darkness that encircled him like a comforting blanket. Out here, no one would try to tell him to remove his feet from the hassock. That's what footstools were for—resting feet. And chairs for bodies, especially tired bodies like his. His mind kept up the litany of complaints as he jerked the cork out with his teeth, dropped it in his hand, and raised the cool bottle to his lips. The first swallow was all he'd dreamed of.

Jude started to replace the cork, but a glance in the direction of the house and those interfering females made him take another.

After a couple more swigs, he edged his way over to the ladder to the haymow and, clutching his bottle to his chest, clamored up. He snuggled his backside down into the pile of hay and leaned back, exhaling a sigh at the silence and the comfort. No one would look for him here.

Soon his head fell back, the empty bottle slipped from relaxed fingers, and gentle puffings deepened into snores.

"What's—" Jude struggled up from the bowels of his sleep. What was the dog barking about at this time of night? He blinked, trying to decide where he was. After rubbing a hand across eyes filled with grit, he looked up to see gold lights dancing on the walls and ceiling above him. Was it morning already? He stumbled to his feet.

His mother would rip him limb from limb if she thought he spent the night drinking in the barn.

"Shut up, you stupid dog," he muttered as he fumbled for the ladder. "You'll wake the whole world if you haven't already."

When Jude stepped from the barn, his heart stopped in his chest. "Oh, no!"

Flames flickered within the downstairs windows of the house, smoke spiraling upward from the open windows.

Jude raced for the back door. His heart pounded in his chest. His mind pleaded for the God he so often profaned to help him get the women out. Surely the barking dog had awakened them, too.

"Ma! Melissa!" His screams rent the air. The wind tossed the sound away, creating instead its own monster song of roaring flames and crashing timbers.

Jude jerked open the door and, arm over his nose and mouth, stumbled through the smoke and heat, searching for the staircase.

Chapter 2

The heat beat Jude back. The dog leaped beside him, barking furiously at the flames. Jude choked and coughed, gagging for air as he leaned forward, nearly toppling to the ground. When he got his breath, he stumbled to the rain barrel at the corner of the house, soaked his shirt in the water, and wrapped the wet cloth around his face. After grabbing a deep breath, he charged through the back door.

The fire wasn't burning as furiously here as he made his way to the stairs. He couldn't call, saving every breath for the ordeal ahead. But the raging flames beat him out again. As his mind dimmed with the heat and smoke, he turned back. He never noticed the pieces of burning wood peppering his back or the heat searing his lungs. His final cry of "Ma" went no farther than his lips as he collapsed on the ground outside.

"Here he is!" the man yelled. "Jude's alive, I think."

"Ma, Melissa." Jude croaked.

"It's gone. All gone." The man draped a wet cloth over Jude's back and offered him a sip of water.

"Gone?" Jude tried to raise his head. Instead he collapsed into oblivion.

"Dag, I think he's coming around."

Jude heard the feminine voice from somewhere down in the chasm where he preferred to remain. At least down there, he didn't hurt so cruelly. His back, his head, his arms—all on fire. He twisted his face to the side. What was he lying on?

"Drink." He forced the word through lips that felt coated with some kind of grease. His throat spasmed around the single word.

"Here." A glass tube appeared between his lips and he sucked greedily.

Where am I? What's happened? The thoughts chased through his mind like the flames had—the flames—the house—Ma and Melissa. The memories seared his mind like the flames had seared his back. A groan tore from his heart and forced its way out his throat.

"Easy now." The voice belonged to his brother, Dag.

"Ma?"

"Send Mrs. Hanson for the doctor." Dag seemed to be talking from far away.

"Ma." Jude put all his energy into the request.

"Easy now, Jude. There's nothing more you can do. You're at my house and burned terribly. It's a miracle you're still alive."

Jude digested the words. But what about his mother and Melissa? Had they gotten out? He could hear the roar of the flames, the dog barking. Were there screams? He tried to remember.

"How about another drink?" The tube appeared again.

Jude drank gratefully. The cool water slipped down like the elixir of life itself. He fought the pain and the fog trying to blanket his mind. "Ma!"

"She's gone, Jude. Both of them."

The simple words sent him spinning back into oblivion. Pain

and searing agony brought him back.

The tube appeared and, as before, he drank, sucking in the life-giving moisture. He tried to figure out what he was lying on, but the effort was too great. Instead, he let himself slip back to that no-man's-land. The pursuing flames of his nightmares hurt far less than the thought of Ma and Melissa dying in the fire.

"How do you think it started?"

Jude heard the voice and fought against the pull back to reality. How did he think it started? How would he know? He'd been out in the barn, slugging down his nightly antidote for living.

"Maybe a lamp?" This voice rang with feminine sweetness.

"We may never know. It was an accident pure and simple." The gruff voice belonged to a stranger. Who was it?

"Thank you for coming, Doctor."

Ah, that's who it was. He'd heard the voice before, sometime during the long, long night.

"You take care of yourself now, too, you hear?" Footsteps faded along with the voice.

While Jude kept his eyes closed, he couldn't shut off his mind. Ma was always so careful. She always banked the stove. Only used candles in an emergency. How did the fire start? Had there been a lightning storm? He tried to shrug his shoulders to relieve the itching. Instead, he bit his lip against the fiery pain.

"Drink." He swallowed and forced his voice to obey the command to speak louder. "Drink, please." The tube appeared at his lips again and he sucked greedily.

"Jude, we have to get some nourishment into you so I'm going to give you some broth by the tube now. Can you manage that?"

Jude knew Clara's voice by now. He nodded.

This time the drink was warm and tasted of beef and onion.

"How long since the fire?" Jude raised his head and turned to the side so he could see. This laying on his stomach was getting hard to handle.

"A week." Dag sat down on the floor in front of his brother so they could look each other in the face. "How are you feeling?"

"Guess I'll live."

"We were afraid you were gone, too, there for a time." Dag crossed his legs and leaned against the wall. "Dr. Harmon says it's a miracle you made it."

"He the one who rigged this bed?"

"No, I did." Dag ducked his head in the old habit of humility. "When he said you couldn't he on your back and you looked like you'd smother on your stomach, I built this. Clara padded it with quilts."

"I allus knew you could make whatever was needed." Jude's voice took on a dreamy quality. It was like looking through a telescope backwards. "Pa said you was one clever boy, even when you was a kid."

"What?"

"That's why I teased you so much."

"Jude, you're talking through your head. Or are you delirious again?" Dag shook his head with a snort.

"Nah. I hated you sometimes ... most of the time, you know."

Jude let his mind float down the telescope. The pain met him halfway down. He slipped off without answering Dag's last question. How would he know how the fire started?

Just before the blackness claimed him completely, he saw the cigar, smoking on the table in his mother s sitting room. His cigar! The one he'd left when he headed for the barn. The pain now searing his heart made the pain from his back seem like a hangnail.

When Jude awoke he wished he were dead. Why didn't they let him die? He wasn't worth keeping alive. He clenched his teeth and arched his back. The pain drenched him and nothing could erase the agony in his mind. His carelessness killed both Ma and Melissa. How could he live? Why bother?

"Jude, what is it? The pain is worse?" Clara knelt in front of him. "Can I get you something?"

Jude shook his head. He couldn't tell her. How could he tell anyone?

"Here. I made you some chicken broth this time. Doc says you can have whatever you can swallow. But I know that position makes eating difficult."

Her caring words drove the nail deeper. He didn't deserve anyone taking care of him like this. He clenched his teeth against the tube she held to his mouth. *God, please let me die.* He felt like roaring at whatever it was had kept him alive and let them die.

"Jude, you have to eat." Dag took his place against the wall. "It's been two days now and you haven't taken even a sip of water. What is it?"

Jude left the land of the screaming voices and raised his headto look at his brother. Couldn't he tell? Wasn't it written across his forehead—MURDERER—in giant red letters.

Jude took a wet cloth and wiped his brother's face. "Doc says you can get up tomorrow if you are strong enough. He says if we don't get you moving, you'll lose all the muscle tone in your back."

Jude clenched his teeth. All right, tomorrow he'd get up. The sooner he got better, the sooner he could leave. Since he wasn't dying this way, he could take care of the matter better when he could ride away. He took the offered drink and grunted his thanks.

From then on Jude gritted his teeth against the pain and forced himself to down all the fluids and nourishment he could stand. He did exactly as the doctor ordered, all except the laudanum. He refused to let his mind dwell in that no-man's-land that the drug brought with it. He didn't deserve the release.

He still couldn't lie on his back, so he slept on the slotted bed Dag had devised, where his head fit into a brace and looked straight down. In that position, Jude found he didn't have to look at anyone unless he wanted to. And he didn't so choose.

One afternoon when he was lying there, he heard Clara, the doctor, and Dag speaking in the other room while they thought he was sleeping.

"But he was doing so much better. I can't understand the change," Clara said.

"Ja, it's not like Jude to be so silent." Dag's voice sounded weary.

"He's been through a lot. Sometimes accidents like this completely change a person." Doc paused before continuing. "Thought for a while there when he quit eating and drinking we was gonna lose him after all."

Ah, if only it were that easy, Jude thought. *After all the meanness I've bothered my brother with all these years, I couldn't quit and die on him in his own home. How can the man treat me with such love and gentleness when all these years...* His mind drifted back, picking out the instances of his cruelty and he winced.

If his mother's ideas of the Maker's judgments were true, he'd not be standing in line for angel's wings, that's for sure. He had to get well enough to get out of here soon. The thought of being a continued burden ate at him like a canker. He studied the healing burns on the back of his hand and arm; his back they said was worse. The angry red welts glistened under the healing salve Mrs. Hanson kept forcing him to apply. At least now when she spread it on his back, he could stand the touch. Soon, he would be able to wear a shirt and then he could leave.

The thoughts of the bustling housekeeper seemed to bring her to him.

"Time for more cold cloths and medicine," Mrs. Hanson said.

Her cheery voice could change in an instant if he didn't respond. He'd learned that the hard way. He knew he was only here on sufferance. While she tolerated him, he could tell from her eyes she wouldn't hesitate to toss him out.

He turned his head when he heard a cane tapping along with a much lighter step and entering his room. Mrs. Norgaard leaned on her cane, but he couldn't raise his head far enough to see her face.

"If we move that chair over by the wall," Mrs. Norgaard said, "I shall be able to converse with our patient more easily." Mrs. Hanson huffed but did her employer's bidding, and Mrs. Norgaard settled herself into her chair in her normal pose, back ramrod straight and never touching the back of the chair.

Silence descended on the room as she studied the man on his stomach. Jude studied the spot on the floor immediately below his face.

Why doesn't she say something? Why don't I say something? The thoughts tiptoed around his mind, fearful the woman in the chair could read them. Jude cleared his throat. Why was she here? Had she come to see him before, when he was unconscious? Had he said anything to her he shouldn't have?

He could feel her eyes drilling into the top of his head. The regrowing hair tingled in response. This was as bad as being called before the class back when he was in school.

Did she suspect the fire had been his fault? That a cigar, the one he'd been warned to not smoke in the house, burned his wife and mother to death. He felt the twisting between his mind, heart, and gut. If she knew, surely she would have thrown him out long ago.

He could stand it no longer. He raised his head, refusing to flinch when the wrinkling skin of his neck and upper back sent pain rippling and stabbing. It wasn't judgment he saw in her eyes. No, they were the eyes of love. Compassion flowed from her to him as if they were bound by golden cords.

He could feel tears burn at the back of his eyes. Tears! *Grown men don't cry.* The order failed to stem the flow. Jude sniffed as quietly and subtly as possible. He blinked not only once but several times, but still one fat tear managed to escape and drip off the end of his nose.

Why didn't she say something? Who turned on the furnace? The room seemed to have heated up twenty degrees or so.

Still, the silence stretched.. .and stretched. But Jude was the one who felt like he was being pulled apart, limb from limb.

"I want to thank—" he cleared his throat and started again. "Thank you for…aah…having me here…in your house."

"This is no longer my home. It now belongs to Dag and Clara."

"Oh." Then the rumors were true.

"They've become my family."

Silence settled in again. Why in the world did he feel like crying?

Jude gritted his teeth. When that didn't help, he bit his bottom lip. Even the taste of blood failed. One didn't yell at a lady. His mother had drilled that into him from the time he was little, but that didn't prevent him from screaming in his head. His body, the fire, the tears, the pain, the heat, the—he ran out of things to scream about.

"It will do no good." The words crept past the damaging words and shut him right down.

"Huh?" He threw his head up as far as possible. "Oh—" He stopped abruptly, but the grimace said more than he intended.

"All the anger you harbor. It will only cause you more pain."

Jude shook his head. If she only knew. The silence seeped in again.

How could she sit so still? He felt his fingers twitch. . .then his toes. He felt like twitching all over. Itching…twitching... Oh, how he could use a drink!

"When you can accept our forgiveness, it will always be here. Dag and Clara can live no other way and neither can I. Always remember that." She rose to her feet and walked to the door. "Remember, too, that Christ died so we might live forgiven. We all might live so. Good evening, Jude." Her footsteps echoed faintly down the hall.

In the morning he was gone.

Chapter 3

Get outa here before I…I —"

"Before you what?" The voice held a trace of a leer that she was sure matched the face hidden in the dimness. "There's no one to hear you. Ma and Pa are gone for the night, remember?"

Rebekka Stenesrude swallowed to dislodge the fear clogging her throat. She could feel the perspiration running down her back under the flannel nightgown. Why hadn't she gone to stay in town when she learned that Mr. and Mrs. Strand were going to be gone? She listened carefully, waiting for the man—if you could call him that—to move again so she could determine where he was standing. Why, oh why, had she drawn the heavy draperies? If only the moonlight were lighting the room. But then he could see her more clearly, too.

A devilish chuckle echoed from the darkened corner. The sound caused the hairs on the back of her neck to stand at attention. Why hadn't she been more alert? She'd noticed his smiles and secret glances, but fighting off advances of young men had never been a problem as there'd never been any to fight off or even brush away.

Her antennae strained to sense the attacking man. What could she do? She felt carefully behind herself, seeking something with which to strike her attacker. Her fingers closed over the handle of the heavy pitcher on the commode.

"You can't run fast enough to get away and if you scream, well, who's gonna hear you?"

The voice sent shivers rippling up her back again, but at least now she knew which way the attack would come from. She took a deep breath in an attempt to slow her thundering heart and then flexed her fingers so she could grip the handle more firmly.

Suddenly, he came with a rush, shoving her against the commode. She swung with all her might. The pitcher crashed against him. Both the man and the shards struck the bare floor at the same time.

The scream died in her throat. She leaped for the door, expecting him to follow, but only silence and her tortured breathing filled the room. Was he dead?

Rebekka grabbed her clothes off the hooks on the wall and ran down the stairs. When she paused to listen, she heard a groan. Relieved in one way but furious that she hadn't permanently silenced the oaf, she darted out the door. "Please, God, let a horse be in the barn." The muttered prayer matched the rhythm of her pounding feet.

In the darkness of the barn, she ripped a bridle off the wall and, with outstretched hands to guide her, made her way to the horse stalls. "Thank You, Lord." She took in a deep breath so she wouldn't panic the horse in the stall. Murmuring gentle words, she shuffled carefully to the animal's head and slipped the bridle on over the halter. Each action seemed to take an hour as she fumbled in the darkness. After untying the slipknot, she backed the animal out of the stall. Then, after retrieving her clothes from where she'd laid them on a bar by the door of the stall, she led the animal outside.

A roar of pain and anger could be heard clear from the house to the barn as Rebekka led the horse over to the edge of the watering trough, stepped up, and swung herself astride the horse, her nightgown and housecoat bunched up around her knees.

Adolph Strand crashed the screen door against the wall and staggered out on the porch, clutching his head.

Rebekka dug her heels into the horse's ribs and galloped down the lane. Where would she go in the middle of the night? Thank God Mr. and Mrs. Strand were driving the team and there was no way

Adolph could follow her.

A mile or so from the farm, she pulled her horse down to a jog. A full moon directly overhead bathed the land in silver and each leaf and blade of grass shimmered with the heavy dew. A sleepy bird called from somewhere, perhaps the brilliant light of the moon confusing his inner clock. Rebekka drew in a deep breath, the aroma of a steaming horse mingling with some night-blooming flower.

"What a shame not to enjoy a night so marvelous as this." She tipped her head back, luxuriating in the feeling, but shivered again at the thought of what had nearly happened to her. Stirred by the breeze and the night scents, she inhaled again. If only she could keep riding forever.

Rebekka shook her head and made an unladylike snort, matching that of the horse she rode. Forever would be a long time, and she had school in the morning. No matter what had happened tonight, all twenty-one of her students would greet her in the morning with bright and shiny faces. And the schoolmarm must be above reproach. Not riding around the country in the moonlight— in her nightgown and housecoat.

She shuddered again at the thought of how close she'd come to losing that purity required of schoolmarms. That. . .that, she couldn't think of a name vile enough. But to whom could she talk? Who would believe her? She clamped her lips together.

Willowford had been her home now for two years and surely, in that time, the parents of her students must trust her. They must—she shook her head. But they could never be told. The Strand family had lived in the area for twenty years or more, and it would be her word against theirs.

She lifted her face to the moon, staring beyond the silver disk to the star-studded midnight expanse of the heavens. "Father God, what do I do? Where can I go? Your word says You look out for widows and orphans. How about an old-maid schoolmarm?"

She waited, her body relaxed and swaying with the moving horse. Would the stars sing for her, bringing the message she needed? She pulled the horse to a halt to listen better. *Moses had his burning bush,* she thought. *How will God talk with me?*

A bird twittered in the brush in the ditch. A breeze lifted the horse's mane and billowed her nightgown and housecoat. She smoothed them down and dropped her chin to her chest. How silly she was being. God didn't talk to people on earth anymore. Did He?

She nudged the horse into a slow jog; its tapping hooves drowned out the night music. A picture of the Widow Sampson's boxy white boardinghouse came into her mind. Maybe she could at least stay there until she spoke with Mr. Larson, the school superintendent for the district.

"One thing sure," she promised the trotting horse, "I won't go back to the Strands', no matter what anyone says. I'll be on that train for. . .for anywhere first." The horse's ears flicked back and forth, and he snorted as if in perfect agreement.

When they entered the darkened town, she slowed the animal to a walk. Music echoed from the saloon and bright light formed a square clear out to the middle of the street. Rebekka edged the horse to the other side of the packed-dirt street and nudged him back into a trot. She couldn't be seen in dishabille like this and still live and teach in Willowford.

After following the picket fence around to the back of the widow's boardinghouse, Rebecca slid off the horse and onto the ground. She tied her mount to the rail and opened the gate. Rebekka froze as the screech of the hinges echoed loud enough to wake the sleepers halfway down the block.

Then, a dog barked on the other side of the street and her horse rubbed his chin on the picket, sending his bit ajingling.

Rebekka tiptoed up the walk, her hand at her throat. She paused again when the first step squeaked beneath her bare foot. How could she rouse the Widow Sampson without waking all her boarders?

She tapped lightly on the back door. When nothing happened, she tapped again more firmly. "Please, please," she whispered to the heavens. But, instead of a welcome from within, she heard someone making his way down the street, singing, if one could call it that, a barroom ditty.

Rebekka formed a fist and raised her hand. She paused just before banging as a disgruntled voice came from within the house.

"Just hold on ta your britches. I'll be there soon's I can." Other grumbles followed, along with the slap of carpet slippers on a wooden floor. "Who's there?" The words were matched by the door's opening just enough for a mobcapped woman to peek around the door.

"Widow Sampson."

"Why, if'n it ain't the schoolmarm. Miss Stenesrude, what are you doing here this time of night—and in your nightclothes? You're not needing a nurse, are you?" When Rebekka shook her head, the door opened all the way. "Get yourself in here before you catch your death."

"Thank you, I…I can explain." Rebekka looked over her shoulder *to* where her horse tossed his head and tried to reach the tips of the grass growing along the fence. She clutched her spare clothes to her body and then handed them to the older woman. "But first I better see to the horse. Do you have a place I can put him for the night?"

Widow Sampson accepted the clothing and pursed her lips. "Why, I s'pose you can put him in the shed there. We're a mite low on coal right now, so there should be room. He your horse?"

"No. I'll explain as soon as I return." Rebekka started down the steps and turned back. "Have you a rope or something I can tie him with?"

"Uh, just a minute." The older woman shut the door.

A shiver attacked Rebekka now that the danger was nearly past. She could hear the singing coming nearer. Did the man have to come down this street? What if he lived in the next house? Rebekka wrapped her arms around her shoulders to quell more of the bone-rattling quakes.

The door reopened and Widow Sampson stepped out on the porch. "Here you go. Think you can see well enough or should I bring a lantern?"

They both paused in response to the off-key serenade. "Oh, that man! He would choose tonight to drink himself silly. How Emma puts up with that, why, I'll never know. You get into the shed and keep that horse quiet until Elmer goes on by. Of course he wouldn't remember if he saw you or not, but best not to take any more chances." She handed Rebekka the coiled rope as she talked and shooed her toward the waiting animal.

Rebekka gladly did as Mrs. Sampson said, keeping her hand over the horse's nostrils when it was inclined to nicker at the man weaving his way past them. As soon as the fellow turned into his own gate and stumbled up the stairs to his house and through the door, she stripped off the bridle and knotted the rope, both into the halter and around a post. "I'll feed you in the morning," she whispered. After a quick hug and pat in total gratitude, she hurried back to the house.

In the meantime, Widow Sampson had lit a lamp and seated herself at the oilcloth-covered table, where she'd set a plate of sugar cookies and two glasses of buttermilk. "Here, I thought some refreshment might be in order since I think your tale may take more than a moment or two." She gestured to the chair,

Rebekka sank into it gratefully. Another shiver shook her frame as she wrapped her feet and legs around each other for warmth. "Thank you for letting me in." She clamped her teeth against a shiver.

"My, my, child, you've gone and caught your death." The widow pushed herself to her feet. 'Til be right back. You need something to warm you right now." Her carpet slippers slip-slapped into a bedroom just behind the kitchen.

Rebekka waited. She could hear the squeak of a chest lid raising and Mrs. Sampson digging around for something. In a minute the woman returned, her cheeks bright red from the effort and her white lawn mobcap set slightly off to the right, giving her the look of a merry elf. "Here ya be," she said as she draped a blanket around Rebekka's shoulders and handed her a pair of hand-knit woolen socks. "These oughta warm you up."

Rebekka leaned forward to slip the socks over her freezing toes. She wasn't sure if her last shudder was from the cold that seemed to penetrate her clear to the bone or if it was the residual fear with the same knifing intensity. How close she'd come to the brink of losing her life the way she knew it. "Thank You, Lord, thank You." Her words kept pace with the carved clock standing sentinel at the door to the dining room.

She drained the last of the buttermilk and set the glass down carefully so as not to disturb the silence. When she looked up, Mrs. Sampson smiled and reached over to pat the younger woman's hand.

"Ja, you are safe here, now. You know you can tell me what happened and it will go no farther than these very walls."

Rebekka nodded. Did she want to tell? She could feel the flush of embarrassment flaming in her cheeks. What words could she use? What really had happened? She chewed on the inside of her right cheek and clutched the blanket closer around her.

"Our Lord says confession is good for the soul and that don't mean only what we done wrong. Now, I know for certain you wouldn't be here in the middle of the night in your nightclothes if something powerful terrible hadn't happened." She studied the face of the young woman before her. "And I know, too, you weren't to be at fault. Not intentionally anyhows."

Rebekka struggled to talk past the chunk of prairie dirt clogging her throat. Dirt, that's what it was all right. What he was. She swallowed again. "I..."

"Take your time, dear, we're in no hurry."

"I'd gone to bed. This is my month out at the Strands', you know, and Mr. and Mrs. are gone to her sister's for a few days." Tears burned at the back of her eyes and down her throat. She squeezed her eyes against the burning and rolled her lips together.

At the feel of the other woman's hand on her own, the tears and fears burst forth and Rebekka laid her head on her arms, the sobs shaking her shoulders. "He…he came at me." Great gulping sobs punctuated her words. She wiped her face on the blanket and tried to sniff the flow back again, but failed miserably.

Mrs. Sampson let her guest cry. She patted the younger woman's arm, "there, there nows" a descant to the guttural sobs. As an occasional sniff replaced the storm, the widow pushed herself to her feet and crossed to the stove to dip a cloth in the warm water of the reservoir on the back of the iron-and-chrome behemoth.

"Here." She handed the cloth to Rebekka. "Now wash your face and hands while I get you a glass of water. Then we'll talk, if you feel up to it."

Rebekka nodded and did as told. How wonderful it felt to be taken care of, like her mother had done back in the good years before—she slammed the door in her mind that had opened just a crack. Stay with the here and now; no good looking back.

The chair creaked as Widow Sampson sat back down. She had set two glasses of water on the table. "I could start up the stove and make coffee," she said as she pushed one glass over to Rebekka, "but the noise might wake up my boarders and that wouldn't be very kind."

"I…I never thought, I mean—I thought you'd have room for another. Are your rooms full, then?" Rebekka's heart took up that erratic thumping again. What would she do if... ?

"Now, now, just don't you worry yourself none. I got a room for you. Why, Mr. Prescott moved out just two days ago. I cleaned it all right nice again, so you can see, it's just waiting for you. Nice corner room it is, too."

Rebekka inhaled a sigh of pure relief. At least something was going right. She wiggled her feet in the wool socks, scooting them back and forth on the floor and then wrapping them together under the chair. She brushed an errant tear from the corner of her eye. Why had this happened to her?

"Well, as I started to say," and the words drifted off as her mind returned to the farmhouse. She clamped her jaw against the fury she could feel exploding in her chest. "He attacked me! That. . .that—" She couldn't think of any words bad enough. "And he thought I was funny. He was laughing. Until he rushed me and I hit him."

"You hit him?"

"With the pitcher from the commode. When he crashed to the floor, I grabbed my clothes and ran out the door." She continued with her story, not leaving out any details.

"Well, I never."

"I never either. And now I don't know what to do. Can I please stay here until I talk with Mr. Larson, the superintendent? I...I can pay." She could feel her mouth drop open. "At least, I can if I can get my things from their house. But I have money in the bank, too, ...some." She raised her gaze from studying her clenched fists.

"Now, don't you worry. Why, when we tell Lars what happened, he'll go out there personally and whip that young pup. Surely the sheriff could do something about this."

"No!"

"No?"

"Don't you see, I can't tell anyone. If this story gets around, I'll lose my position. Teachers are fired for a lot less reason than this."

"But it wasn't your fault." The words exploded from the widow's lips. She caught herself. "I know. I know. The snickers. The men will all get together and say you enticed him. That's what Adolph'll tell anyone who asks."

"I know. And those who don't. What can I do?"

"Let me think on this, child. You go on and get a good night's sleep and we'll let the good Lord tell us what to do. He never makes mistakes." The older woman sighed and shook her head.

"You ... you believe me, don't you?" Rebekka pushed her cuticle back with a trembling finger. She looked up to see Mrs. Sampson smiling at her.

"Yes. Have no doubts in your mind about me. And God, who knows your heart, will work this out. God has a plan in mind, you can be sure of that."

"I know…I think." Rebekka caught herself on a yawn. She pushed herself to her feet. "And you. . .you won't tell anyone? Not ever?"

"Come along, my dear. That question don't even bear an answer." Mrs. Sampson picked up the kerosene lamp and led the way up the stairs. She opened the second door on the right. "The bed's all made up. I'll bring up warm water in the morning, but usually my guests come downstairs for their own. Breakfast will be at seven, prompt. Mrs. Knutson has to open her shop at eight." She set the lamp down on the five-drawer oak dresser and dug a spill from the drawer to light the room's lamp from the one she brought in.

Rebekka stared around in delight as the warm glow of the kerosene lamp brought to life thc rainbow colors in the log cabin patchwork quilt on the spindle bed. A hand-crocheted doily kept the matching pitcher and bowl from scratching the top of the commode; a braided rag rug lay by the bed, ready to keep feet off the cold floor on a winter morning.

"Oh, this is beautiful." She looked around to find brass hooks on the back of the door and hung up her dress.

"I have an armoire in the storage room that I could bring in here for you to hang up your clothes. If you decide to stay, that is."

She chuckled at the sight of the younger woman trying to disguise another yawn. "You go on to sleep now. Nothing can hurt you here." She picked up her lamp and closed the door behind her with a quiet click.

Rebekka felt the bottom of her night dress and realized it was damp. But, she had nothing else in which to sleep. She'd just pulled back the covers when she heard a tap on the door. "Yes?"

Mrs. Sampson peaked through the crack in the door and held out a faded flannel nightgown. "Here, yours is still damp, I'm sure. Don't want to take a chance on you coming down with something."

"Thank you." Rebekka crossed the room and accepted the offering. "You are so kind."

"Ja, well you need some kindness right now." She harrumphed her way back out the door.

"Oh, Lord above, what am I going to do?" Rebekka either prayed or pleaded, she wasn't sure which, after she snuggled down under the crisp sheets. If she told Mr. Larson exactly what had happened, would he believe her or throw her out? If she didn't tell him, how would she explain the need to leave the Strand farm before the school year was up? Where would she go? She allowed her gaze to drift around the peaceful room, where the moon cast bright spots upon the waxed floor and the sheer curtains fluttered in the night breeze. She gulped back a leftover sob. Resolutely, she climbed from the bed and knelt on the rug.

"Heavenly Father, I have to leave this in Your hands. I don't know what to do. I thank You for sending Your angels to protect me." She shuddered again at the memory. "Please, if it be Your will, I would be pleased to stay in Willowford. Thank You again. Amen." She rose to her feet and slipped back into the cooling bed. The idea of closing her eyes and letting the memories surge back was about as frightening as the actual event.

She rubbed her cold feet together and then snuggled them up into the folds of the nightgown. Warmth stole around her, rich and comforting, like the sense of peace that crept along into her heart. On a gentle sigh, her eyelids drifted closed. When they fluttered open one last time, she smiled at the thought. There were two smiling angels sitting at the foot of her bed. What a wondrous dream.

She greeted the morning cockcrow with a catlike stretch, starting with her arms and working down clear to her toes. "Thank You, Father," she breathed at the thought of the restful sleep she'd had—no nightmares…no memories. She sat straight up. But what about the angels? She chuckled as she left the bed and went to stand in front of the window.

Dawn had bowed out, giving way to sunrise and the glorious birdsongs greeting the new day. The aromas of freshly turned earth and the green shoots sprouting up to meet the sun drifted in on a teasing breeze.

A tap at the door caught her attention. "Just your warm water, dear." The cheery voice brought a smile to Rebekka's face.

"Come in, Mrs. Sampson." Rebekka hurried across the floor to open the door. "Thank you so much." She stepped back to let the bustling housekeeper in.

"And how did you sleep? Was the bed all right?" She set the pitcher in the bowl on the oak stand and placed the towel draped over her arm beside the bowl. "There's soap there. I made it myself. I add rose petals for the fragrance." She peered into her guest's face. "You look rested, in spite of all you went through." She patted Rebekka's arm. "Breakfast in half an hour." And out the door she went.

Rebekka clapped her mouth closed, sure now that she understood how one felt after being whirled around in one of the summer tornadoes. Then she took her white blouse and dark skirt down from their hook and shook them to dislodge both horsehair and wrinkles. After laying them across the bed, she poured water into the bowl. As she picked up the soap, she inhaled its faint fragrance. What a luxury after the lye soap she'd been forced to use on the Strand farm.

After washing, Rebekka stared from her nightgown to her skirt and blouse, then to her feet. She had no underthings and no shoes. How could she call on Mr. Larson like this?

She combed her fingers through her hair and wished for the brush and comb sitting on her dresser at the farm. All of her things. She had to retrieve them, but how?

Teeth clenched against the surging anger, she pulled the nightgown back over her head and picked up the white blouse. Noticing smudges on the front and sleeves, she took the garment over to the washstand and applied the soap and water and some hard scrubbing to remove the stains. She dried the blouse as much as possible and smoothed the damp surface with her fingers. All the while doing this, she brooded over the injustice of it all.

It wasn't her fault! But if it wasn't, why did she feel so guilty? Why did she feel like she should wash again and keep on scrubbing?

She shoved her arms into the sleeves and buttoned the pearl buttons, then put on her walnut brown serge skirt. Standing in front of the mirror, she finger-combed her hair again and braided it, clamping the end with her fingertips until she could ask Mrs. Sampson for some pins.

As she made her way down the stairs, she could hear two women's voices coming from the kitchen. A canary trilled when they laughed, adding his music to the homey scene. Rebekka paused in the doorway.

The round table was now set for three, a pot with bobbing pink cabbage roses set between the cut-glass salt and pepper shakers and a gleaming golden mold of butter.

The gold-and-black canary hopped about his cage in the front of the window, pipping his song as if he were responsible for the coming of the new day.

Rebekka cleared her throat. "All, good morning."

"Oh, there you are." Widow Sampson turned from stirring her kettle on the gleaming black stove. "Mrs. Knutson, you know

Rebekka Stenesrude, the schoolmarm, don't you?"

A diminutive woman, as slim as Widow Sampson was round, nodded and smiled at the same time. "Of course. I. . .ah—" She ducked her chin and made as if to sit down then paused from fussing with the chair. "If there's anything you need..."

Rebekka tore her gaze from the other boarder to stare helplessly at Mrs. Sampson. When the older woman barely shook her head, Rebekka breathed again. Thankfully, she hadn't told the secret.

"I mean, Alma said you had to leave your things. Whatever I have that you can use, you are welcome to it." Her voice faded into a whisper. "I don't want to be presumptuous…or anything."

Rebekka felt like circling the table and wrapping the bitty bird of a woman in her arms. Instead, she clamped her fingers over the back of the chair in front of her. "Thank you." She picked up the end of her braid. "You wouldn't by any chance have extra hairpins, would you?"

"Oh, yes." A bright smile lighting her face, the little woman darted out the door and up the stairs.

"Never worry, your secret is safe with me, but I had to tell her something." Mrs. Sampson placed a filled bowl of oatmeal at each place. "I have a plan. We'll talk when she leaves for her shop."

Abigail Knutson returned and placed pins and a comb and brush by Rebekka's place. "There, and now, let's eat. I mustn't be late."

After grace, the three women chatted happily while eating their biscuits and jam besides the oatmeal and coffee. Rebekka wiped her mouth with the napkin she'd spread on her lap and tucked it back into the carved wooden napkin ring. "Thank you. I haven't enjoyed breakfast like this in a long time." She raised a hand and shook her head when Mrs. Sampson tried to refill the coffee cup.

Mrs. Knutson left immediately after placing her breakfast things in the sink. "Now you remember, if I can help with anything, you be sure to tell me."

Rebekka nodded and rose to take her things to the sink, also.

"Now." Mrs. Sampson sat back down after the front door closed. She lifted her coffee cup to her mouth and, after a sip, she pointed to the other chair. "Sit down and I'll tell you my plan."

Chapter 4

Well, what do we do?" Rebekka asked.

Mrs. Sampson took another sip of her coffee and smiled at Rebekka over the rim. "First of all, we take a buggy out to the Strand farm, return the horse, and pick up your things."

"But what about Adolph?"

"By the time we get out there, he should be out in the fields with spring planting. When did you say Mr. and Mrs. Strand are coming back?"

"Tomorrow, Sunday, on the evening train. And you're right. Adolph is behind in his work, so he'll be pushing hard." Rebekka raised stricken eyes to her benefactress. "I don't ever want to see him again."

"I know, my dear." Mrs. Sampson patted Rebekka's hands, clenched on the tablecloth. "That's the beauty of my idea. This way you can return the horse. Adolph is such that he'd probably turn you in for stealing the animal."

"Oh, no. He wouldn't." Rebekka shoved herself to her feet with such fury, the chair rocked behind her. She stormed across the kitchen and back. "Yes, he would. Let's go. I need my shoes and other things so I can go talk with Mr. Larson."

"And I'll be right behind you. You won't get any resistance from him with me along. I know a thing or two about what's going on in this town that just might come in handy right about now."

Rebekka whirled from her pacing and stopped at Mrs. Sampson's side. "You are a jewel among thousands. I can't wait to begin."

"Well, you wash up those dishes while I go get a team at the livery. Then we'll be on our way." Mrs. Sampson paused at the door. "And Rebekka, remember, I'm behind you all the way."

The young woman tried to smile through the film that suddenly covered her eyes but sniffed instead.

The drive out to the Strand farm passed quickly as the two women used the time to get to know each other better. Instead of a wagon, they rode in the comfort of a well-sprung buggy with a flashy chestnut horse trotting between the shafts. The horse that had brought Rebekka to town kept pace behind the buggy, shaking its head now and again at the lead rope.

As they drew nearer, Rebekka slipped into silence. The sight of the house in the distance sent terror coursing from her toes to the top of her head and back down again at breakneck speed. She could feel the fear gnawing at her stomach. What if he was up at the house? She couldn't even bear to use his name.

Mrs. Sampson kept the reins in one hand and used the other to pat Rebekka on the knee. "Now, now. This'll be all over in just a few minutes. There's no need to be afraid. I just know our Father will make this go easy."

Rebekka couldn't force an answer from her dry throat if her life depended upon it.

But for the creaking of the windmill above the well house, the farm lay silent in the sunshine. Rebekka watched the windows carefully to see if the dog's barking brought anyone to peer out. As soon as the dog realized that Rebekka rode in the buggy, he yipped and leaped in apology. *At least the dog likes me,* Rebekka thought, bringing a smile to her quivering lips.

Liking you is just the problem, her inner voice remonstrated with her other thoughts. *If he hadn't liked you so much ...* Rebekka turned to Mrs. Sampson. "Why don't we pull up at the barn and I'll take the horse inside. Then we can go to the house."

Ten minutes later they were out the door and trotting back down the lane. Rebekka allowed herself both a prayer and a sigh of relief. With her personal items stuffed into a carpetbag and her school things in a box she found on the back porch, she dared breathe in a breath of freedom.

"Maybe I should have left them a letter or something." She looked over her shoulder at the slumbering farm.

"You can always mail them one." Mrs. Sampson flicked the reins over the chestnut's back and he picked up the pace.

"I know what I'd like to tell them."

"Ja, I know."

"I just wish there were some way to…to..."

"Get even?"

"No, I mean, yes." Rebekka paused and drew in a deep breath. "I mean, there should be some way to punish him for what he did and to keep him from doing so again."

"I learned a long time ago that the best revenge is letting God handle the situation. There's a verse, 'Vengeance is mine…saith the Lord,' and since He sees more than we do, I'd kinda rather let Him dole out the punishment."

Rebekka thought awhile on the widows words. "But it seems He takes so long to go about it."

"That's true." Widow Sampson flicked the reins again. "Git up there now. We got plenty important business to tend to."

Widow Sampson looped the reins around the whip pole and descended to the ground in time to lift the box out of the back of the buggy. After tying the horse, the women made their way into the boardinghouse and carried Rebekka's things upstairs to her room.

Rebekka felt herself smiling at the curtains billowing in the fresh breeze. *I already think of this as my room,* she thought in amazement. After two years of moving from home to home, she hadn't thought of any place as her own in a long time.

Mrs. Sampson bustled back out of the room and left Rebekka to redress and redo her hair. Staring in the mirror, Rebekka let her mind wander. Not since she was little had she had a room of her own. After her father started drowning his sorrows in the bottle at the local saloon, she and her mother had been moved from pillar to post with never a place to call their own. And rarely a moment's peace,

But at one time, she'd had a room with a quilt and rug and bright white curtains and a picture of Jesus on the wall. Jesus with the lambs. Rebekka laid her brush back on the dresser. Back at her grandmother's house, she'd had a real home. Back in her grandmother's house, life had been altogether different.

She wound the braid into a scroll at the base of her skull and pushed in the pins to secure it. After dampening a finger, she smoothed back the tendrils about her face that resisted confinement. Now she must present herself to Mr. Larson as her true self. *The old-maid schoolteacher who couldn't*—she amended the thought, *wouldn't—stay with the Strands any longer.* And she wouldn't, nay, couldn't tell him why.

The two women climbed back up in the buggy with nary a word between them. Mrs. Sampson slapped the reins over the horse's back and clucked him forward. They turned right on Main Street and trotted past the mercantile, the Lutheran church, and the doctor's dispensary. Mr. Larson lived up on the bluff overlooking the Missouri River. The horse dug in its feet to gain footing on the grade.

"He should be home for dinner about now. Good a time as any to be the bearer of good news."

"Good news?"

"Ja, you're still here." Mrs. Sampson tightened the reins and tied them around the whipstock as soon as the horse stopped. "And you're only asking for a permanent place to live. Not too big a request, considering."

"But…but, I can't tell him what really happened."

"No need. Just tell him what you want." She climbed down from the buggy and tied the horse to the rail fence. An apple tree in full bloom filled the air with the fragrance of spring and spread protective arms over the rope swing hung from its branch. A rag doll leaned against the trunk as if comforted by the support.

Rebekka paused at the picket gate. Two of the Larson children attended her school and she knew there were two more at home. How could she talk to the father with his children around?

Mrs. Sampson took Rebekka's arm and led her up to the steps. "Don't be afraid. You have nothing to fear."

Ja, sure. Rebekka felt like ripping her arm from the firm clasp and running back down the road. What would she say if he asked her why? She'd never learned to lie. It was a sin, remember. Her mother had sent her to bed without any supper when she told just a little white fib. What would she say?

She tucked a stray wisp of hair back into the severe coil and squared her shoulders. After one last glance at the woman beside her, Rebekka raised her hand and tapped on the door.

The door opened and Mrs. Larson greeted them with a wide smile. "Come in, come in. Why, if I'd knowed you were coming, we could have set another two places at the table for dinner." She wiped her hands on her skirt-length white apron and gestured them toward the sitting room. "Can I get you some coffee? We'll be having dessert in just a minute. Lars, look who's here, Miss Stenesrude and Widow Sampson."

After exchanging a conspiratorial glance, Rebekka and Mrs. Sampson followed their hostess. Nothing had changed. Give Mrs. Larson a moment and look out. When she started talking it took stronger hearts than theirs to stop her.

She bustled them into sitting on the horsehair sofa in the sitting room and met herself going out again.

"I. . .I need to talk with Mr. Larson," Rebekka called to the retreating back. The woman bustled on.

"Whew," Mrs. Sampson drew the back of her hand across her forehead as if to wipe away a flood of perspiration. She leaned back against the stiff sofa and turned to warm Rebekka with a smile. "Can't say as I ever am prepared when I see Elmira after a time. She talks faster than a tornado spins." She kept her voice to a whisper.

Rebekka clamped her bottom lip between her teeth and forced herself to sit perfectly erect, her feet primly together, her shoulders back and chin high. That was the only way to keep from turning into a mound of mush. Surely this couldn't be worse than facing a class of twenty brand-new students, ranging in age from five to fifteen. She bit her lip. Yes, it could. What if she had to lie? Why, oh, why couldn't Adolph keep his hands and lascivious thoughts to himself? Only with sternest self-control did she keep herself from shuddering.

Mr. Lars Larson sported the sunburned face and pure white forehead of a man who spent his days in the blazing Dakota sunshine. No ruler could have drawn a more perfect line than the one his hatband had done, dividing his face. He wore the sober look of a proper Norwegian upon learning that women were calling upon him in his professional capacity as school superintendent.

"Now, what can I do for you ladies?" he asked after all the proper greetings were exchanged.

A movement at the door caught Rebekka's attention. Two shining faces with smiles fit to crack a rock, peered around the corner. The girl, braids pulling her hair into some semblance of order, waved and then hid her giggle behind her hands.

"Come, children, say hello to your teacher and then go about your chores." Mr. Larson shot an apologetic glance at the women sitting on his sofa and beckoned the children. Two smaller replicas tagged behind the boy and girl who were her students.

"Hello, Inga and Ernie." Rebekka reached out her hands to clasp those of the towheaded children and draw them to her side. "Maybe you could introduce me to your brother and sister."

"This is Mary and Johnny. They're twins." Inga took over as the oldest.

"They're babies. They don't go to school like us big kids." Ernie puffed out his skinny chest, visible under the straps of his faded overalls.

The two little ones clung to the chair where their father sat. When Rebekka greeted them, they each stuck one finger in their mouths and ducked their heads in perfect unison.

"They always do everything the same." Ernie turned his serious blue-eyed gaze on his teacher. "Ma says that's 'cause they was borned at the same time."

Rebekka nodded. She dredged up every bit of schoolmarm control to keep from ordering the children out to play so the adults could talk.

Mr. Larson must have sensed her feelings for he patted the twins on the bottom of their matching overalls and sent them out of the room. "Inga, Ernie, enough now. You go help your ma."

The children filed out of the room, sending smiles over their shoulders.

Mr. Larson turned as they left. "And Inga, close the door behind you."

Rebekka breathed a sigh of relief at his consideration. All of a sudden, the coming interview didn't seem quite as frightening. Surely a man as considerate of his children as this would be sympathetic to her plight.

"Now, you want to talk with me. How can I help you?" He looked from Rebekka to Mrs. Sampson and back.

The silence deepened as the discomfort level in the room rose. Rebekka looked toward Mrs. Sampson and received a nod of encouragement. "I…I—" She pictured herself in front of a classroom of students and took a deep breath. "I cannot remain at the Strands' any longer. The situation there is totally untenable and I must have another place to live." The words gained strength and purpose as they followed one another, starting at a stagger and ending in a march.

Mr. Larson leaned back in his chair, rubbing the line of demarcation between summer and winter on his forehead. "Well, you know, we've always done things for the schoolteacher this way. He or she, you in this case, moves from home to home throughout the school year. We excuse those folks who absolutely can't afford to feed the teacher or who don't have room for one."

"I know." Rebekka lifted her chin a mite higher.

"What else can we do? Now, if you were married, you'd be living in your husband's house and then there wouldn't be no problem."

Rebekka bit her lip on a retort to that nugget of information.

"Just what's the problem with finishing out your stay at the Strands'?"

Rebekka refused to cringe at the blunt question. Instead, she looked Mr. Larson straight in the face and answered, "I'd rather not say." Now she knew what a witness must feel like in court.

Out of the corner of her eye Rebekka could see Mrs. Sampson straighten herself, an act that reminded her of a hen all fluffed up and ready to attack anyone who disturbs her chicks.

Mr. Larson raised a hand. "Please don't think I'm not concerned about this. I am only trying to get to the bottom of a problem."

Mrs. Sampson cleared her throat.

Rebekka felt a burst of strength, as if she were inhaling confidence. "We have worked together now for the good of Willowford's children for nearly two years. Wouldn't you agree that it's been a productive two years, Mr. Larson?"

"Well, of course."

"Wouldn't you like to continue the progress that we've made?"

Without giving him time for a response, she sailed on. "At this time, we have all the school-age children in the district enrolled in school and two of our eldest are preparing for college. Now, wouldn't you say those are major accomplishments?"

"Yes, I—"

Mrs. Sampson leaned back just a trifle.

"I would be sorry to see the education of Willowford's children suffer even the smallest of disruptions, wouldn't you?" Rebekka asked.

Mr. Larson nodded.

"I hear there's a shortage of teachers coming out of Normal School the last couple of years." Mrs. Sampson nodded sagely. "The folks of Willowford do appreciate having a trained teacher over in the schoolhouse." While unspoken, her "for a change" rang through the quiet of the room.

Mr. Larson rubbed his forehead again. "Now, look. This is the way we've always done it. And it's worked. Now, why should we change?"

"Remember that incident one night last summer?" Mrs. Sampson tossed the question out, casually, as if she were pitching a pebble into a pond.

Mr. Larson's lower face matched his forehead. He closed his eyes. "Oh, my."

"Now, the ways I see it, Miss Stenesrude would be much closer to the school, were she to live in my house. Beings we're just across the creek from the schoolhouse."

"But we have no money."

"And that way she could go over on cold mornings to start the stove earlier. Keep Willowford's children warmer, you might say."

Only a groan rose from the other chair.

"You can be sure I would do my part for the children of my community and give you a real good rate. In fact, it might be that Miss Stenesrude would be willing to help me out some, to help pay her expenses, you know."

Mr. Larson leaned forward. "I'd have to clear this with the rest of the school board, you realize."

"Like you did the well?" Mrs. Sampson smiled, but the whisper penetrated to the bone.

"I take it this would be agreeable to you?" Mr. Larson turned to Rebekka. At her nod, he continued. "When would you like me to go with you to pick up your things at Strands'?"

"We've already done that," Mrs. Sampson said, "I know you won't regret this, Lars. You've made a wise decision and the fewer people who know about this, the better. Don't you agree?"

Mr. Larson mumbled something as he pushed himself to his feet. "Let me see what is keeping Elmira with that coffee."

Rebekka breathed a sigh of pure relief. She hadn't had to lie. But on the way home, she was surely going to ask Mrs. Sampson what had happened last summer.

By Monday morning Rebekka felt like she'd lived at the widow's boardinghouse all her life. While she'd had a nightmare on Saturday night, Sunday night she slept through and woke up to face the new day with joy and a sense of adventure.

Rebekka felt a smile tug at the corners of her mouth as she lay in bed relishing the peace and loveliness surrounding her. While dancing in the early morning breeze, the sheer curtains struggled against the ties that looped them back When she planted her feet on the braided rug, she resisted the urge to dance along with the curtains. Stretching her arms over her head to banish the last yawn, she crossed to the window and knelt to place her crossed arms on the sill.

"This is the day that the Lord hath made, I will rejoice and be glad in it." Her verse was certainly easier to live up to today than it had been in the days past. "Thank You, Father, for bringing me here to live. It's been so long since I felt like I had a real home. What would it be like to have a home of my own?" She thought of the Larsons, their fine home on the hill, and their towheaded brood. Would she ever have a home like that? Was there a man out there somewhere who would invite her to share his home? Who would love her with the kind of love Christ talked about? Whom she would love the same way?

A robin pipped his early morning love song to the heavens from the tree in the corner of the backyard. Rebekka searched the branches until she saw him, his red breast puffed out and beak open wide. "Hope you find her, Mr. Robin," she whispered. "Everyone needs that perfect mate." She swallowed the lost feeling that crept over her and pushed herself to her feet.

"How silly, mooning around like that." She scolded herself all the way through her morning wash and even while brushing her hair. Long, wavy strands that shaded from wren brown to deep sienna snapped in the electricity from her brush, creating a cloud about her head that reached halfway down her back.

She smiled at the heart-shaped face in the mirror. What would it be like to wear her hair free but for two combs to catch it back from her face? She laughed at the sight of her hands trying to harness all that wildness. What was the matter with her this morning? She wet the brush and slicked the unruly strands straight back and into their usual braid and the braid into its coil at the base of her head.

She checked the mirror again. There now, the schoolmarm was back in control where she should be. The old-maid schoolmarm who would always teach other peoples' children to the best of her ability.

She quickly made up her bed and, picking up the slop jar, made her way downstairs for breakfast.

The feeling of anticipation returned as she crossed the bridge that spanned Bryde Creek. The creek flowed full and brown, swelled with runoff from the spring rains. At the sound of her feet tapping on the planks, Rebekka gave a little skip and four quick heel smacks to add to the stream s spring song. Soon the summer would be here and what would she do then?

She continued the thought. Eight more days of school and then the big picnic. Everyone was already having trouble studying and the older boys had left weeks earlier to help with spring planting. Other years she had returned to stay with her mother in Minnesota, but since her mother died, she had no family — no immediate family that is. Somewhere she might have relatives on her father's side, but no one knew for sure. Her mother had a sister somewhere, but they had lost touch through the years of her father's dragging them from pillar to post and back again.

"And that's what being married gets you," she warned the creek "So stay the way you are." Her heels clicked a rhythm of their own as she headed on toward the schoolhouse. She looked around to see if anyone had heard or seen her—talking to the creek no less. Surely they'd think she'd been addled by the sun or something. Definitely not a good example for a teacher to set.

She looked over her shoulder, a grin peeking out around her admonishments. So was the creek male or female and was it really single? Or would you call it a marriage when two creeks flowed together and then into the river? She shook her head. Maybe she had been addled by something. Or maybe she'd been around her pupils too long. Those were the kinds of questions she encouraged from them.

She'd written the instructions for the first lesson of the day on the blackboard before some pupils arrived giggling at the door. Rebekka put all thoughts of her own questions out of her mind and concentrated on her pupils. She checked the small watch she wore pinned to her plain white blouse. Ten minutes until school began.

"Mith Thtenthrude," a small charmer with two missing front teeth lisped. "Our cat had kittenth."

Rebekka squatted down to be on eye level. "How many did she have?"

Emily wrinkled her forehead and began raising fingers until she showed four on one hand and one on the other. "Five."

"Very good. Is she taking good care of them?"

"Yeth. Thee had them in Bernie'th bed." She clapped her hands over her mouth to stifle the giggle. Her blue eyes sparkled, and when Rebekka laughed with her, they both looked back to see Bernie plunking his lunch pail down on his desk. Emily whispered between her fingers. "Bernie wath mad."

Rebekka rose to her feet and checked her watch again. "Bernie, would you be so kind as to ring the warning bell?"

Bernie nodded his pleasure and scampered out to the cloakroom, where the heavy rope hung from the bell tower. As the bell pealed its warning across the town, she could hear the children shouting and laughing as they ran toward the school.

Yes, this would be another high-spirited day and there was so much she wished to teach them before the end of the year. She waited for them at the door as they lined up, boys on one side and girls on the other, starting with the youngest in front and ending with the oldest. The boys' line was regrettably short since all those over twelve were helping their fathers in the fields.

"Bernie, the final bell." She waited while the tones rang out again. It was precisely eight o'clock. "Elizabeth, will you lead the morning prayer?" At the girl's nod, Rebekka opened the Bible she carried. "Today we will read from Psalm Twenty-three. 'The Lord is my shepherd; I shall not want.' Now, let us repeat that together." All the voices raised in unison at the familiar verse. At Rebekka's nod, Elizabeth bowed her head and waited for the shuffling to cease. Her musical voice joined with the bird choruses from the trees planted on each side of the school.

"Father in Heaven, we thank Thee for this day. Thank Thee that we can go to school and learn so many things. Please help us to do our best." Elizabeth paused, then finished swiftly. "And let everyone come to the picnic. Amen."

Rebekka rolled her lips together to keep from smiling. She and every child there knew Elizabeth was hoping that James Johnson would be in attendance. Elizabeth and James had been making eyes at each other for the last year.

"Thorlief, will you lead the flag salute?" At his answering grin, she turned and led her charges into the schoolroom.

When all the feet ceased shuffling, the boy's voice began, "I pledge allegiance to the flag. . ." At the finish, they all took their seats and folded their hands on their desktops.

Rebekka sat down at the piano and sounded the opening chords for "America the Beautiful." As the voices rose in song, she felt shivers run down her back. The children sang so wonderfully.

After the singing, she walked to the front of the room. "Today we'll start with reading. Take out your books, please."

By the end of the day, Rebekka felt like she'd been whipped through the eye of a hurricane—twice. After the last child departed, she had yet to sweep the floor and wash the blackboards. These were all chores the older boys did when they were in attendance, so she missed their presence doubly. She also needed to work on her lesson plans for the rest of the week.

When she finally closed the schoolhouse door, she sank down on the steps and wrapped her arms around her knees. At least she didn't have to walk two miles home again like she had done for the last month. And other places had been farther. She breathed in deeply of the soft air, content to be right where she was at that very moment.

Rebekka was as ready as her pupils were for the school picnic.

They'd planned games and contests for every age group from the three-year-old race to the horseshoe pitching for the older men, with the school board providing awards. Everyone in town and the surrounding area was invited.

That Saturday dawned with a thundershower, but by ten o'clock, the sun shone brightly and folks began to gather. Trestle tables had been set out and they groaned under the array of food brought by the women.

Rebekka stood on the steps and surveyed the colorful crowd. If numbers were any indication, this would be the very best school picnic that Willowford had ever seen. Only one cloud floated on her horizon—would Adolph Strand have the gall to appear? She checked every wagon and buckboard that drove up and tied up in the grove down by the creek.

"Anything else you need?" Mr. Larson appeared at her side.

"No, nothing. Just enjoying the excitement. The children have been looking forward to this day nearly as much as Christmas." Rebekka returned a wave from a newly arrived family. "Thank you for the prizes you brought. And also for the extra gifts. It means so much to the little ones to be part of the school program."

"Well, you met my two. They'd be crushed if everyone got something and not them, so I brought plenty. We'll save the left-overs for next year." He picked a stalk of grass and nibbled on the succulent stem. "Ah," he muttered as he chewed the stalk and spit out the tough section. "Umm," he started as he studied the toe of his dusty boot.

"Yes?"

He looked up at the tops of the trees bordering the creek. "There…ah…been any problems, I mean anyone hanging around or anything?"

Rebekka could recognize the flush creeping up Mr. Larson's neck because it matched the one on her own. "No, no problem. And thank you for your concern." She bent down to answer a question from one of her young students, grateful for the distraction.

When she stood up again, Mr. Larson was striding across the schoolyard. *Bless you,* she thought. *You really care and yet it is so hard for you to show it.*

By late afternoon parents were loading tired and even some sleeping children into the wagons, gathering up their things, and heading home to do evening chores. If the enthusiasm of those departing meant anything, the picnic had indeed been the success Rebekka dreamed.

Now it was time to close the school for the summer. Since several of the women had already helped clean while the children were running three-legged and sack races, the building had the smell and sound of summer slumber. The last remaining pupils policed the yard, cleaning up every scrap of paper, and then charged off to their homes.

"Bye, Miss Stenesrude. See you in the fall. Have a good summer." The calls went back and forth. Mr. Larson locked the door for the final time and pocketed the key.

"What are you figuring to do this summer?" he asked as they stopped at the rail fence bounding the schoolyard.

"I don't rightly know, besides helping Mrs. Sampson, that is." She looked up at him with a smile. "But I'm sure the good Lord knows. He promised to provide."

"Ja, that's right." He tipped his hat. "Be seein' you then." He started off, then turned. "You want a ride back to town?"

"No, thank you. I like the walk." She waved him off and, after picking up her bag loaded with books and papers, ambled toward the boardinghouse. When she paused on the bridge and looked down, the creek had retreated to its summertime ramblings, burbling over stones and babbling around tree roots. The song it sang seemed to promise good things ahead.

Even though she was tired from the rigorous day, Rebekka found herself smiling with the stream and singing its song on her way home.

"There's a letter for you," Mrs. Sampson called when Rebekka walked in the door.

Chapter 5

"Next stop, Willowford."

The conductor called. *Next stop, home,* thought Rebekka as she stared out the window, trying to catch a glimpse of a familiar landmark. Two months was a long time to have been gone. She leaned her head back against the seat and thought of all that had happened since she had opened the letter…the letter from her grandmother, her father's mother.

She still couldn't believe how they had found her. And now she had family. She, who had no one, suddenly had a grandmother, an aunt, three cousins, and various other in-laws and almost in-laws. People in Minneapolis certainly did live differently than her friends in Willowford. Why, she'd never seen the contraptions called horseless carriages, electric lights, and indoor privies. Granted, she'd read about those things in newspapers, but now she'd seen them with her own eyes.

She brought herself back to the present and peered out the window, checking if she could see the Missouri yet. Instead she saw smoke.

Smoke across the prairie, as far as she could see! Prairie fire! Fire between here and Willowford. Which way was the wind blowing? Would the train be trapped? The thoughts raced through her mind like flames driven before a gale-force wind.

"No worry, folks," the conductor announced in his sonorous

voice. “The wind is coming from the east, blowing due west, so we’re in no danger.”

Unless the wind changes, Rebekka let her thoughts drift to the cataclysm on the prairie. While the train slowed down, she leaned forward, as if she could encourage it to forge ahead. What was happening in Willowford? There was nothing to stop the fire between here and there. She’d seen the Willowford Volunteer Fire Department practice. Had they put their skills to use?

As the train covered the remaining miles, the prairie on each side of the tracks lay charred and blackened. Some fence posts still smoldered, and here and there a haystack sent tendrils of smoke skyward. Farm buildings off to the north lay in an oasis of green where the farmer had set a backfire to save his home. Plowed firebreaks kept the rampaging inferno from gobbling up another farm. A third lay in smoking ruins.

“They was some good, the soddies like I lived in as a child,” one of the passengers said. “Prairie fire burnt right on over us. All we had to eat that year was potatoes. Good thing the livestock lived in a soddie barn, too. I’ll never forget us runnin’ to herd the cows and chickens inside.”

Rebekka shuddered. But people didn’t live in soddies anymore, usually.

Smoking piles of animal dung dotted a pasture. She hated to look in case there were also dead animals lying around, but so far she didn’t see any.

The train whistle sent its haunting call ahead of them. Rebekka leaned her forehead against the grimy window. The feeling of relief at the sight of buildings still standing caused a lump to rise in her throat. But where was the creek, the trees that lived along its bank? And that smoking ruin she could barely see for the tears streaming down her cheeks. The schoolhouse lay in smoldering rubble.

Her schoolhouse. All the books for which they’d saved and scrimped. The flag, the bell. . .had she left any of her personal things in the desk? She thought of the shelves of books donated for a library someday. All gone.

She drew a handkerchief from her bag and wiped her eyes. As the train crossed the railroad bridge over the creek, she understood why it was hard to see from a distance. The men had cut the trees to use the creek as a firebreak. The trunks and limbs not under water still smoldered. The men of the town leaned on shovels or tossed dirt on stubborn patches. Black with soot, they stared at the train, their weariness evident in the drooped shoulders and slackjawed faces.

Rebekka blew her nose. She couldn't cry anymore now. At least they'd saved the town. They could rebuild the school. But until then, where would they meet? The church? School was due to start in three short weeks. What would they use for books?

Her mind raced ahead as she stepped down on the station platform and thanked the conductor for his assistance. Had anyone been injured? Guilt stabbed her as all she thought about was her school. Buildings could be rebuilt, but what if someone had died or was severely burned? Were the children all right?

She set off down the street to Widow Sampson's boardinghouse. Men congregated at the saloon where the owner had rolled out a keg and was handing out free beer.

"Miss Stenesrude, Miss Stenesrude." A young boy, blackened and unrecognizable, came running across the dusty street. "Did ya see? The schoolhouse burnt right down."

"Yes, I saw. Is everyone all right?"

"Ja, just some burns from blowing stuff. And everybody's coughing. You never had no tiling hurt like breathing smoke. Pa says we'll prob'ly start school in the church until they can build a new school."

"Thank you, Kenny." Rebekka felt relieved she'd finally figured out who her bearer of bad tidings was.

"Can I help you with your bag?" The boy fell in step beside her. "I'm plenty strong."

With a flash of trepidation, Rebekka relinquished her bag to the boy's sooty hand. How would she get the soot off the handle? She pushed the thought back as unchristian. Her "Thank you" sounded more fervent because of her doubts.

"Ah, my dear, I am so glad you are returned and safe through all this." Mrs. Sampson wiped her hands on her apron and grasped one of Rebekka's in both of hers. "How was your family? Ain't it awful about the school? But thank the good Lord, He spared the town. They was all ready to send the women and children to the other side of the river by boats and the ferry, but we was fightin' the fire right alongside the men."

Rebekka felt a stab of guilt. She should have been here helping. "Were they able to save anything from the school?"

Mrs. Sampson just shook her head. "And no one's been out to the farmers yet to see how they fared. We just came home and washed up. My hair's still damp." She patted the coronet of braids she wore.

"Have you had any new boarders?" Rebekka asked from halfway up the stairs.

"Nah, your room is still the same one. You make yourself at home and I'll have the coffee ready shortly. Mrs. Knutson went over to her shop to check and make sure everything is all right there. We'll have supper soon's I can set things out. If you still would like to help me, we need to wash everything down tomorrow to get rid of the soot. Like spring cleaning all over again. I closed up the rooms afore I left to help on the fire line, so this house ain't bad as some."

Rebekka shuddered. The smell of smoke permeated *everything* inside and out, and the odor made her eyes water. What they needed now was a good rain to wash things clean again.

That night she fell asleep with her windows wide open and the breeze trying to blow away the fire's residue. How good it felt to be home, in spite of the fire. But what would she do about school?

In the morning the three women were aproned and wearing

kerchiefs tied over their heads to protect their hair as they dragged the rugs out to the line for a good beating, washed and hung out the curtains, and scrubbed down every surface in the house. Since she was the tallest, Rebekka stood on a stool to wash the outsides of the windows.

"Good afternoon, Miss Stenesrude," Mr. Larson called as he opened the picket gate and strode up the walk. "Seems everyone in town is doing the same thing today. Scrubbing and counting our blessings. Good to see you back."

"Good to be back. Although I wasn't too excited about my welcome." She climbed down from her stool and wiped her hands on her apron. "What can I do for you?"

"Could you come to a school board meeting tonight at the church at seven?"

"Of course."

"Good. I have two more members to call on. I'll see you then." He turned and strode back to his horse. "See you tonight."

The meeting that night had one item on the agenda. How would they get the money to rebuild the schoolhouse?

Within a week the bank had loaned the school district enough money to begin the building. Rebekka spent a good part of every day driving the buggy to the outlying farms to invite the people to a school raising.

"You mean like a barn raising?" one woman asked.

'Just like that." Rebekka nodded. "Plan on the second Saturday in September. Most people will be done harvesting by then, so we'll make it into a school building and end of harvest celebration. If enough people turn out, we should be able to frame the walls and put on the roof by Sunday night."

"Count on us."

Rebekka missed only one farm and that was intentional. As she drove by the Strands', she kept her eyes straight ahead. But ignoring the goosebumps chasing each other up and down her back wasn't as easy as looking the other way. Why did she feel that the whole situation wasn't resolved yet? She hadn't even heard hide nor hair of Adolph. She tried to put a lid on her worry box. "Remember, you ninny, that God says He watches over us like a hen with her chicks. And you know how fierce that little hen can be." The horse flicked his ears at her voice.

The lumber came in on the train, and the townspeople hauled it in their wagons to the school site. Rebekka walked among the stacked lumber piles, inhaling the scent of freshly milled timbers and siding. Wooden kegs of nails, crates of window glass, and the sawhorses belonging to Lars Larson lay in readiness. The flat river rocks used for support under posts and beams had been measured and placed in the proper positions.

Off to the side, the cast-iron bell salvaged from the burned building rested, cleaned and repainted and ready to lift into the new tower. Rebekka stopped at the bell and tapped it with the toe of her boot. A hollow thunk made her smile. Like everyone or everything, the bell needed to be hung in the right position to make music. "Soon," she promised the inert object. "Soon you'll be calling the children to school again." She turned in place, taking in all the supplies, ready for the morning. All that was needed were the people.

The hammering and sawing started about the time the first rooster crowed in Willowford. Rebekka bounded out of bed and rushed through her morning toilet as if she were afraid she might miss out on something. Downstairs, Mrs. Sampson was already taking three apple pies out of the oven.

"How can we find room on the table?" Rebekka moved bowls of food around to make room for the steaming pans. "You trying to feed all the builders yourself?"

"Nah. Just doing my share."

Rebekka dished herself a bowl of oatmeal from the kettle on the back of the stove. “You’d be up there nailing if they’d let you.”

“Ja, I would. But since theyd drum an old woman like me...” Rebekka gave a decidedly unladylike snort. Mrs. Sampson gave her a look and then continued, “Off the roof, I want to make sure the workers come back the next day to finish the job. Our children need that school.”

“And I need my job.” Rebekka poured a dollop of molasses on her cereal, then some milk, and sat down to eat. “But what are we going to do for books and desks? The library? Oh, and our piano?”

“Won’t the insurance cover some of that?”

“I hope. But it all depends on how much the rebuilding costs. I sent a letter to the state teachers’ association requesting their help and Mr. Larson contacted the State Board of Education. But all that takes time.”

“We used to have the parents pay for their children’s books. So there still might be books in peoples’ homes that can be used. If you tell everyone to bring any books they have at home, you’ll have something to start with.” Mrs. Sampson lifted the full teakettle off the stove and filled the dishpan in the cast-iron sink.

“Thanks. I’ll start passing the word today. Do you have someone to help carry all this over to the schoolyard?”

“I’m picking up the wagon at the livery at ten. Then Mrs. Knutson and I’ll go around to some of the other houses to help them. I’m bringing my washtubs for the lemonade.”

Jude Weinlander let his horse drink from the river’s edge. He leaned his forearms on the saddle horn and stared upriver. The town lay shimmering in the September heat, and even from this distance he could hear the pounding of hammers.

He stared across the blackened prairie, where shoots of green could be seen poking up through the ashes toward the sunlight. Drying goldenrod nodded in the breeze across the river, where leaves already sported the tinges of fall. But on this side, all lay desolate.

When his horse, Prince, raised its head, ears pricked toward the sound of building, Jude nudged the animal forward. "That's the way we'll head then." He spoke for the first time since he mounted up, just before sunrise. The horse flicked his ears as if truly interested in what was being said. "Hope you know what you're doing." The horse snorted and broke into a trot. When he raised his head and whinnied, a horse answered from the town ahead.

Jude sat on his horse at the edge of the beehive of activity. Floor joists and flooring were already in place and different groups were framing up the walls. The north wall stood while men nailed the plate in place. Hammers pounding, saws buzzing, people laughing and swapping stories, children running and laughing along a creek where the willows had been cut for the firebreak—it looked more like a party than a building site.

Across the creek, Jude could see the town. He strained to read the sign on the train station—WILLOWFORD. He shrugged. Good a place as any. Maybe they could use another hand on the building.

He watched the busy scene to determine who was in charge. A tall man, fedora pulled low on his forehead, seemed to be answering questions and keeping his laborers busy. Jude stepped from his horse and tipped his hat back before searching in his saddlebags for hammer and pigskin gloves. Before leaving his mount, he loosened the saddle cinch and wrapped the reins around a willow stump.

Two barefoot, overalls-clad youngsters charged by him, their speed outclassed only by the volume of their shouts.

"Need anything to drink?" A tall woman dressed in a white blouse and ankle-length serge skirt moved from helper to helper offering drinks from a bucket on her arm.

"You got something stronger than that lemonade?" One of the sweating hammer wielders asked.

"Now, you know better than that." The woman grinned, changing her face from plain to pretty. Auburn highlights glinted from hair imprisoned in a coil of braids at the back of her head. Springy tendrils of hair framed her heart-shaped face in spite of her determined efforts to tuck them back into their prison.

As if feeling his gaze, she turned and stared straight at him. With one hand she brushed back a lock of hair before going on to the next man to offer him a drink.

He watched the way she moved about the yard, her long-legged stride, free of feminine artifice. Funny, he hadn't noticed something like the way she moved, since, well, since... He clamped a lid on the memories of his other life. Nothing mattered now but the next job… the next town…the next meal. And maybe working here for a few hours would at least give him that.

He kept his eye on the man in charge, following him around the corner of the building before getting his attention. "Ah, sir."

The man waved at a man nailing boards in place on a wall frame and then strode over to answer another's question.

Jude paused by a man busily sawing boards laid across the sawhorses. "Who is the man in charge here?" he asked.

"Ah, that'd be Lars Larson, the man getting a drink from the schoolmarm."

"Thanks." Jude tipped his hat and, stepping across a couple of beams, made his way around the building. So that's who she was, the schoolmarm. "Mr. Larson." He walked closer. "Mr. Larson."

Lars Larson turned from a laughing comment exchanged with the tall woman Jude had noticed before. "Ja?" At the sight of a stranger, he offered his hand. "I'm Lars Larson. What can I do for you?"

"I wondered if maybe you could use another hand." Jude concentrated on keeping his gaze from swinging to the woman. He forced himself to look Mr. Larson in the eye instead.

"You know how to use a hammer?"

Jude nodded, his mouth set in a firm line.

"I can't pay you. This is a community project. The school burnt in a prairie fire a few weeks ago." Mr. Larson studied the man in front of him. "But there'll be plenty of food, if'n that appeals to you."

Jude nodded. "That'll be fine."

"You go on and join that crew on the front wall."

Jude tipped his hat to Mr. Larson and then to the woman standing off to the side with a slight smile on her face. "Ma'am." He turned and pulled on his gloves while crossing the schoolyard.

As he reached the men raising the wall, he drew his hammer from its place in his belt in the back on the right side.

"Who is he?" Rebekka stared after the man. She turned to Mr. Larson, who shrugged.

"Just a drifter, I imagine. At least he'll get a good feed for his labors." Mr. Larson took another sip from the dipper and wiped his mouth with the back of his hand. "Thank you, Miss Stenesrude. That lemonade tastes mighty fine."

He didn't even say his name and I heard everything they said. Rebekka allowed her thoughts to drift as she continued around the building with the lemonade bucket. Again she saw and felt the shock of his gaze. Did she know him from somewhere else? She tried to think. No, she'd remember someone with a gaze so summer-sky blue. Eyes so blue they seemed to pierce like shards of ice on a winter day. Now why did she think of winter? Today when the sun was so hot that she'd had to wipe her face with a handkerchief twice already.

She returned to the washtub to refill her bucket and she felt it again. How could the gaze from a man she'd never even met before send shivers up and down her spine?

Rebekka handed her half-full bucket to her oldest pupil, reminding her to stay out of the way of the men while they worked, and then she went over to help the women setting up the tables for dinner. From the looks of the groaning boards, no one would go hungry. In fact, there'd be plenty left for supper, too. That way those that didn't have animals to care for could work through until dark.

"Who was that man talking with you and Lars?" Mrs. Sampson paused in the act of cutting her pies.

"I have no idea." Rebekka felt the urge to look over her shoulder again. If she did, she was sure she would see him watching her. "He didn't give his name, just said he knew how to use a hammer."

"Well, he wasn't just blowing smoke. I been watching him. You mark my words, he's used that hammer plenty. Has an air of mystery about him, wouldn't you say? Or maybe it's sadness."

"I wouldn't say at all. I don't know the man and probably never will." Rebekka turned to her friend. "You sure have strange ideas. He's just a drifter."

"I wouldn't be too sure."

Just then someone came up to ask Rebekka a question, so she had no more time to pursue the discussion. But something niggled at her just the same. Who was he?

At the stroke of noon Rebekka rang the triangle, calling everyone to eat. The Reverend Haugen came down off the ladder where he'd been nailing on the upper plate and, after wiping his face on a bright red kerchief, bowed his head. "We thank Thee, O Lord, for the gifts Thou hast given us, for the food the women have prepared, for the progress on our building, and for the protection Thee offers us all. Hear our prayer and now give us strength to continue through the day before us." At the universal "Amen," he raised his hands. "Let's eat."

The men formed two lines and moved down the length of the laden tables, loading their plates as they went. Another row of tables had benches on each side ready for the men to slide first one foot and then the other under the table and sit down. As soon as the men had filled their plates, the women and children did the same.

Rebekka had switched from carrying lemonade to carrying coffee and made her way down the table with a huge pot. At her "Coffee?" the seated men held up the mug from on the table in front of them.

"There's more lemonade, too," she said as she poured coffee and offered praises for jobs well done.

"Coffee?" she said again, stopping just before the stranger.

He turned without a word and held up his cup.

Rebekka felt her hand shake as she poured the dark brew. When the cup was full, she raised her gaze to see the man studying her over the rim of the cup. He lifted the steaming mug and, after one swallow, turned and set the cup down. Without a word, smile, thank you, or by your leave, he resumed eating.

Rebekka paused as if giving him a chance to remedy his bad manners. But when he continued to fork potato salad into his mouth without another glance, she stepped to the next man at the table.

"Coffee?" Now her voice shook, too. She cleared her throat and took a tighter grip on the pot holders with which she held the pot. Of all the...

She stayed away from him after that—far away—and did the slow burn. What an ingrate. Had his mother not taught him common decency? No manners? Everyone was taught to at least say "Thank you." Weren't they?

Obviously not. She stopped after her last round with the water bucket and gazed up at the new schoolhouse.

As the sun was setting, the men on the roof were nailing the last rafter in place.

"That's it for tonight," Mr. Larson called. "We'll start again at first light. Reverend Haugen has agreed to lead the worship service tomorrow right here so those who want can attend without much of a loss of time. We can use the good Lord's blessing." He waved toward the tables, set now with plates of sandwiches and the left-overs from dinner. "Now, come and help yourselves. These women would be mighty hurt if anyone left here hungry."

Rebekka kneaded the aching muscles of her lower back with her fists. If she had to carry one more coffeepot she was sure her shoulders would come loose from their sockets. She could hear others groaning, too, but everyone laughed off the pains and dug into the food.

Jude pounded in the last nail and, after sticking his hammer back into its usual place, he climbed down the ladder. He pulled off his gloves and tucked them into his back pocket, then crossed to where the men were washing their hands and faces in a row of buckets of water lined up on a bench.

He tipped his hat back and, sloshing water up in cupped hands, he washed his face first, then hands, and finally his arms up to his rolled-back sleeves. He could feel someone watching him but, when he turned around, no one seemed to be paying him any attention. Then why that creepy crawly sensation up his spine? He lifted his hat and ran damp fingers through the waves trapped beneath the hatband. The slash of silver that began at his upper temple on the left side caught a glint from the setting sun.

The glint caught Rebekka's gaze, in spite of her efforts to not look at the man. What was wrong with her? She'd never in her life paid so much attention to one man, and a drifter at that.

After the crowd finished eating, they slowly left the school grounds and headed for their homes. Lars Larson sat down beside Jude on the bench and leaned his elbows on the table. "You sure got a way with that hammer of yours. Been building long?"

Jude shook his head. "Nope, just the last year or so."

"You from these parts?"

"No." Jude cut and levered another bite of pie into his mouth.

"You plannin' on coming back tomorrow?"

"If nobody minds."

"You got a place to stay?" Mr. Larson leaned on his elbows.

"Down by the river'll do."

"You're welcome to my barn. You can put your horse out in the pasture and leave him there long as you want." Mr. Larson swiveled around like he was getting ready to leave. "What'd you say your name was?"

"Jude Weinlander. And I appreciate the offer." Jude accepted a cup of coffee from the woman pouring and thanked her. Then he turned back to Mr. Larson. "Just where is your barn?"

Mr. Larson pointed out his house on the knoll on the other side of Willowford and pushed himself to his feet. "See you in the morning then and thanks for your work on the school today."

Jude nodded. He watched as the man gathered his family into a wagon and drove off. He slapped at a mosquito buzzing around his head and sipped his coffee. This was a good town, he could tell already. The townsfolk made even drifters feel welcome, at least this one who could nail up a wall with the best of them.

He turned and studied the bare bones of the new school. Siding covered most of two walls, the rafters were ready for the nailers, and two men had been splitting cedar shakes to finish the roof. Tomorrow would make a big difference if as many people turned out as today. He inhaled air redolent of freshly sawed wood. Even the ache in his back only added to the contentment. He started to reach in his pocket for a cigar but remembered he didn't even have a nickel to buy one. He'd have to find a paying job pretty soon.

Bedded down on soft hay that night, he thought back again to the day. Glints of auburn off a tall woman's hair and a laugh that floated like music on the air brought a smile to a face that had found little reason to smile in a long while.

Stretched out on her bed after helping Mrs. Sampson boil potatoes and eggs for salad again the next day, Rebekka thought over the day. She'd never realized how friendly and caring the people of

Willowford were. All those who pitched in to raise the new school building and not a cross word heard all day. She deliberately kept her mind away from the stranger with the black hat and the slash of silver in his hair. He didn't look old enough to be going gray already.

She rolled over and thumped her pillow. Who was he? Where had he come from? She could ask Mr. Larson tomorrow. Sure, just go up and say, "Mr. Larson, I saw you talking with that stranger. Tell me his life history." Even the thought of such outrageous actions sent the heat flaming up her neck.

If she waited long enough, Mrs. Sampson would find out plenty. If she had the patience to wait. A mighty big word, "if." Would he be back tomorrow?

Chapter 6

You think he'll be back today?" Rebekka asked.

"Who'll be back?" Mrs. Sampson removed a pot of baked beans from the oven.

"You know. The stranger," said Rebekka while carefully spreading frosting on the chocolate layer cake in front of her. She leaned over to make sure frosting covered every spot; that way she didn't have to look up at Mrs. Sampson or Mrs. Knutson. She wondered if they noticed the flush she could feel creeping up her neck.

"Need more eggs for that potato salad?" asked Mrs. Sampson, crossing over to taste the mixture in the bowl.

"No, I don't think so." Mrs. Knutson pushed her friend's fingers away from the food. "And yes to you, Rebekka. I heard him tell Lars that he'll be back."

"Oh."

"Why?" Both women stared at Rebekka as she scraped the bowl for the last bits of frosting.

"I. . .ummm. . .well, it would be a shame to lose a good carpenter like him."

"How do you know that?"

"What?"

"That he's a good carpenter." Mrs. Sampson flashed a grin at her longtime boarder.

"Anyone could see that." Rebekka flipped new curls into the top of the cake.

"Anyone who was watching, that is." The two widows turned to focus totally on Rebekka.

Rebekka wished she had never started this discussion. She kept her gaze on the cake, but her flaming cheeks refused to cool. *One would think you're interested,* she chided herself. *You know better than that. He, whoever he is, is just a drifter, a man passing through. Be grateful he helped on the school and let it go at that.*

She mentally shrugged off the thoughts and, with a grin tugging at the corners of her mouth, asked, "Either of you catch his name?"

The three of them were still laughing as they loaded the wagon to bring the food over to the schoolyard.

They arrived just in time for the church service. Reverend Haugen stood in front of the impromptu altar and raised his hands for silence. People found places to sit on the benches, the remaining stacks of lumber, or the ground. A hush fell, broken only by a bird's song.

"This is the day that the Lord hath made," Reverend Haugen began the service.

"Let us rejoice and be glad in it," the scattered congregation responded.

"Let us pray." The Reverend bowed his head and waited for the rustling to cease. "Lord God, bless us this day as we worship Thee and bless the fruits of our labors. Open our hearts to hear Thy word. Amen." He raised his head and looked over the people gathered. "Today we'll sing the songs we know best since we chose not to bring the hymnals. Let's start with 'Beautiful Savior.' " As his rich baritone rang out the opening notes, everyone joined in.

Rebekka felt the sun warm on her back while a playful breeze tickled the strands of hair that refused to be bound into the coil at her neck. As she sang the familiar words, she let her gaze roam around the gathering. Her pupils, their families, the townsfolk, some who came to church regularly, and some who didn't. She kept her eyebrows from rising when she recognized the saloon owner and exchanged a wink with Mrs. Sampson when they both noticed two of the older youths making calf eyes at each other.

I wish we could worship outside like this every Sunday, Rebekka thought, *at least as long as the weather is nice. Seems to me people feel closer somehow. Maybe it's because we're all working together on something truly important.*

As the Reverend read, Rebekka forced herself to concen-trate. "From 1 John, chapter four, 'Beloved, let us love one another: for love is of God...' "

Here, today, her thoughts continued with a mind of their own. *It is easy to love one another.* A black cloud of remembrance dulled her joy. Well, maybe not everyone.

When they raised their voices in the final hymn, she allowed herself a glance around the group again. Now, why was it that the sun seemed to shine brighter when she saw the stranger, leaning against the corner of the schoolhouse?

And why was her neck warm when she caught a grinning Mrs. Sampson watching her?

By the end of the day, the building looked complete—from the outside. A roof, windows glinting in the dying sun, and die door hung above three steps, all there but the bell hanging in the tower.

"Looks pretty good, if I do say so myself." Lars Larson joined her in staring up at the men coming down from nailing the cap along the roof's peak. "Sure is farther along than I thought possible."

"Just goes to show what a determined group of people can do when they set their minds to it. When do you plan to rehang the bell?" Rebekka turned to watch two children playing tag under the ladders. When their mothers called them away, she looked up at Mr. Larson.

"Soons we're done with supper. Thought we'd use that as a good way to finish the day."

"Wonderful."

"Excuse me, Miss Stenesrude, I need to talk to Jude before he gets away," Mr. Larson said as he left her side to stride across the yard to where the man in black, as Rebekka called him in her mind, was leaving the yard.

"At least now I know part of his name," Rebekka said to no one in particular.

"Here, how about pouring coffee?" Mrs. Sampson handed her the heavy pot. "And it's Weinlander."

Rebekka took the pot and scurried off. There it was, that blush that crept up her neck. She'd never flushed so much in her whole life as these last two days. What in the world was wrong with her?

"Weinlander, wait up."

Jude turned at the calling of his name, and he watched as Lars Larson caught up with him.

"You're staying for supper, aren't you? That's the least we can do after all your fine work. I think you're a good part of the reason we got so much done."

"Ja, I'll stay. I was just going over to look at the creek. Pity you had to cut down all the trees along it." Jude tipped his hat back.

"It was that or lose the town. You know, with that fire and all, there's lots of building needs doing before the snow flies. Might you be interested in staying on and working for me?" Mr. Larson caught his suspenders with his thumbs. "I know how good you are. You could run one crew and me another."

Jude lifted his hat and ran his fingers through his hair before using both hands to place his hat back in place. He looked off to the horizon on the other side of town. When he nodded and said, "Guess I could," Mr. Larson let out his breath as if he'd been holding it. "Guess I could."

"You could probably get a room at Mrs. Sampsons boarding-house. I heard she has a vacancy."

"Well, I better—"

"If it's a case of money, I could give you an advance, and since you're working for me, I know she'll let you pay the rest later. The food's good there, too."

Jude thought of the beans and no coffee he'd subsisted on for the past week. One morning he'd even borrowed a cup of milk from a cow in the barn where he'd slept. When he'd gone to look at the creek, he'd been hoping to see fish. Fried fish had sounded mighty tasty. And how long had it been since he'd slept in a real bed?

He looked back to the waiting man. "All right. But if you don't mind, I'd as soon sleep in your hay barn till it gets colder."

Mr. Larson grabbed his new employee's hand and shook it. "Good. That's Mrs. Sampson over there, the lady with the white hair and white apron who's been overseeing the food serving. Just tell her I sent you." Before Jude could walk off, Mr Larson put a hand on Jude's arm and dropped his voice, "I'll just pay the room for now."

Jude nodded his thanks. He'd pretty much used up his store of words in the last two days. Everyone had been so nice to him. If they only knew who he really was. The thought caused the two slashes between his eyebrows to deepen. If they only knew, they'd never speak to him again. They'd just run him out of town.

He joined the last of the laborers at the wash bench and, after sluicing down, took a seat on the benches by the laden tables. While some folks had left to attend their evening chores, many more laughed and joked around the tables. Jude listened to the jokes as the two young men beside him flirted with all the young women bringing refills of potato salad, fried chicken, sliced ham, and baked beans down the row.

Mrs. Sampson brought him a piece of apple pie and sat down beside him. "Lars told me you need a room?" She spoke in a low voice, only for his ears. "By the way, I'm Widow Sampson with the boardinghouse."

"Glad to meet you." Jude picked up his fork. "You make this pie?"

She shook her head. "That chocolate cake is my doing. Yesterday

I noticed you seem a mite partial to apple pie, so I snagged you a piece before it was all gone."

"Thank you. I'm sure the chocolate cake is good, too," Jude said as he cut off a bite of pie and lifted it to his mouth.

"I have a proposition for you. I need some things done around my place that you could fix if you had a mind to. You could work off some of the board if you'd be so inclined."

Jude turned and looked at the cheery woman beside him. "But you don't know me."

"I know what I see."

Jude wanted to ask her what it was she saw but instead took another bite of pie.

"Well?"

"I'd be so inclined," he nodded. "And thank you."

"It's the big white house off Main Street on Sampson Street."

Jude turned and looked at her. "Sampson Street?"

"Mr. Sampson was well liked by the founding fathers." The twinkle in her eyes invited him to smile back.

Jude scooped up the last bite of pie as he said, "I have a horse."

"I know. I have a fenced pasture behind the house and a shed that could be called a small barn. You can get feed and hay at the Every after you get back on your feet."

Jude swung one leg over the bench so he could face her.

"Why are you doing this?"

Without flinching and looking away, Widow Sampson met his gaze and said, "I don't really know. It just seems what I am supposed to do." The two stared at each other, both measuring and weighing the person in front of them. "Is there anything else I should know about you?"

"Not that I can think of," Jude answered without batting an eye. Inside his head he finished, *If you only knew.*

"Then we'll see you back at the house when you've finished here. You can bring your horse tonight or pick him up tomorrow."

Mrs. Sampson rose to her feet. “Stay here. I think I see a piece of chocolate cake with your name on it.”

They sure got chummy fast, Rebekka thought as she carefully avoided looking at Jude and Mrs. Sampson. She absolutely refused to let herself amble over to see what was happening.

“All right, folks, let’s gather ‘round. The pulley is installed for the bell. All you children, Miss Stenesrude, come over here. It’ll be your job to pull the rope that will raise the bell.” Lars Larson waved his arms to encourage the children to make a line by the rope lying on the ground.

“Miss Stenesrude, you take the end. John, Elizabeth, you bigger kids, start right here.” Mr. Larson handed them the heavy rope. “You little ones, line up on both sides. Now, when I count to three, you’ll all pull together, understand?”

Children came from every corner, laughing and giggling as they grabbed the rope.

Rebekka looked up on the roof where two men sat on the edge of the tower, ready to secure the bell when it reached its new home. One waved at her.

“We’re ready when you are,” he called.

“Mith Thtenthrude, can I be by you?” Emily Gordon pleaded with her round blue eyes.

Rebekka stepped back and shared her rope with the little one. “Of course. Now you be ready to pull.”

“One,” Mr. Larson’s voice rang out. Silence fell. “Two.” Giggles erupted along the rope line.

“Stop shoving me!” a small boy demanded.

“Get off my foot!” yelled someone else.

“Three! Now, pull steady, don’t jerk. You want the bell to rise nice and easy.” Mr. Larson walked along with his pulling team as the rope stretched from the tower clear to the ground and along the caterpillar of pullers.

“Good, good!” A man inside of the building who was guiding

the bell called. “Easy now.”

The line of children snaked back, each one carefully pulling on his section of rope. Rebekka watched as the older ones looked out for the younger and they all worked together to raise the bell.

“There it is!” The cry rang out as the top of the bell cleared the ledge. The two men waved. The line stopped.

“Ith almotht up,” the lisper beamed up at Rebekka.

“Sure is. You did a good job.” Rebekka leaned down and laid a fingertip on the little one’s button nose.

“Don’t drop your rope,” the charmer cautioned.

Rebekka nodded solemnly. “I won’t.” She raised her gaze to the bell tower as one of the men called out.

“Easy now. Only an inch at a time.”

The children stared up at him, waiting for the signal and then barely moving back. The bell inched upward.

“That’s it.” The two men secured the bell and raised their hands for the cheer. “Okay now, on three. Pull the rope for the bell to ring. One, two, three!”

The children pulled; the bell rang out, the *bong, bong* sounding joyous and richer for the cleaning. They pulled again and the bell sang for them all.

“Yeth,” the little one said, clapping her hands and turning to Rebekka, who lifted the child into her arms. Together they and all the crowd clapped and cheered.

Reverend Haugen walked up the schoolhouse steps and turned to face the gathered people. “A fitting end to a wonderful day. Let us bow our heads and thank the Lord for watching over us.” He waited for the rustlings to cease and bowed his head. “Dear Lord, we dedicate this building to Thee. Be with our children who learn here and the teacher that teaches them. We thank Thee for keeping us all safe and in Thy care. Now, please give us safe travel and good rest. Amen.”

Rebekka shook hands and wished everyone good night, thanking them for their efforts. As the last wagon was loaded and left, she and Widow Sampson folded tablecloths and picked up the stray napkins.

"What a day," Rebekka said as she rubbed the small of her back with her fists. "Mr. Larson said we would be able to open school next Monday. They'll be finishing the inside of the building this week." She turned to catch a secret smile that Widow Sampson tried to hide. "All right. What's that for?"

"You'll see." The older woman packed the last box into the wagon. "Are you riding with me or walking?" she asked as she climbed up on the seat of the wagon.

"I'm coming," said Rebekka as she stepped up and pulled herself onto the wagon seat. When the horse started off, she looked over her shoulder to the schoolhouse, gleaming faintly in the dusk.

"Thank You, Lord," she whispered.

"What's that?"

"Just happy, that's all."

"That's enough."

"You want me to take the horse back?" Rebekka asked when they pulled to a halt at the boardinghouse.

"That would be nice, dear. Then I can get these things put away. When you get back I have something to tell you." The Widow Sampson stepped to the ground and tied the horse to the fence. Together, the two women unloaded the wagon, carrying baskets and tubs to the back porch.

"I wouldn't mind if you told me now." Rebekka paused before returning to the horse.

"Just hurry back. I hate to see you out after dark."

Rebekka hummed along with the horse's *clip-clop, clip-clop* trot back to the livery. Since no one answered her call, she tied the horse to the hitching post in front and swung off back to the widow's house. As she walked the quiet streets, lights glowed from windows, a dog barked, and another answered. Since it was Sunday night, the saloon was closed and dark.

But there were plenty of lights at Widow Sampson's boardinghouse and Rebekka looked across the yard in surprise. She'd have thought Mrs. Knutson would have gone up to her room and Mrs. Sampson would be finishing up in the kitchen. The gate creaked as she opened it; a horse nickered from somewhere out in the pasture.

Rebekka froze. Who's horse was out there? Had an animal gotten loose and found its way to their pasture? She locked the gate behind her and strode up the walk. Surely she wouldn't have to take a strange animal back tonight.

At the sound of voices, she paused on the back porch. One voice was a man's. Perhaps someone had come for his horse. She breathed a sigh of relief, opened the back door, and crossed through the pantry to the kitchen.

"What?" she said as she saw the stranger, sitting perfectly at ease at the table in Mrs. Sampson's kitchen.

"Rebekka Stenesrude, I'd like you to meet our new boarder, Jude Weinlander." Mrs. Sampson shot Rebekka a look of apology.

"Miss Stenesrude." Jude rose to his feet and tipped his head in the time-honored greeting of male to female.

"Mr. Weinlander." Rebekka knew her manners. What she didn't understand was how one man's eyes could look so…so…sad wasn't nearly strong enough. Not blank, not dead, just filled with deep-down, soul-searching sorrow. Whatever had happened in his life to bring that darkness to eyes that should have sparkled like the sun, dappling a Minnesota lake in the summer?

Again the slash of silver in his dark blond hair caught her attention. Did he ever smile? What would it take to make a smile light his eyes and crease his face? *Silly,* she chided herself. *He's a drifter. He'll be here and gone before you know it.*

"Mr. Weinlander will be working for Lars," Mrs. Sampson said as she reached for the coffeepot on the stove. "Would you like a cup before you retire?"

Rebekka shook her head. "No, thanks. I think I'll go on up."

The usual camaraderie seemed to have fled the kitchen. Would things ever be the same?

Jude watched her leave the room, her back straight, her head high. He wondered how she could hold her head so straight with that thick braided coil at her neck. It looked heavy enough to tip her all the way over. Tonight she wasn't smiling. In fact, the temperature had dropped ten degrees in the room when they'd been introduced. But he'd seen her smile at the children today. And all the others helping at the school. She had a wonderful, heart-catching smile when she allowed it out to play. Must have something to do with being a schoolmarm.

He picked up the cup of coffee set before him and sipped. No matter. He wouldn't be here long enough to get to know her anyway.

Mrs. Sampson sat down across from him and, with a sigh, stretched her shoulders and leaned back in the chair. "This has certainly been a busy two days. Glad we don't have doings like this too often."

Jude set his cup down and ran a calloused fingertip around the edge of the mug. He could feel a war going on inside him. Why in the world did he have this desire to tell the woman across from him his life's story? Surely if she knew, she would send him packing in an instant. He cleared his throat. He could hear footsteps overhead.

That must be Rebekka's room. Why in the world was he thinking of her as Rebekka? Miss Stenesrude.

He took another swallow of coffee. "I need to tell you some things."

Mrs. Sampson studied him across the top of her cup. "Not if you don't want to, you don't."

Jude pulled at the collar of his shirt. "It's been awhile since I told anyone—in fact, I never have." *Why do you want to do this?* his mind cautioned. *What is there about this woman that invites you to tell all?* He looked across the table into the most compassionate eyes he'd ever seen.

"You don't need to do this."

"Ja, I guess I do." He took a deep breath and began. "I been a no-good all my life, deviling my older brother and making life miserable for my wife and mother. But I can't make my wife and my mother sad anymore because they are dead and it's all my fault." He continued with his story without a break. "And now you know. So if you want me to leave, I'll understand."

"Do you play an instrument?"

The question surprised him. "What?"

"I asked if you played an instrument."

"I know what you said. I heard you." He stared at the woman across the table. Her smile warmed him clear down to his ankles. He shook his head, feeling a laugh starting down in his middle. "Yes, I play, if you call a mouth organ an instrument."

"Good. That means we'll have nearly an orchestra right here. Miss Stenesrude plays the organ and piano, Mrs. Knutson the fiddle, and I do a fair-to-middlin'job on the gutbucket…banjo some, too. I think we'll have some real high times, come winter." She pushed herself to her feet. "More coffee?"

Jude shook his head. "No, thanks." He stared at the woman who had just given him his life back. "Is that all you have to say?"

She poured her coffee and turned to look at him. "No. There'll be no smoking or drinking or playing cards in my house!" Then her eyebrows raised in question.

"Of course not."

"And it's high time you understand that God forgives us when we ask…and even before. You need to plug into that. Breakfast is at seven, earlier if you need, I make your dinner bucket, and supper is served at six o'clock sharp. You needn't worry that I'll tell tales on you. Your life is safe with me." She walked over to the sink and set her cup into the dishpan. "I'll show you to your room." She picked up the kerosene lamp and led the way up the stairs.

Rebekka heard them come up the stairs. What on earth had they been talking about all this while? She turned over and thumped her pillow. She missed sitting in the kitchen discussing the day with Widow Sampson. Why had he come along and ruined everything? Now this house that had felt like home felt more like just a place to live.

Chapter 7

Everywhere Rebekka went, Jude was there.

"Howdy, Miss Stenesrude," said Johnny J., her oldest pupil, as he waved at her from his painting ladder when she approached the school on Monday morning. "Sure is looking good, wouldn't you say?"

"I certainly would." Rebekka stopped to admire the sparkling white paint. "You're doing a fine job." She opened the door to find Jude nailing up the thin boards and the chicken wire for the plasterers who were coming next. "Mr. Weinlander," she said as she tipped her head in acknowledgment.

"Miss Stenesrude." Jude continued nailing, the hammer ringing in perfect rhythm.

Now he was here, ruining her joy in the new building. How could anyone else be happy when he stared out at them with such sad eyes? She slanted a peek in his direction. There was no indication he cared whether she was in the room or not; he just continued with his work.

Rebekka paced the room, picturing the blackboards for the wall, where her desk would go, and if she would change the configuration of the children's desks. She'd seen a school building with movable desks, and since the school was also used as the town's meeting hall, theater, and dance hall, movable desks would be a decided advantage.

She took a paper and pencil from her bag and began a list of supplies, including the changes she would like to make. But where could they get the money? She'd have to talk with Mr. Larson to see if there was any left from the bank loan. As she paced, she tapped the pencil end against her teeth.

When finished, she put the things back in her bag and walked toward the door. "Good day, Mr. Weinlander." She kept her voice cool and terribly proper.

"Ummm." The hammering continued without a break.

As she stalked the path homeward, she fumed at the snub. Didn't he even have the grace to be polite?

After having talked with Mr. Larson and called on two families who had recently moved to the area, she walked into the boardinghouse and found him sitting at the table drinking a cup of coffee.

"Supper in half an hour," Mrs. Sampson said as she turned from the pot she was stirring on the stove and smiled at Rebekka. "There's a letter for you on the entry table. And a box arrived. Must be books, it's so heavy. Jonathan brought it over from the train station."

"Wonderful. Thank you." Rebekka crossed through the kitchen and went out without looking that man in the face. Two could play at his game. She stopped at the oak secretary to pick up scissors and knelt by the box. As she cut the strings, she read the address.

"Who are they from?" Mrs. Sampson followed her into the sitting room.

"A school in Fargo." Rebekka folded back the top of the box and peered inside. "Arithmetic, history, reading," she said as she shuffled through the books, setting them outside the box as she dug deeper. "What a gift. This gives me at least something to start with." She opened a letter taped to the inside of the box top.

She read aloud, "Dear Teacher, We are sorry these aren't brand-new, but we planned on sending these to the Indian Reservation after we received new textbooks. Please send them on when you are finished with them. Please accept our sympathy on the burning of your school." Rebekka looked up to Mrs. Sampson. "Isn't that wonderful?"

Jude, who was standing behind Mrs. Sampson, saw Rebekka's shining eyes and felt like a mule had kicked him in the gut. Why, she wasn't plain at all, like he'd first thought. When she smiled like that, her eyes could teach the sun something about shining. And all it took was a box of hand-me-down books for her school, no less.

Jude turned and left the two women talking. He needed to wash before supper anyway. As he pumped a bucket of water at the outside well, he thought back to the school in Soldahl. They had plenty of books. There was even a library in town, at the school, of course. And Mrs. Norgaard had a whole room full of books.

But was he ready to write to them? He sluiced water over his head and shoulders and scrubbed with the bar of homemade soap left on the bench beside the bucket. As he rinsed again, he shook his head. "How can I ask them for something when they've already given me so much? And all I ever did for them was cause trouble."

But this wasn't asking for something for himself, his argument continued. Rebekka's, Miss Stenesrude's—he even caught himself correcting his thoughts—happiness wasn't for herself either. What she needed was books and supplies for her school so she could teach the kids who would be coming to her. Cute kids like the little girl with the lisp…and the two young lovebirds.

Jude dried himself with the towel Mrs. Sampson had hung on a nail above the wash bench. He would write the letter tonight. It was for the children of Willowford, after all.

After repacking her box of books, Rebekka sat down in the sitting room to read the letter from her aunt. What a joy it was to have family again. She who had felt alone for so long. She smiled at the news that one of her cousins was getting married, a second was increasing her family, and her grandmother wished Rebekka could come for another visit soon.

Rebekka tucked the letter back into its envelope. Maybe she could go see them for Christmas. What would it be like to spend Christmas with people who were her real family, not only friends, but related? Her mother said they'd had Christmas with her mother and father, back when Rebekka was little, but Rebekka couldn't remember them. Most of her memories were not worth dragging out.

"I'll carry that over to the school for you on Friday," Jude said as he stopped in the arched doorway. "Should be done with the walls by then."

Rebekka started. She hadn't heard him walk across the floor. "Why…why, thank you." She looked up in time to catch a fleeting glimpse of something lighten his eyes. No, she'd been mistaken... only the dark remained. But she couldn't pull her gaze away. Such deep, dark eyes. All she could call it was sadness.

"Supper's ready," Mrs. Sampson called from the kitchen.

Rebekka let the conversation between the two widows flow around her, answering only when asked a question. She concentrated fully on each bite, but if someone had asked her what she was eating, she couldn't have said. She didn't dare look up for Jude sat right across the round oak table from her, and she knew for certain that if she looked into his eyes again, she would blush enough to light up the room.

"Please pass the bread." His voice, deep and rich like maple syrup flowing over steaming pancakes in the morning, played bass to the women's soprano.

At the sudden silence, Rebekka looked up. "Oh." She passed the bread plate that had been sitting directly in front of her. But she didn't look across the table. No, sirree. She only looked to Mrs. Knutson, who sat on her right and who passed the plate to Jude.

But his hand caught Rebekka's eye . . . tanned, long, blunt fingers. She forced her gaze back to her plate. What was the matter with her?

When she finally escaped to her room, Rebekka gave herself a good talking to. She tried to sit down at the table beside the window to write her letter but instead ended up pacing the floor. *You ninny. You are the schoolteacher, remember? You can't talk to anyone. You have a respected position in this town and that man is only a drifter. Besides that, he doesn't care a bit for you and you don't want him to.*

She kept her shoulders back and her spine straight. When she felt she'd said and heard enough, she sat herself back down in the chair and took out paper and pen and uncapped the inkwell. She dipped the pen and began, "Dear Aunt Sofie..."

Her mind floated down the stairs and into the sitting room, where she could hear Mrs. Sampson and Mrs. Knutson and Mr. Weinlander talking. A black blot spread across the white paper. *"Uff da."* Here she was the schoolteacher, who was supposed to teach penmanship, and shed blotted the paper.

Only women's laughter drifted up the stairway. Did that man have a personal law against laughing?

Rebekka took another sheet of paper from her packet and began to write again but stopped when she heard the stairs creak under a heavier tread.

Then she stared down at the newly spreading black smear and wrinkled the page, dropping it next to its mate in the wastebasket by the table. Now she'd not only not finished the letter, but she had wasted two sheets of paper. And paper costs money.

After asking for paper and a pen, Jude climbed the stairs to his room. He sat down at the table by the window and after uncapping the ink, wrote in a bold, firm hand to his brother, Dag. He pictured his brother reading the letter aloud at the supper table in the big house in Soldahl. They would all be sitting at the long oak table in the dining room—Dag, Clara, Mrs. Norgaard, and Mrs. Hanson, who would be jumping up to serve. Gaslight from the chandelier above the table would bring a brilliance to the room, impossible with kerosene lamps like the one sitting on the edge of the table.

The house was grand, for certain. And his brother had grown into the grandness himself, changing from the shy, filthy blacksmith to one of the leading businessmen of the town, even though he was still the blacksmith. Jude chewed on the end of the pen. Where was the anger and jealousy he'd felt all these years? There was Dag with all the trappings Jude had dreamed of and here he was, a drifter in a town far from anywhere, and he... he didn't hate anymore. Had it, too, been burned away?

He finished the letter and addressed the envelope. He'd pick up a stamp and . . .he shook his head. He couldn't even buy a stamp until payday. How could he ask for one more thing from Mrs. Sampson? He put the envelope aside. He'd mail it next week.

As he closed his eyes in bed, his mind flitted back to the sitting room and Rebekka. He gave up. He couldn't call her Miss Stenesrude in his mind any longer. Rebekka, kneeling in front of the box of books. Rebekka, with such joy and delight, he'd almost smiled at her. Almost—until he caught himself.

He turned over and folded the pillow under his head. He'd ask for a stamp in the morning. After all, it was only three days until payday.

By the end of the week, Rebekka had collected two more boxes of books from people in the community. On Friday, while she sorted her papers and books into the desk the doctor in town had loaned the school, she heard a team draw up by the school.

"Hello, Miss Stenesrude," a male voice paged her from outside. Rebekka pushed back her chair and crossed to the window. Jonathan Ingmar, the stationmaster, tied his team to the hitching post planted to the side of the schoolhouse and walked to the rear of his wagon. A flat, wooden crate lay in the wagon bed.

"I'll be right there to help you," Rebekka told him from the open window then dashed out the door and around the corner. But Jude got there first, and the two men were lifting the crate out by the time she arrived.

"That must be the blackboard. I can't believe it got here so quickly." Rebekka walked beside them, ready to lend a hand if the tall, skinny crate leaned too far to the side. The two men carried it to the front of the room and set it on the floor, leaning against the desk.

"I'll get my hammer," Jude said as he strode across the room and out the door.

"I need to get home to my dinner," Mr. Ingmar said. "You need anything else, Miss Stenesrude?"

"No, Mr. Ingmar, and thank you so much for delivering this."

"No trouble. I brought my team in for a shoeing this morning." He cast a glance out the door. "You're sure you're all right with…?"

Rebekka caught his meaning. "Nothing to worry about. Mr. Weinlander and the others are finishing up the school building. Mr. Larson went on home and—" She felt like she was blathering. "So, thank you again." She walked him out to his wagon and waved him off.

When she reentered the school, she heard the screech of nails being pulled. Jude picked up the top section of the crate and put it off to the side as she reached him.

"Brand-new. Can you beat that? I'll be the first person to write on the new blackboard." Rebekka squatted down and ran her fingers over the dusty black surface. When she looked up at Jude, she thought she caught a smile...almost. At least his right cheek had pulled back a mite. She was sure it had. She smiled in return—just in case.

"If you give me a hand, we can lift it out right now or wait until the others return."

"Let's do it now. I can't wait to see it on the wall." She paused. "Shouldn't the wall be painted first?"

"We can take it down again. Might not get at the painting until a cold snap anyway."

"All right." Together they lifted the blackboard out and stood it against the wall. "It's heavy."

Jude removed his yellow measuring stick and unfolded it to measure the height and length of the blackboard. Then he measured down from the ceiling and marked on the plastered wall. Lightly tapping with his hammer, he located the studs and drove home the nails needed to hold the heavy blackboard.

Rebekka watched as he accomplished each task with an economy of movement and the sureness that comes with practice and pride in his work. She wanted to offer to help but had no idea how.

"Ready?" He shoved his hammer back into his belt and leaned over to pick up the blackboard. "This'll be heavy."

"I know." Rebekka prepared herself and, with one eye on Jude and the other on the blackboard, hoisted it up and set the back of the frame over the line of nail heads. When it was in place, she gave the oak frame a pat and turned to smile at Jude.

"Thank you. Oh, that's wonderful." With a swirl of her skirts, she spun back and stroked her hand down the frame again.

The smile she gave him lit up the room…and his heart. Jude felt like clutching his chest. What could one do with a smile like that but treasure it and keep it safe? Keep it to take out again on a cold winter's night and warm himself when he was far away down the road.

"You're welcome." He forced the words past a lump in his throat.

When she turned back, he had his usual expression in place. But he could literally feel his face cracking.

He picked up the pieces of the crate. "If you need anything else, just holler." Crate pieces on his shoulder, he strode out the door.

Rebekka watched him go. Funny, but for a minute there he had seemed almost friendly. She finished up her work and dusted off her hands. Tomorrow the men were slated to build the desks. They'd be crude until later on in the winter, Mr. Larson had told her, when finishing work would be done. Right now he had a house and barn to frame and enclose before the snow fell since both of them had burned in the prairie fire.

Rebekka closed the door and set off for home. She could hear the hammers and saws at work behind her. The men were finishing the privies and the coal shed.

On Monday morning, she arrived at the school early, too excited to eat breakfast. When she opened the door, the fragrance of new wood greeted her and she stopped just to look around. The American flag hung from its stick in one front corner, a globe donated by the mercantile dominated the other. While the children's desks and benches were still unpainted wood, they at least had places at which they could sit and write. Her desk appeared to be the only real piece of furniture in the room.

She left the outside door to the cloakroom open and walked softly to the front of the room. After laying her satchel on the desk, she turned to face the benches. "Please, Father," Rebekka whispered, "bless this year and all of us who come here to learn and to teach. We ask Thy special protection on this place so that all who come here may be safe and feel wanted. Fill me with wisdom and love for all my children. I thank Thee in Jesus' precious name. Amen."

When she opened her eyes she thought she saw a shadow crossing the door. Had someone been there? Immediately she heard two male voices in the schoolyard—Jude's and Mr. Larson's. By the time Rebekka walked to the window and looked out, Mr. Larson was climbing back into his wagon to drive away.

He looked up and caught her wave. "Have a good day, Miss Stenesrude," he called and waved again at her. "Thank you." At his bidding the horse trotted out to the dirt road and turned left, away from town.

Rebekka checked the time on her brooch watch—seven-thirty. Still half an hour until school started. She wandered to the window overlooking the back of the school. Jude stood on a ladder, nailing the shingles onto the roof of the boys' privy; the girls' was already finished. Hat pushed back on his forehead, shirt sleeves rolled back to his elbows, he laid a shingle, nailed it in place, and laid down the other, all with a rhythm born of long practice.

She'd never enjoyed watching a man work before, in fact, she'd never much watched a man do anything. A child's laughter drew her away from the window and back to her desk. The day was truly beginning…a whole new year was beginning.

"Miss Stenesrude, see the books I brought." Yes, school had begun.

"That's wonderful." Rebekka walked across the room to stand at the door. Buggies and wagons brought children from the farms farther out; those from town walked across the bridge or ran up the lane. Two tied their horses in the shed.

"John, will you ring the bell?" She checked her watch—five minutes to eight—right on time.

The *bong-bong, bong-bong* rang out across the schoolyard, over the river, and out to town. The children cheered, their voices loud and high with delight. At eight o'clock they were lined up in two lines for the final bell. Rebekka turned and led her charges into their new schoolhouse. Elizabeth led the pledge of allegiance, another child recited a Bible verse, Rebekka led the prayer, and the day was begun.

As Rebekka assigned places at the bench/desks, she collected all the books that the children brought, carefully writing the family's name in each book so they could be returned when finished.

She introduced three new pupils, children of the recent arrivals to the area. All the while concentrating on the children and the beginning of the day, she kept one ear on the hammering coming from outside the building.

"Now I know it will be hard to concentrate with all the noise around us, but I expect you to pay attention just like you always have."

All the children nodded. "Yes, ma'am."

"Now, we all know we are short of supplies, so we will share books. I expect those of you in the fourth grade and above to help with the younger ones."

"Yes, ma'am."

Giggles erupted from a smart comment from the left side of the room, and Rebekka nailed the guilty one with a stern look. "Andrew, would you like to say that so we all can hear?"

A dark-haired boy with faded overalls rose to his feet. "No, ma'am."

"Then we'll hear no more such outbursts?"

"Yes, ma'am. I mean, no, ma'am." He shuffled his feet and looked up at her from under indecently long, dark eyelashes.

Rebekka shook her head and then checked her watch—ten o'clock. "There will be a twenty-minute recess. When you all come back in, I expect you to pay attention. And keep out of the way of the men working."

"Yes, ma'am."

"Excused." The horde leaped to its feet and turned to pound out the door when Rebekka raised her voice. "Order!" The pupils walked sedately to the door, but once through it, broke into shouts of laughter.

Rebekka sank down into her chair. Why did she feel like it should be time for school to be out rather than only morning recess? *It's just the first day,* she reminded herself. *Every year's first day is just like this—except for the pounding and sawing going on outside.*

As her usual habit, she started reading a book to the entire school the last half hour of the day. "We're going to read one of Mark Twain's lesser-known stories to start this year. It's called *A*

Connecticut Yankee in King Arthur's Court. Have any of you read it?" When they all shook their heads, she opened the book and started to read.

Her voice floated over the enraptured children and out the windows to the ears of the man working on a window frame. Jude paused in his measuring. He'd read the story way back when he was in school, but no one with such a musical voice had ever read to him. Schools, they were a'changin', that was for sure.

That night at the supper table, Mrs. Sampson and Mrs. Knutson kept asking questions until Rebekka related her entire day. The only thing she failed to mention was her awareness of a certain carpenter working outside the building.

When she fell into bed that night, she didn't even have to roll over before being sound asleep.

"Was there a rainstorm during the night?" she asked at the breakfast table in the morning.

"Thunder, lightning, the works. You mean you slept right through it all?" Mrs. Sampson set the bowls of oatmeal before each of her boarders.

"I guess so. I'm not sure I even remember crawling into bed." When she glanced for a second time at the empty chair across from her, Mrs. Sampson chimed in.

"Mr. Weinlander ate at six. Said he needed to get a head start on the day, what with so much to do and all. That man, he's a real hard worker, he is."

"Oh," Rebekka said as she sprinkled brown sugar on her cereal and then poured milk over the top. She hadn't really wanted to know where he was, had she?

By Thursday things were settling into a pattern at school. Everyone seemed to ignore the nailing outside and was reading, writing, and working their arithmetic on the no-longer-brand-new blackboard.

After the last child ran out the door that day, she swept the room, washed the blackboard, and settled at her desk to correct some essays she'd assigned during the day. She chuckled as she read one child's highlight of her summer. She'd fallen in a patch of poison ivy on a picnic and spent days soaking in oatmeal baths. "Now I know what poison ivy looks like," she wrote at the end. "And it's not pretty."

Rebekka turned to the next paper and checked the pile of those remaining. She had six or seven papers to go when she heard someone walking up the three stairs to the cloakroom. She raised her head, ready to answer any question one of the workmen would have.

The man paused in the door. Shivers started at her toes and shuddered their way to the top of her head. The last time she'd seen him, he'd been out cold, knocked unconscious by the pitcher she had slammed against his head.

Chapter 8

Thought I'd find you here about now." Adolph's voice wore the sneer shed heard hissed through the night of months before.

"Will you please leave?" Glacier frost couldn't have been colder.

"Now, don't act thata way. You know we got unfinished business, you and me." He swaggered down the center row, between the benches.

"If you don't leave, I'll—"

"You'll what?" He placed his hands flat on the desktop and leaned toward her.

It was all Rebekka could do to keep from gagging. He'd borrowed his swagger from a bottle down at the saloon, just like that night he attacked her.

"Get out!" She hissed from between clenched teeth. When he leaned closer, she raised her voice, putting all the authority she'd ever learned into the words. "Get out! Don't you ever come near me again!"

Her command ended on a shriek as his hand snaked out and grabbed her by the neck to pull her into a kiss.

Rebekka screamed again and flailed at him with her fists. Suddenly, there was nothing there to hit. Adolph, with Jude's strong hands at neck and seat, was tap-dancing back down the aisle, and then Jude flung him out the door.

Rebekka could hear the thud when he hit the ground.

"And if you ever come near her again, this is only a taste of what you'll get, you hear?" Jude was yelling.

"I'll get you!" Adolph said as he clambered aboard his horse and rode away.

Jude turned and strode back into the schoolroom. Rebekka met him halfway down the aisle, her eyes wild and tears streaking down her cheeks. When he opened his arms, she threw herself into them. Her braid tumbled down her back and sobs shook her frame.

"Easy now, easy." Jude held her close, murmuring words of comfort, in spite of the hard line of his jaw. By all the saints, he'd felt like killing the young fool. "Did he hurt you?"

Rebekka shook her head and burrowed closer to his shoulder. "I got...*hiccup*...away last time, too."

"Last time?" Now Jude was sure he'd go after the fool.

When Rebekka finally quit sobbing and calmed down, Jude felt reluctant to let her go. When she pulled back and dug in her sleeve cuff for a handkerchief, he stepped back. "Are you all right now?"

"I...I think so." She blew her nose and mopped her eyes.

"Did he hurt you?"

"Do you mean physically or emotionally?"

"Either."

"Or my pride?"

"That, too."

Rebekka took in a deep breath and let it out. "All three."

"That brute!"

"No, no. He just pulled my hair and jerked my neck. He didn't really injure me physically. But why should any man think he can treat a woman that way and get away with it?"

"Did you tell the sheriff last time?"

Rebekka gave him the same look she gave a pupil who'd repeatedly made a dumb statement. Then she studied the knuckle on her right thumb. "I couldn't tell anyone he'd attacked me. He said he'd tell them I en—" she choked on the words, "I enticed him. That I was asking for it. And even if no one believed him, my name would be dragged through the mud and no respecting school system would hire me."

Jude tried to think of an answer to refute her statements but he couldn't. She was right.

"It's the liquor that does it. It's always the liquor." Rebekka shook her head. When she realized her hair was hanging down her back, she reached up to coil it again.

Jude stepped back farther and tightened his jaw. If she only knew. How many times had he teased a woman? How many times had he taken kisses rather than asking? How many times had he been drunk and had no idea the next day of what he'd done?

"I need to finish up outside. Will you wait and let me walk you home? That way we know he won't bother you again."

Rebekka fought a battle with herself, but it never showed on her face. Yes, she wanted to walk home with him. No, she didn't want to come to depend on a man, especially this man who would one of these days be going on down the road. No, she didn't want Adolph to attack her again. Yes, she'd...

"I'll be here correcting papers whenever you are ready."

She had to force herself to concentrate on the essays. Whenever she thought of the close call, she started to shake all over. She'd never felt so vulnerable in her own school before. The more she thought about it, the more furious she became. Anger at Adolph, at the liquor, at the men who serve liquor, at those who drink it, smoldered deep within her.

The walk home with Jude passed in silence, both of them caught up in anger at the same situation but from different angles. Jude plotted ways to take care of the young Mr. Strand. Rebekka dreamed of destroying the saloon.

"I'll be ready to leave when you are in the morning." Jude laid a hand on her arm to stop her at the gate to the boardinghouse yard. He continued before she could quit sputtering. "I know you hate having to accept my help but, please, think of the children. If you let me walk you over and back, you'll always be there for them."

"But I...I have to go early to start the stove once the cold weather hits."

"I could do that."

"And shovel the steps off and—"

"Some of those things you could ask the older boys to do."

"I do, but they come from so far and have to get home to do their chores. Mr. Weinlander—"

"Jude. I think after what we've been through, you could call me by my given name."

"Jude, then. I really can't ask this of you."

"You aren't. I'm offering." He leaned over to unlatch the gate. "And Miss Stenesrude—"

"Rebekka."

He said her name, as if tasting it on his tongue. "Rebekka, at least try it my way for the next week or so. If Mr. Larson needs me on another job, we'll discuss this. All right?"

Rebeklca nodded. "All right. And thank you. I—"

"That's enough. You go on in, I have to wash up."

Rebekka stepped through the gate he held open and walked on up the back steps and into the kitchen.

"Child, what happened to you?" Mrs. Sampson dropped her long-handled spoon and crossed the room to stand in front of Rebekka. Gently, she grasped Rebekka's chin and turned it to the right. "You have bruise marks on your neck. And your hair is down. What happened?"

Rebekka sank down into a chair at the table and poured her story into the widow's sympathetic ear. "I thought Jude was going to kill him there for a minute, but he threw him out the door instead. Thank God he was there or...or—" Rebekka closed her eyes against the horror of it.

Mrs. Sampson set a cup of coffee in front of the younger woman. "Here." She dumped two spoonfuls of sugar in it and stirred. "Drink this. You'll feel better."

That evening they all gathered in the sitting room as if in unspoken agreement that no one wanted to be alone. Rebekka sat down at the piano and lifted the keyboard cover. She ran her fingers lightly across the keys, letting the notes seep in to relax the fear and anger from the afternoon. As she drifted into a Chopin sonata, she could feel the tension drain out of her shoulders. Closing her eyes, she let her mind float, feeling the beauty of each measure. Her hands continued to work their magic as she flowed into "Beautiful Savior" and then to "Sweet Hour of Prayer."

Jude watched her from the wing chair in the corner. Lamplight glowed in the auburn highlights of her hair, now slicked back into its tight restriction. Her lashes lay like dark veils on the high rise of her cheeks. The music drew them together, wrapping them in a magic net. But she didn't know that, and he wasn't about to tell her. What would it be like to have a woman like her in his life? He took the idea out and toyed with it, all the while watching the straight back of the woman on the piano stool, swaying in time with the music. But he put it away. He didn't deserve a woman like Rebekka. He didn't deserve any happiness at all. He had killed it long before.

"Why don't you go get your harmonica?" Mrs. Sampson leaned across the intricately carved table between their chairs and whispered so as not to disturb the player. "Mrs. Knutson will get her fiddle and I'll get my banjo. Let's see how we all sound together."

The three left the room at the same time.

Rebekka opened her eyes, finally aware of the near-trance she'd been in. Music did that for her. "Hey, did I play so badly you have to leave?"

"You know better than that." Mrs. Sampson turned at the newel post on the landing."Were just going to join you. No sense you having all the playing fun."

The two women tuned their strings to the piano while Jude practiced a few trills on the mouth organ. Rebekka spun the stool around, a wide smile replacing the former somberness. "So, what'll we start with?"

"You know 'Turkey in the Straw?' " Mrs. Sampson strummed an opening chord then looked at Jude. When he nodded, she strummed again and away they went. The lively music had all their feet tapping. They played on with each of them calling out tunes.

"That's enough," Mrs, Sampson said, laying her banjo down. "I haven't played for so long, my fingers are near to bleeding."

"Me, too." Mrs. Knutson agreed as she blew on the end of her fingers on her left hand. "These strings are murder. We'll just have to do this more often." She laid her fiddle back into it's case. "I haven't had so much fun since…since I don't know when."

Rebekka closed the keyboard cover. "You would have thought we've been playing together forever. There won't be a shortage of musicians for the dances this winter."

"How about a cup of coffee? And there's still some of that pie left, Jude, in case you're interested."

Jude stuck his mouth organ into his shirt pocket. "Never could turn down a piece of pie." He stood and stretched his hands above his head. "Lead me to it."

When Rebekka said her prayers that night, she had an extra thank you for the music played in the sitting room. What had started out as a way to let go of the anger from the afternoon turned into a party. "Father, that was such fun. And I think Jude even smiled a time or two. Shame I had my back to them. I'd like to see him laugh some time. Thank You he was there to…to..." The anger swelled up unbidden, tasting bitter on her tongue, and she couldn't say the words. She rested her forehead on her clasped hands on the edge of the bed. The hard floor beneath the rug made her knees ache.

"What can I do about Adolph, so he doesn't attack anyone else?" The remembered smell of liquor on his breath made her gag. She waited for more words to come, but she saw only black. "Please help me. In Jesus' name. Amen." She shivered in the breeze lifting the curtains at her window. The bite to it made her think of frost and fall.

She pushed herself to her feet and slipped beneath the covers. This night she was grateful for the quilt to pull over the sheet and blanket.

In the morning, Jude was already gone by the time Rebekka had finished dressing and had entered the kitchen for breakfast.

"He said to wait for him; he'd be back to walk you over." Mrs. Sampson turned the bacon with a long fork. "How many eggs you want this morning? I thought to make you a fried egg sandwich for your dinner."

"Two, I guess," Rebekka answered as she pulled out her chair. "And that sounds fine." She sat down and placed her napkin on her lap. "But he doesn't need to do that. I'll be just fine."

"Don't think it'll do you any good to argue. Seems like when he makes up his mind about something, he don't let nothing get in his way." Mrs. Sampson set Rebekka's plate in front of her along with two pieces of toasted bread. She poured herself a cup of coffee and sat down. "That was some fine playing last night, if I do say so myself."

"You can say that again." Rebekka spread ruby-red choke-cherry jelly on her bread. "Do you think—" She didn't have time to finish her question as the sound of male feet on the back porch cut her off.

"You about ready?" Jude took off his hat as he entered the room.

"You don't have to do this, you know," Rebekka said after swallowing the food in her mouth.

"I know. Finish your breakfast. I'm due for a cup of coffee anyway." He crossed to the cupboard and took out a cup, filled it, and sat down at the table. "Any of that pie left?"

"You know you finished the last piece last night. Will molasses cookies do?"

"Ja, sure." He leaned back in his chair.

Was it just her imagination or had he winked at Mrs. Sampson? Rebekka finished her eggs and wiped her mouth with her napkin. "I'll be right back down."

The walk to the school passed without conversation. Every time Rebekka tried to think of something to say, she thought it sounded silly. Since when did she have trouble thinking of topics to talk about?

"Thank you," she said as she started up the steps.

"Don't leave until I'm ready this afternoon."

Rebekka sucked in a breath, ready to lambaste him for giving her an order, but he was already off around the corner of the building before she could come up with the appropriate words.

The walk home passed without words also. He tipped his hat at the gate and turned back to the school. "Tell Mrs. Sampson I'll be here at six."

Tell her yourself, was what Rebekka wanted to say. Instead, she blustered into the kitchen and did as he asked. Guilt at taking up his work time kept her quiet.

But he doesn't have to do that, she argued with herself, her heels tapping out her ire on the stairs to her room. *But you did feel safer, didn't you?* The other side of her argument won.

By the end of the week, Jude and Rebekka had progressed to discussing the day's events on their way home from school. He asked her how the children were doing and, by the time she told him, they were already at the boardinghouse's gate.

"You read real well," he said as he tipped his hat and then strode back to the school.

Rebekka watched him go. Now what had he meant by that? She thought to the open schoolhouse windows. He must have been listening to the story she read at the end of the day. She felt the heat begin at her collar and creep upward. What an unusual man.

On Monday, James Olson returned to school and by Wednesday the other three older boys joined the row in the back of the room. Harvest had finished early due to the extra long hot weather.

On Friday, Jude announced that he was finished with the outside work on the school and would be moving on to the barn Mr. Larson was building for Ed Jameson. They hoped to have both the house and barn usable by the time winter set in.

"I've asked John Johnson to walk with you." Jude tipped his hat and turned away as usual. "He'll be here at seven-thirty Monday morning. He'll also walk you home in the evening."

Rebekka fumed as she strode up the walk. He could at least have asked her instead of telling her. But now that darkness was coming earlier, she knew she'd be grateful for the escort. She could have asked one of the older children herself. *But would you have?* the voice from within asked her. No, she had to admit, she wouldn't have.

Saturday, she saw Adolph Strand at the mercantile and the look he flashed her spelled pure hatred. Rebekka ordered her hands to stop trembling but it did no good. She left without purchasing the writing paper for which she'd come.

That night, the nightmare returned for the first time since the incident at the school. Hands grabbing for her…foul breath…the smell of liquor gagging her…eyes so filled with hate she felt like she'd been stabbed…a voice screaming. She sat straight up in bed, her heart pounding enough to jump out of her chest.

The room lay dark around her. Without the friendly moon to light it, all the shadows seemed to hover, strangling her every breath. Rebekka coughed, the sound chasing the shadows back to their corners. She drew in three deep breaths and let them out, feeling her heart slow back down and take up its normal pace again.

She lay down against the pillows and created in her mind the picture of Jesus the shepherd, carrying one of the sheep. "Jesus. Jesus. Jesus." She repeated the name aloud until she could feel the warmth creeping back into her bones. The name faded into whispers and silence as she drifted off to sleep.

When she arrived at the schoolhouse on Monday morning, the new heating stove resided in its place of glory, all shiny black and chrome. After the frost of the last few evenings, the heat would be welcome in the mornings.

"I think we should have a celebration on Saturday night the week after this," she announced at the close of school. "We'll celebrate both the new school building and the end of harvest. What do you think?"

"Will it be a dance?" one of the older girls asked.

"Of course. But I've been thinking. What if we have a box social first to help pay for the new desks?"

As the cheers erupted, Rebekka raised her hands for quiet. "You all make sure to tell your parents, now. I'll post a sign down at the mercantile and tell everyone I see. We'll have a real party."

"When will our desks be finished?" one of the younger children asked.

"Not until after they can't work outside anymore. Maybe we'll have them done for Christmas. I think Mr. Weinlander will be doing them."

"I saw some desks in the Sears catalog. They was real nice."

"Were, Elmer, were nice."

"That's what I said, they's nice."

"All right everyone, let's have a grammer review right now."

Groans resounded back to her. "I am, past tense, now."

"I was." The class answered back.

"She or he?"

"Was." One "were" was sounded from over by the window.

"They?"

"Were."

"Now do you understand, Elmer?" He nodded. "Let's all repeat it together." The declension echoed from all their throats. Rebekka smiled. "Class dismissed."

At supper that night Rebekka announced her plans. "And I think we could provide some of the music for dancing. This way the same musicians won't have to play all night and not get to dance."

"I'd like that. We need to find another piano player, too," Mrs. Sampson said, passing the bowl of stew around once more.

"We won't have to worry about that. The school piano burned in the fire, remember?" Rebekka dished herself out a small helping. "And I hate to borrow the church organ. Every time we move it, it gets wheezier."

"Organ music just doesn't do for dancing like a piano anyway. We'll do without. There are enough fiddles, guitars, and such," Mrs. Knutson said, setting the bowl down in front of Jude. "Help yourself, young man. You need plenty of fueling for the work you're doing." She patted his arm. "I been hearing mighty good things about you."

Jude looked at her with a raised eyebrow.

"Mrs. Jameson was in today to order a new winter coat since hers burned in the fire. She says the barn's about done and you've started framing the house. This time she'll finally have two more bedrooms. And for their brood, that'll make a big difference."

Jude nodded. "They need more room all right. They've been living in tents since the fire." He helped himself to another of Mrs. Sampson's rolls. "That Jameson has two fine sons. Not afraid of work, let me tell you."

Rebekka listened as the conversation flowed around her. Each night the four of them talked together more, with Jude taking part rather than sitting silently, watching them with those sorrowful eyes. While she hadn't seen him smile yet, at least there was animation in his face. What would his laugh be like? Rich like his voice?

"…don't you think?" Mrs. Sampson waved her hand in front of Rebekka's face. "Hello, there."

"What? Oh, I guess I was off gathering wool somewhere." Rebekka shook her head. "What did you say?"

Mrs. Sampson grinned a knowing grin. "I asked if you thought we could have this party without any liquor being served?"

Rebekka looked up to find Jude watching her, as if aware her thoughts were of him. She swallowed. She could feel the warmth start below her neck and work its way up. One would think an old-maid schoolmarm like her would be past the blushing stage.

"I certainly hope so." She folded her napkin and slipped it back into its ring by her plate. "In fact, I shall make sure everyone knows that that is the rule." Now she even sounded like an old-maid schoolmarm.

"The men won't like that much." Jude pushed his plate back and leaned his elbows on the table. "And if you want to make money for the school, you want plenty of men there to buy dinner boxes."

"Surely, they can do without for one party." Rebekka leaned her elbows on the table, directly across from him. She could actually feel the steel setting into her jaw.

"Now, now." Mrs. Sampson stood and began clearing the plates. "Anyone for spice cake? I made it this afternoon from a new recipe I got from Isabel down at the post office."

Jude leaned back, breaking eye contact with Rebekka. "Make mine a big piece, please. My mother used to make the best spice cake."

Rebekka felt her jaw drop. The steel melted. This was the first time he had ever mentioned family. She stood and helped Mrs.

Sampson clear the table. When she looked a question at her friend, the older woman just nodded.

"Here, you can pass these around." She handed Rebekka the dessert plates. "I'll pour the coffee."

But when Rebekka went to bed that night, she couldn't get over the idea that all men thought there should be booze at every social event, and when it wasn't served, they brought their own. She thought of an article she'd read in a newspaper. Maybe prohibition would be a good idea. The suffragettes were marching both for the end of liquor and the beginning of the women's vote. What would happen in Willowford if the women got together and made their views known?

Friday afternoon the school received its first cleaning by all of the pupils and their teacher. They washed windows, swept and cleaned all the building debris out of the schoolyard, and cleared an area outside for dancing. Since it would be a harvest moon and if it wasn't too cold, the dancing would be outside.

Rebekka lifted her face to the late afternoon sun. Indian summer brought its own kind of warmth—crisp nights, cottonwood and willow leaves turning autumn yellow, the few maples and elms splashed with russet and gold and all the shades in between. But the days called to her, inviting her out to enjoy the last warm slanting rays of sun, yet with a tang that sang of coming cold.

"Mith Thtenthrude." Emily tugged on her skirts. "Look what I brung you." She handed Rebekka three nodding black-eyed Susans she'd found in the ditch.

"Thank you. I'll put these in water on my desk. They're just right for the party." The little girl smiled, her grin stretching rounded cheeks until her entire face glowed at the compliment. Rebekka squatted down and wrapped Emily in a hug.

Jude saw the two of them, towhead to mahogany head, as he rode his horse back from the Jameson farm. The slanting sun lit the tableau with a golden light, catching him right in his heart.

He pulled on the reins, bringing his mount to a halt, and crossed his arms on the saddle horn. But the moment disappeared as Rebekka rose to her feet and patted the little one on the shoulder. Emily ran off and the teacher looked up to see the rider on the black horse. She waved and turned back to the schoolhouse.

"All right, everyone, I think we're finished. Would you rather leave early or hear another chapter of *Connecticut Yankee?"*

"Read to us. Read to us."

"Everyone find a place to sit, then. I'll get the book and be right back." She turned and entered the schoolhouse, returning in a minute with the book. As she took her place on the top step, children clustered around her like she was a hen with too many chicks.

Jude dismounted and walked his horse into the schoolyard. He folded his legs and sat Indian fashion on the ground, just like the children who turned and welcomed him with smiles as if this were an everyday event.

Rebekka caught her breath. She hadn't expected an adult to join her audience—especially this particular adult. She found her place and began reading. At first her tongue stumbled over the words, but, as she got into the story, she forgot Jude and read to entertain her children.

The night of the party the harvest moon climbed over the edge of the earth and into the sky, huge and golden. While the breeze carried a nip, the warmth of the earth rose to help spread fog veils in the hollows. Laughing people greeted each other as they walked, rode, or drove their wagons and buggies into the schoolyard. When the yard filled, they pulled up along the road.

Rebekka watched as it seemed the entire county turned out for the box social. The tables inside groaned under the fancy boxes, ready to be auctioned off to the highest bidder. Every woman, young and old, had prepared her box in secret, yet hoping a certain someone would buy the right one so they could enjoy the meal together.

She'd brought her box in her bag so no one would see which was hers. Wrapped in blue-and-white checked gingham with a bright red bow, it lay underneath several others. Wouldn't it be something if Jude bought her box? She watched the door, but that certain man hadn't come through it yet.

Lars Larson had volunteered to be the auctioneer for the evening, so when it looked like most of the people had arrived, he stepped to the door to announce the start of the bidding. Everyone crammed into the school building, and even with all the windows and the door wide open, the temperature rose like a thermometer stuck in hot water.

"All right folks, let's start with this little beauty here." He held up a red box with a blue ribbon, ran it past his nose, and declared, "Whoever gets this box will have some good eatin'." He held it high. "Now, what am I bid? Remember folks, this is all for a good cause. Our children need new equipment to go with their new schoolhouse."

The stack of decorated boxes dwindled as the basket of coins filled. Rebekka kept one eye on the table and the other on the door. When Jude finally walked in, she breathed a sigh of relief. When he bid on another box, she felt a stab of... She considered the feeling. It couldn't be jealousy, could it? She shook her head.

"Something wrong?" Mrs. Sampson asked from beside her.

"Oh, no, no. I just remembered something."

"Jude arrived."

"I know."

Mrs. Sampson chuckled. Her box went on the block next and Jude bid on it. The price rose all the way to a dollar before he dropped out and Ed Johnson from the mercantile claimed his dinner partner.

Mrs. Sampson fluttered her hand as she left with her partner and the box.

The three remaining boxes looked lonely on the tables that had been so full. Two looked almost the same, both had blue-and-white gingham but one sported a blue bow, the other a red.

Mr. Larson waved his hands over them and picked up Rebekka's. "Now, what am I bid for this lovely creation? I know there are some of you out there without a supper partner. Let's make these last boxes count."

Rebekka kept her eyes straight ahead. She didn't dare look back at the man in the full-sleeved white shirt and dark pants. Without his fedora, his hair gleamed deep gold in the light given off by the myriad of flickering kerosene lamps set around the room. The silver streak caught the light and…she refused to look again.

"I'm bid one dollar. Who'll make it one and a quarter?" Mr. Larson continued with the singsong chant of a born auctioneer. "One—there, one and a half."

Rebekka wanted to see who was bidding, but she daren't even look. When she heard two dollars, she swallowed—hard.

Jude's voice rang out, "Two and a half."

Down in her middle, Rebekka felt a little shiver begin. Had someone told him which was her box? She looked to the back where Mrs. Sampson shook her head.

"Three dollars," young Johnson sang out.

"Too rich for my blood." Jude bowed to the younger bidder.

Rebekka felt her heart bounce somewhere down about her toes, but she made sure a smile showed on her face as she stepped forward.

John looked from her to the young woman standing beside her, and Rebekka could see the consternation on his face.

"Why he thought he was bidding on Elizabeth's box." Rebekka looked back to Jude, who shrugged and bid two-fifty on the other gingham box. As he came forward to claim his partner for the supper, he offered Elizabeth his hand. The two young people tried to look happy, but their smiles, even to those who knew them, were forced.

"Well, now," Mr. Larson slammed his hammer down. "It appears to me we had a slight mixup with the boxes. I thought no one was supposed to know which was which."

"Obviously they didn't," a jocular voice called from the back. "But fair's fair. You go with the partner who paid for your box."

"Easy for you to say, Jameson," Jude called back. "You peeked."

Laughter floated around the room.

"I have a suggestion," Jude gathered the three of them together. "Why don't we all go outside and eat together? That way we'll all get extra helpings."

The two young people grinned at each other and at Jude. Rebekka's shiver changed to a warm spot. What a thoughtful thing for him to do.

On the other hand, it would have been nice to share a box, just the two of them. *Don't be silly,* she scolded herself. *Put a smile on your face and have a good time.* "Let's go," she said as she picked up one box and handed it to John while Jude lifted the other. "I'm starved. And if we don't hurry, the dancing will start before we're finished."

She followed Jude out the door. Barn lanterns hung from poles around an open area cleared for dancing. She stopped so quickly, Elizabeth ran into the back of her. "A piano," she said, staring at the wagon off to the side. It's load—a piano. "Where did it come from?" She looked from Jude to the wagon and back.

"Well, Nels over at the saloon wanted to give something to the party, so a bunch of men loaded it up and drove it out here," Jude said.

Rebekka stopped like she'd been slugged. "From the saloon? I certainly hope that's all he donated for the night's entertainment."

"Now, Rebekka. Don't look a gift horse in the mouth. You wanted a piano, you got one. Now, come on, let's eat."

Rebekka looked around for John and Elizabeth.

"I thought they'd rather be alone. I remember what it was like to be young and in love," Jude shrugged. "So arrest me, I gave them the right box."

The warm spot in her middle melted and flowed out to her fingers and her toes.

The box could have been packed with sawdust for all the attention Rebekka paid to it. What she really wanted was to make Jude laugh. But, a smile would do.

Jude did a respectable job of demolishing the contents, all the while exchanging remarks with Rebekka about the evening, the people present, and the amount of money earned. What he wanted to say, he couldn't, and a sincere "Thank you" had to suffice. He just wanted her to keep laughing. The rich contralto joy that flowed through the music of her laugh, warmed him clear down to the icy spot that hadn't melted in two years.

He watched a dimple come and go on the right side of her wide mouth. He didn't, no, couldn't deserve her. Slowly, carefully, he drew his cloak of guilt back around him and shut her out.

Rebekka watched him pull back. There would be no smile this night. What had happened to him that... ?

"Time for the music to start," Mrs. Sampson announced, appearing out of the circle of light. "You two ready?"

Rebekka nodded. At least this way she could contribute something to the evening herself. And she didn't want to dance anyway. Earlier she'd been looking forward to whirling around the packed-dirt dance floor. But in her dream Jude had been her partner. Something told her for sure that wouldn't happen now.

They played jigs, reels, and hoedowns, sprinkled with waltzes and a square dance or two. They'd just swung into a Virginia reel when a gunshot split the air.

Chapter 9

Rebekka crashed the chords.

"Call the doctor!" The shout came from behind the schoolhouse.

"What's going on? What's happened?" someone screamed.

Pandemonium broke loose with children crying, men shouting, the sound of a fight, fists thudding on flesh. A crash, the sound of a table or some such shattering under the force of a falling body.

Rebekka sprung to her feet and jumped down from the wagon. Lars Larson grabbed her arm. "Get back up there and start playing again. We'll do a square dance, 'Texas Star.' I'll call."

Rebekka, torn between going to see what was happening and listening to the wisdom of Mr. Larson, nodded. She accepted Jude's hand to pull her back up on the wagon bed. After sitting back down on the piano stool, she looked over the heads of the teeming crowd. The doctor with his black bag in hand disappeared behind the building.

"Please God, protect my school. Please don't let them break up what we've worked so hard to replace," she murmured under her breath as she sounded the opening chords. Then, aghast at her concern for the school and not the men involved, she amended her prayer. "And please take care of those who are hurting."

But if they've been drinking. . . She didn't finish the thought, trying instead to think back over the evening. Had men been sneaking out back for a snort or two? She couldn't be sure. She'd been too busy playing and helping all the dancers have a good time.

"We can do this," Mrs. Sampson said over the twang of her banjo. "Jude, you take the melody."

Mr. Larson joined them in the wagon bed. "All right folks, form your squares. Partners ready?"

At their assent, he swung into the call. "Alamen left with your right hand..."

Rebekka followed the words, her mind anywhere but on the tune. At least her fingers knew what to do.

"Now, bow to your partner..."

What was happening behind the school?

The dance whirled to a close. Applause followed the final chord and Mr. Larson raised his voice again. "Last waltz, folks. Find that special partner for the last waltz." He turned to the musicians. "Choose what you will. I'll go see what's happening and be right back."

Mrs. Sampson took the lead. At her nod, they joined in and played through the tune. After the applause, Mr. Larson again took over.

"That's it and thank you all for coming. Remember to take your lantern or you won't have anything to light your barn with in the morning. Thank you for supporting our school." He waved his arm and the musicians swung into "Good night, ladies, good night, gentlemen..."

Rebekka sang along with the others. At the close, she shut the cover over the keyboard and spun the top of the stool around. "Now, Mr. Larson, what happened back there?"

"A couple of young bucks got into it. Nothing serious."

"And the shot fired?"

"Just a flesh wound. Doc took care of it. Now, now, I know what you're thinking. We couldn't search everyone who came tonight. Yes, they brought booze with them. And yes, they'd been drinking."

Rebekka clamped her jaw shut. She could feel the sparks

shooting right off her hair she was so furious. If she said anything, it would be too much. Men and their booze. Couldn't they live without it?

Jude watched her burn. The fire flashing from her eyes threatened to scorch anyone and anything in its path. In his other life, he would have been right back there, carousing with the drinkers, making a joke out of anyone who tried to force them to stop.

Now he was on the other side. Now he wanted a life not dependent upon booze to have a good time. He'd been having a great time this evening and he'd felt a part of a group bent on making other people have a good time. But what had it cost to change him?

He hitched the livery team to the wagon and turned around in the schoolyard. "Ladies," he pulled up even with the two widows and Rebekka. "Can I give you a ride home?"

Without looking at him, the three boosted themselves up onto the back of the wagon bed and sat with their feet hanging over the edge. He could barely hear their discussion over the groaning of the wagon wheels under the weight of the piano, but he knew he didn't really want to know what they were saying.

He stopped at the gate to the boardinghouse and let them off. Their "Thanks" came in unison, but no smiles accompanied the word. Instead, they continued their discussion on up the walk and into the house. Jude flicked the reins and the horses walked on. After telling Nels thanks for the loan of the piano, he left the loaded wagon in front of the saloon and trotted the team back to the livery.

While he had a gentle hand on the reins, he kept a tight hand on his thoughts. Too many memories clamored to come forward and be recognized.

Playing the organ in church the next morning kept Rebekka's mind occupied because she had to read the music. When her fingers faltered, she commanded them to find the right keys. When her feet failed to pump the correct pedal, she ordered them on. But the Scripture, the sermon, and the prayers went right over her head.

She'd seen Jude saddle his horse and ride out first thing this morning. Where was he going? He couldn't be working on Sunday because Mr. Larson felt strongly about honoring the Sabbath. He and his family lined the second pew on the right. Didn't the man believe in going to church? It wasn't like other towns where the pastor had just the one church. Willowford had church only every other Sunday because they were part of a two-point parish. Reverend Haugen lived in St. John, where the other church was located, and he traveled to Willowford.

Right now, she would have liked to travel someplace. Anyplace would do, just away. What were they going to do? She played the closing hymn and continued with a postlude. How could they get the women together? Other than sewing or quilting bees, the women let the men lead. And look where it had gotten them—someone shot in a fight at a fund-raiser and party for the schoolchildren.

She pushed in all the stops on the organ and tucked the sheet music inside the bench. She really needed to practice more if she was to be the church organist, but right now she didn't even want to be that. Why hadn't God taken better care of the evening? After all, she'd asked Him to.

By Monday morning a plan had begun to form in Rebekka's mind.

"You look like the cat that ate the cream," Mrs. Sampson commented when Rebekka sat down at the breakfast table.

"I'll tell you about it when I finish thinking it through," Rebekka promised.

A blustery wind buffeted her and her escort all the way to the school. *At least winter held off until after our party,* she thought as they crossed the bridge. Dry leaves blew before them, the trees denuded by the storm that had sprung up during the night. Rebekka shivered and walked faster.

"We have to get the stove started and the room warmed before the children get here." She looked up to the gray clouds scudding across the sky. "It could even snow."

"My pa says winter's come. He had to break up ice on the stock tank this morning," John said, his nose matching the red of his stocking cap.

Rebekka looked up again. The roof of the schoolhouse caught her attention. Smoke rose from the chimney and blew away on the wind. When they opened the door, warmth flowed outside and invited them in.

Rebekka hung her coat in the cloakroom. "Were you already here?" she asked.

John shook his head. "I bet Jude—ah, Mr. Weinlander, did this."

Rebekka nodded. He'd said he'd take care of the fire in the mornings. A little nettle of guilt stung her mind. And here she'd been downright rude to the man ever since the dance. And all because he was a man. He'd had nothing to do with the fight or the drinking. All he'd done was be male.

She rubbed her hands together over the warmth of the stove. Now she had time to work on her lesson plan. Christmas would be here before they knew it, and what should they do for a pageant this year? But who wanted to have another celebration anyway?

Snowflakes drifted down like lace doilies when Rebekka and John left the schoolhouse that afternoon. Huge, wet flakes clung to their clothes and even their eyelashes.

"You hurry on home," she said as she turned into the street along the boardinghouse. "And thank you for all your help, John. You have no idea how much I appreciate it."

"I don't mind. And thanks for the book." He raised a hand in farewell, his treasured book rucked under his jacket so it wouldn't get wet.

Rebekka nodded. The extra time with John was paying off in more ways than one. He'd become a reader for sure, if she had anything to say about it. And his requesting to borrow a book was certainly a step in the right direction.

She shook the snow off her coat and hat, unwinding the scarf around her neck as she kicked off her boots at the doorsill. After hanging her things up on the back porch, she walked into the kitchen, redolent with the aromas of baking chicken and its dressing. Her stomach growled in anticipation.

"And hello to you, too," Mrs. Sampson said with a laugh at Rebekka's consternation.

"Pardon me." The young woman laughed along with her friend. "Mrs. Knutson home yet?"

"No, and neither is Jude." She peered out the window.

"Looks like it's coming down harder."

"Good thing they got the roof on the Jameson house," Rebekka remarked as she went to the sink and washed her hands. When she got the dishes out of the glass-faced cupboard to set the table, they heard boots being kicked against the doorstop on the back porch.

"Well, at least Mrs. Knutson is home safe."

The sparrowlike woman flitted in, still brushing snow from her hair. "Even my hat didn't suffice," she said as she smoothed her hair back up into the pompadour that crowned her head, adding an inch or two more to her meager height. "What a day! Seemed everyone in the county needed something before the snow fell. As if they haven't known it was coming for weeks now." She set her bag of tatting in the dining room. "Three dress orders for Isabel. I think she must be planning a trip or something."

While they discussed the happenings of the day, Rebekka divided her attention between the conversation and the back door where, to her relief, she again heard the thump of boots on the step.

"Good, Jude's here, and supper's ready soon as he gets a chance to wash up. Bet he's near froze after that long ride in. I don't doubt they stay out there during the week if the weather stays bad."

"Sorry I'm late," Jude called as he hung up his things. He stopped at the stove to rub his hands in the rising heat. "Brrrr. When winter comes around here, it doesn't just pretend. This is the real thing. Evenin' everybody."

Heat poured into the room when Mrs. Sampson opened the oven door to remove the roasting pan. Jude leaned over and inhaled the rich aroma of baked chicken. "Now, that alone is worth the cold ride. Gimme five minutes, all right?" He opened the lid on the reservoir and dipped hot water into the pitcher waiting on the counter. Pitcher in hand, he left the kitchen.

"Oh, Rebekka. I almost forgot. There's a letter for you on the hall table," Mrs. Sampson said, brushing back a lock of hair with the back of her hand.

"Thanks," Rebekka said, then went to get it. Compared to the kitchen, the rest of the house felt chilly; perhaps the coal furnace needed stoking. She picked up her letter and ambled back to the warm kitchen. Sitting down at her place, she slashed the envelope with her dinner knife and started reading, mumbling softly. "Dear Rebekka," her aunt wrote in a firm hand. "We are all fine here, but I thought I'd better get our invitation out early. We would love to have you come for Christmas and stay until after the New Year. Grandma especially asked me to invite you."

Rebekka raised her gaze to find Mrs. Sampson watching her.

"Is everything all right?" She set the platter of sliced roast chicken on the table.

"They want me to come for Christmas." Rebekka felt a lump form in her throat. She hadn't celebrated a holiday with family in ten years.

"Are you going?" Mrs. Knutson brought the stuffing bowl.

"I don't know."

"Going where?" Jude entered the kitchen in his stockinged feet so no one had heard him coming.

"To Minneapolis…for Christmas with my family."

"Sounds wonderful." He pulled out his chair and sat down. "When will you leave?"

But I don't want to leave this family either, Rebekka thought as she looked around the table at the dear faces, these people who were becoming so much more than just friends. This was her family, too. "I don't know." She folded the letter and replaced it into the envelope. *Please ask me to stay here.* She bit her tongue to keep the words from tumbling out. What in the world was she thinking? Of course she wanted to spend Christmas with her relatives, really she did.

But when she went to bed that night, she wondered whom she was trying to convince. Especially since they'd had another musical evening.

She was prepared to wake up to a dark and blustery day, but instead, the rising sun reflected off the crystallized world outside. The elm tree outside the window wore frosting branches and the spirea bushes laid down under their pristine blanket. By the time she and John followed the already-made tracks across the bridge, the sun was glinting off the snow, hurting their eyes. Rebekka looked thoughtfully at a drift off to the side. She hadn't made snow angels for a long time. Perhaps they could do that during recess.

That afternoon, the stationmaster delivered three boxes to the school. "You boys come on and help me," Jonathan Ingmar said as he lugged one box in and set it down by the stove, where everyone was gathered to eat their dinner. Two of the big boys followed him out the door and returned with two more boxes that they set down by the first.

"Who are they from? What are they? Can we open them

now?"

The questions flew fast and furious.

Rebekka retrieved her scissors from a desk drawer and handed them to one of the newer children. "Go ahead, cut the twine."

His grin didn't need an interpretation. As he cut the strings binding the boxes, the other children ripped off the wrapping.

"Go ahead." Rebekka answered the question before it could be asked. "The address was for Willowford School. Just save me the return address so we know who we must thank."

As the children peeled back the carton flaps, a letter lay right on top. Emily handed it to her teacher. "Thith ith for you."

Rebekka read the perfect script. It was addressed to Jude Weinlander. She tucked it into her pocket to deliver tonight.

"More books. Look. *Tom Sawyer, Huckleberry Finn.* A whole set of encyclopedias, *McGuffey's Readers*. . .ten of them." The children piled them out on the floor. "Who sent them, Miss Stenesrude?"

"I don't know," she answered. "But I'll find out."

"Chalk, pencils, paper, even glue." The children sat back in delight. 'And colored paper." Down in the bottom of the third box lay three sets of watercolor paints. One of the older girls picked one up reverently.

"I've always wanted to paint," she whispered as she traced a gentle finger over the brightly colored squares.

"And now you shall," Rebekka said, rising to her feet. "Why don't you pack all that back in the boxes for now? As soon as we have shelves, we can put them out."

That evening, when Jude saw the letter, a shutter closed across his face. Rebekka watched it happen. One moment he looked at her with interest, the next he was gone. He stuffed the letter into his shirt pocket and continued with his meal.

Rebekka left it alone until they'd finished supper. When he asked to be excused, she followed him to the base of the stairs. "To whom shall I send the thank you letters? The children are so thrilled with the supplies and would like to thank the sender."

"I'll give you the address in the morning," Jude said then climbed the stairs without another look back. The curve of his shoulders, though, spoke volumes to the woman watching him. She put her hand to her heart; the ache there pulsed for the pain of the man for whom she cared so deeply. Was it the love one has for the wounded or some kind of deeper love? Rebekka wished she knew.

Up in his room, Jude read the entire letter for the third time. While Mrs. Norgaard penned most of it, there were personally written messages from Dag and Clara, pleading for him to come home to Soldahl. They missed him, prayed for him, and were thankful he'd finally written.

Mrs. Norgaard asked if there was anything else the school needed. She volunteered to collect more books and send them on, but Jude would have to let her know.

Jude put the paper down on his desk. She was a sly one, that Mrs. Norgaard. Here she made it impossible for him not to respond. The school needed so much and the thought of a piano flitted through his mind. No, that was a want, not a need. The children sang like larks anyway, with or without a musical instrument to lead them.

He walked to the window and peered out. Much of the snow had already melted. When they finished up out at the Jamesons' he could go home. Mr. Larson hadn't mentioned any other jobs. He listened to the music float up from the sitting room.

"Come home, come home, all who are weary, come ho-o-o-me." The words of the age-old hymn, sung in harmony by the three women downstairs, tugged at his heart. Home, where was home anymore?

In the morning he left the address for Rebekka and told Mrs. Sampson he would be gone for a while. They would be staying at the

Jamesons' to finish up as quickly as possible.

When he mounted his horse in the early dawn and rode down the street, he felt a compulsion to look over his shoulder at the two-storied, slightly Victorian house, smoke rising straight up from the chimney in the still air. If anywhere was home at this time in his life, that was it. Was Rebekka up yet? Was this home because Rebekka lived and played and sang there? He already missed the evenings at the boardinghouse and he wasn't even out of town yet.

The week seemed to drag its feet, like those who plowed through the mud that followed the snow. Early mornings the ground crackled beneath their feet as John and Rebekka broke through the frost cover. But by afternoon, the mud clung to their feet — gumbo they called it. Usually North Dakota soil turned to gumbo only in the spring.

At school one afternoon Rebekka opened the *Old Farmer's Almanac* and read the prediction. This was to be an unusually cold winter, with plenty of snow and blizzards, and an early spring with an excess of rain. *Wonderful,* Rebekka thought. Her pupils would go stir-crazy for sure. Could be this would be a winter when they had to close down during the worst weather. Last year had been mild, so they only missed a week in January.

She rapped on her desk for attention. "Children, finish what you are working on and we'll take time to talk about the Christmas pageant. We'll plan it together, so come up with good ideas."

When she dismissed them that Friday, the pageant's planning was well under way. But she still hadn't answered her letter. Would she go to Minneapolis for Christmas?

Even though the three women didn't overwork themselves, that Saturday equaled three normal ones in the amount of things they had accomplished. Rebekka had just gone to bed when she heard shots ring out. She threw on her wrapper and ran down the stairs.

"Sounds like it's coming from the saloon," Mrs. Sampson said as she opened the front door so they could hear better. Shouts, another gunshot. "That one was the sheriff's shotgun." Mrs. Sampson clutched her wrapper more tightly around her.

The sound of running feet announced the emissary before he arrived at the boardinghouse. "Doc says come quick," he panted. "He needs a nurse."

Mrs. Sampson whirled back into the house to grab her boots and coat. "What happened?" she asked as she shoved her feet into the ice cold rubber.

"Two men down. There was a fight, somethin' awful." He grabbed her arm and hustled her down the walk.

Rebekka closed the door and leaned her forehead against the stained wood. The booze won again.

Chapter 10

Mrs. Sampson dragged herself in the door at seven o'clock the next morning.

"What happened?" Rebekka leaped up from the table where she and Mrs. Knutson had gathered for coffee. Neither claimed to have slept a wink. She poured Mrs. Sampson a cup of coffee, while Mrs. Knutson took her friend's coat and hat and hung them up.

With the three of them around the table, Mrs. Sampson took a sip of her coffee and rubbed her tired, red eyes. "It was terrible. One man I didn't know was already dead. Shot through the heart. Two more were injured. One we patched up and sent home. The other, Ole Johnson, Doc worked over all night. But it wasn't enough. He died an hour ago."

"But Ole Johnson has four children at home. Two of them are in my school." Rebekka swallowed the tears that already burned the back of her throat. Those poor babies. What would Ethel, their mother, do now? The family was dirt-poor already.

"I know. We did the best we could. He was shot in the gut. Couldn't stop the bleeding." Mrs. Sampson spoke in the monotone of weariness and despair. "Two men died tonight because two others got in a fight. Ole wasn't fighting. He caught a stray bullet."

"But he was drinking at the saloon when he should have been home with his family. They don't have enough money for food and clothes, but he can spend the night drinking at the saloon." Rebekka felt the fury burn out her tears. "When will they learn?"

"Never," Mrs. Knutson said quietly. "Some men never learn."

Rebekka looked up at her. "You, too?"

The other woman sat straighter in her chair. "My Claude froze one night in a snowbank coming back from the saloon. He said he had a right to have some fun once in awhile, and drinking and playing cards with the men was his idea of the best time."

Rebekka reached across the table and clasped the widow's hand. "For me, it was my father."

"Well, something should be done. More and more I think that closing down the saloons and stills is a good idea. Make booze illegal, that's what." Mrs. Sampson rubbed her upper arms with work-worn hands. "I hate the stuff."

"I hate what it does to people." Rebekka rose to her feet to begin making breakfast. She fetched the frying pan and the eggs from the pantry and the side pork from the safe out on the porch.

"You don't have to do that. Give me a minute to rest and I'll be fine." Mrs. Sampson started to rise, but Mrs. Knutson laid her hands on her friends shoulders, gently pushing her back in her chair.

"Let us. You've already done your share for today."

"Thank you, both. Thought I'd go out to see Ethel this morning and help with washing the body and readying him for burying." Mrs. Sampson shook her head. "What kind of a Christmas are those poor folks goin' to have now?"

"The funeral will be tomorrow?" Mrs. Knutson sliced the bread and set two slices in the rack over the coals.

"I'm sure, since that's when the reverend will be here. Otherwise he'd have to make another trip." She yawned fit to crack her jaw. "Think I'll take a little lie down before I go."

The three went about the duties of women everywhere who reach out to their sisters in grief. Rebekka fried sausage for scalloped potatoes while Mrs. Knutson baked a cake. When the food was ready, Mrs. Sampson got out a bar of her special soap and several towels. Her box of mercy complete, she walked out to the horse and buggy Rebekka had fetched from the livery.

"We'll take care of things here, don't you worry." Rebekka helped tuck a rug around the widow's knees. "Give her our thoughts and prayers and hug the children for us."

"Will do." Mrs. Sampson flapped the reins and the horse trotted down the street.

The next day after church, the congregation remained for the funeral service. Reverend Haugen said all the proper words but Rebekka had a difficult time sitting still and listening. During the prayers she gripped the back of the pew in front of her to keep from leaping to her feet. This man's death wasn't God's will. If he'd stayed home where he belonged he'd still be singing with the rest of them, rather than leaving his wife to weep and his children to sob for their father. She bit her tongue to keep from shouting the words aloud.

"Dust to dust," the reverend intoned the words at the cemetery. But after Ethel Johnson and her oldest son each tossed a handful of dirt on the pine box, she straightened her shoulders and turned to the other mourners.

"Please, do something about this evil in our town. Good men can't be safe when the booze takes over. Do something before other tragedies happen." She wiped her eyes. "Please. Do something."

Rebekka clamped her hands together. The idea that planted itself in her mind after the fight at the box social had matured. Like wheat nodding in the field, the plan was ready for harvest.

"Tell every woman in town that we will be meeting at the church tonight at six o'clock. If we hurry, we can catch some of the farm wives also."

Quickly, the word spread. When anyone asked a question, the answer rang the same—just be there.

That night Rebekka stood at the front of the pews watching as the women filed in. She closed the doors when it looked like every woman in town and the surrounding area had arrived. After taking her place again at the front of the room, she raised her hands for silence.

"I know you are all wondering why we called this meeting, but after the sad afternoon and Ethel's, Mrs. Johnson's, plea, I think you can guess what we are about."

Gaining courage from all the nods and assents, Rebekka continued. "Many of us have suffered because our men drink. If I polled the room, I'm sure you all have stories to tell. My father was the drinker that ruined my young life. My mother died, I think, of a broken heart. He died because his body couldn't handle any more liquor." She continued with her story and finished with, "I never told anyone this before because I was too ashamed. I thought other people would look down on me because my father had been the town drunk, one of them anyway. And wherever we went." Rebekka looked out over the heads of the women gathered. "Now is the time to do something about this problem in Willowford."

Silence lasted but for a moment when a woman in the back rose to her feet and started clapping. Others joined her, and soon all of the women were on their feet, clapping. The applause soon became as one pair of hands, the steady beat from the heart of each woman.

Rebekka nodded and smiled. When she raised her hands again, the women fell still. "I have a plan. You want to hear it?"

The answer came as one voice. "Yes!" The women took their seats.

"We start with the legal process by talking with Sheriff Jordan. We'll ask him to close the saloon."

"He won't do nothin'. He's a man." The comment came from the back of the room; laughter greeted the sally.

Rebekka went on to outline steps two, three, and four of her plan. The women applauded again. "Now remember, this plan is our secret. The good Lord sees in secret, but the men won't."

"Unless someone blabs," a woman off to the right called out.

Mrs. Sampson rose to her feet, stretched herself as tall as she could, and ordered, "No one will blab." She stared around the room, daring someone to argue.

Nobody said a word.

"Now, who will call on the sheriff with me?" Rebekka asked after the silence stretched to give anyone a chance to comment.

Three hands went up. Mrs. Johnson from the mercantile, Mrs. Sampson, and, Rebekka caught her breath in surprise, Mrs. Larson.

"Good. We will let you all know what happens. And if that fails—"

"Like we know it will," another voice interrupted. "We'll see you all on Friday night. You know where." The women stood as one and filed out into the night.

The next afternoon after school, the four women met at the boardinghouse. "Ready?" Mrs. Sampson looked at each of them directly. For a change Mrs. Larson didn't have much to say.

"Who wants to do the talking?" Rebekka asked.

"Let me start." Mrs. Sampson pulled her red knitted hat down over her ears. "I have plenty I want to say to him—and all the men."

As they entered the sheriff's office, Sheriff Jordan pushed his chair back and rose to his feet. "Well, hello, ladies." Steam rose from the coffee cup at his left. "What can I do for you?"

Rebekka clamped her lips together at the syrup dripping from his voice. He surely wouldn't be so sweet when they finished with him.

The women took up their places as if assigned. One on each side of the desk and Mrs. Sampson in front.

"Sorry I don't have enough chairs to go around. I wasn't expecting company," he said, his smile faltering slightly at the corners.

"We want to talk about the shooting on Saturday night."

"Now you know I can't discuss a case like that. I have the two men in lockup who accidentally did the shooting. Or rather who are accused of the crime."

"And when their lawyers post bail, they'll be out on the road again." Mrs. Sampson leaned her arms on the desk.

"Well, ja. That's the way our legal system works. Everyone is innocent until proved guilty. We'll have a trial and —"

"And the most they'll get is manslaughter because, after all, it was only a fight and no one meant to do any harm."

"Well, now, Alma—"

"Mrs. Sampson."

He looked at her for a moment and tightened his jaw. "Mrs. Sampson, that's for the judge and jury to decide."

"A jury of all men."

"Now you know the laws, Al . . . Mrs. Sampson." The sheriff leaned on his straight arms, towering above the woman across the desk. "Now, what can I do for you ladies?" He cut the end of each word like a sharp cleaver through chicken bones.

"You can close down the saloon so there won't be any more such 'accidents.' "

"Now you know I can't do that. The Willowford Saloon is a reputable business. Nels pays his taxes just like everyone else. Why, he even loaned out his piano for the school party. . .out of the goodness of his heart. You know that, Miss Stenesrude." He shook his head. "What you're asking, I just can't do that."

"In spite of all the fightings and killings caused by the liquor served there?"

"Now, that was an accident, I told you—"

"That leaves us no alternative but to deal with this ourselves. Good day, Sheriff. Ladies?" Mrs. Sampson turned and strode out the door, the three other women following like soldiers behind their general.

Evenings, the three women at the boardinghouse plotted and planned. During the day, other women were seen coming and going. While all their errands looked legitimate, the boardinghouse hadn't seen such activity in years.

It's a good thing Jude isn't here, Rebekka thought one night as she finished her prayers and crawled between the icy cold sheets. *He'd have tried to stop us for sure.* But oh, when she thought of it, how she missed him. They hadn't had a musical night since he had left.

Friday night at eight o'clock the women gathered at the church. Whispers sounded loud in the dark, as they huddled together both to keep warm and to receive their instructions one last time. Axes, hatchets, and a buggy whip or two were drawn from satchels and from under coats.

"Now, remember," Rebekka spoke in a low, but carrying voice. "Be careful you don't hurt yourself and do not do the men harm. Just the saloon."

"All right. May God be with us." She raised her voice in the old marching hymn. "Onward Christian soldiers, marching as to war…" Fifty women, young and old, marched out of the dark church and formed a line, four abreast, to sing their way down the street.

They sang their way the three blocks to the saloon, up the wide wooden stairs with their feet in perfect rhythm, stomped across the wooden porch and through the double doors, now closed against the winter's cold.

They sang as they laid the whips about, driving the men from their gaming tables like cattle in a drive. They sang while they smashed all the bottles lining the glass shelves behind the bar and chased the few diehards with their axes. The third verse swelled while they made kindling of the tables and chairs. "Forward into battle..." The words sung from fifty throats could be heard above the crashing, the smashing, and the yelps as men ran out the door.

The shotgun roared as Sheriff Jordan slammed the doors open.

Rebekka and her platoon of ten lined up behind the carved walnut bar with a marble top and, on "Three," they all shoved, tipping the entire bar over on its side. The front was already splintered by the swinging axes.

"That's enough!" Sheriff Jordan roared, loud as his gun.

"Onward Christian soldiers, marching as to war. . ." The women swung into the chorus and, shouldering their axes, marched out the door.

"Just keep on marching right to the jail," the sheriff boomed his order. He stood to the side as the marchers left, eyes straight ahead like good soldiers. "Oh, no. Ann, Mary, what are you doing here?" His wife and seventeen-year-old daughter faced forward and marched with their sisters.

The singing women turned right into the jail and marched in. Those who couldn't force their way through the door marched in place and sang in time on the porch and in the street. Their marching and singing kept them warm, in spite of the night wind that growled across the plains, promising snow and cold to freeze one's bones.

"Let me through. Excuse me. Sheriff!" Nels pushed his way into the packed jail. When he finally made it to the sheriff's desk, he leaned on his arms, panting and glaring like a mean hound who'd just been whupped.

"I. . .want. . .to file charges. These women destroyed—" His voice rose to a shriek. He took a deep breath and started again in a lower key. "These women destroyed my saloon. The only thing left in one piece is the piano." His voice rose again. He heaved and puffed, trying to get his breath again.

"I know, Nels. I was there, remember?" Sheriff Jordan stood at his desk.

"Well, you didn't come quick enough. They broke everything—"

"I know, except the piano." The sheriff raised his voice to be heard over the singing. "Cut it out. Quiet!"

The women sang on, their faces forward, looking neither to the right nor the left.

"Alma!"

"Mrs. Sampson." Her voice cut through the air like the buggy whip she'd used earlier.

"I want to press charges." Nels thumped his fist on the table. "Put them all behind bars. Look what they did to my saloon." He thumped again.

Sheriff Jordan swung around, his fists clenched. "Just get outside right now, Nels, before I throw you in the clink. I got fifty women here to deal with and I ain't got enough jail cells for ten. You got any better suggestions, you just tell me now or leave. I'll talk with you later."

"Well, I never!" The saloon owner looked around the room until he was impaled on Mrs. Sampson's glare. "I'll be back." He pushed his way out of the room, no "Please" or "Excuse me" left in his gullet.

Mrs. Sampson and Sheriff Jordan faced each other over the desk again, like a replay of the Monday before.

The women kept on singing.

Out of the corner of her eye, Rebekka watched the standoff, careful to keep on singing even though her throat felt raw like a ground-up piece of meat. She tried to keep a grin from cracking her face. The orders had been to keep a straight face and keep on singing. She tried to hear what they said but, short of moving out of her place, she couldn't distinguish the words.

Their faces said plenty however. Glare for glare they stared and stormed like two bears over a kill.

Sheriff Jordan threw his arms up in the air. "All right, ladies, about face. Go on home. And stay there!" His roar matched the shotgun that he used for crowd control.

The singing stopped.

"And what are you going to do about the saloon?" Mrs. Sampson cut through the silence.

"I don't know."

The women turned as one and marched out the door. Out on the street, they let themselves smile for the first time.

Rebekka watched them head for their homes. *But what will they face when they get there?* The thought wiped the smile from her face.

"Don't you worry none about us," Mrs. Jordan said in a low voice, as if having read Rebecca's thoughts. "We know how to handle these men of ours, most of us anyway."

Chapter 11

Nels won't be rebuilding."

"What? You mean that?" Rebekka asked as she dropped her satchel on the table. "How did you hear?"

"Sheriff Jordan came by to say there are no charges being filed. Gave me a lecture on civil disobedience, however." Mrs. Sampson spread the frosting on a chocolate layer cake in front of her. "Said if he'd had a bigger force, he'd a'clapped us all in jail until we rotted." She turned the cake, her eyes twinkling above the smile that came and went. "But he'da needed a bigger hoosegow, too."

"But what will Nels do about the saloon?" asked Rebekka as she dipped a finger in the bowl and licked off the frosting.

"Well, the building wasn't his, he rents it, so I 'spect he'll build a place somewhere on the outside of town." She checked the cake to make sure she hadn't missed any spots.

"Then we failed." Rebekka felt her shoulders slump.

"No. We stood up for what we believed and now the men of this county know their women can accomplish something when they all get together. But unless prohibition goes through, there'll always be places men can drink and play cards. You gotta remember, some women like to join them."

In mid-November, the setting sun was slanting across the snowdrifts when Jude was returning to the boardinghouse. As he rode past the school, he wished it were earlier so he could have given Rebekka a ride home or at least walked with her. The snow in the schoolyard had been trampled by many feet, a circle for "Run, Goose, Run" packed by the game players.

Just past the school he saw three angels formed in the snow, one large and two small. "Who do you think made those?" he asked the only live creature around, his horse. The black gelding tossed his head and snorted. Jude shook his head. Here he was, the man who'd rather not talk with anyone and now he was so starved for conversation, he even talked with a horse.

"It's all her fault, you know." Prince nodded then tugged on the bit. Home lay just across the wooden bridge. "What am I to do?" Prince lifted his tired feet a bit higher. He pulled at the bit again, his ears pricked toward the town ahead.

The horse's feet thudded across the bridge. Beneath, the creek lay frozen, drifted snow filling the creek bed nearly to the tops of the banks. Snow muffled the *clop, clop* of the hooves on the timbers.

The stillness of the schoolyard and winter silence of the creek made the jangle of the bit ring loud on the crisp air. Somewhere ahead a door slammed. Smoke curled up from chimneys and lighted windows beckoned a traveler home.

Prince turned on Sampson Street and broke into a trot. "I have to tell her, don't I?" Prince shook his head and picked up the pace.

Before he headed up the walk to the house, Jude led the horse into the barn, threw in some hay, and dumped a pan of oats in the manger. By the time he hit the back porch, he was nearly running. He leaped up the steps and kicked snow off his boots. His coat caught the hook along with his hat, and his saddlebags hit the floor. He pulled off his boots at the jack and padded to the door to the kitchen. Heavenly smells assailed his nostrils, and the sounds from inside said supper wasn't yet on the table.

As he opened the door, he knew why he was so excited—he was home! Rebekka jumped up from grading her papers at the table and took a step toward him, her smile wide as the sun on a summer day.

"Welcome home, stranger." Mrs. Sampson spun around and gave him a hug.

Jude stopped as if he'd been struck.

Mrs. Sampson patted his cheeks with both her hands. "Does you good, boy. You need more affection in your life. Just want you to know how much we've missed you." He looked over her shoulder to Rebekka.

What he wouldn't give to have her in his arms instead. He returned the older woman's hug and squeezed Mrs. Knutson's hand. When he straightened, his gaze refused to leave Rebekka's. The two looked deep into the other's eyes, all the while separated by five feet of kitchen floor and a lifetime of sorrows and fears, hopes and dreams.

"Hello, Rebekka," his voice cracked.

"I. . .we're glad you're back." She clamped her fingers around the back of the chair so she wouldn't throw herself in his arms. Why could Mrs. Sampson hug him? What would happen if she just walked across the canyon separating them and into his arms? What would he do? What would she do?

"I hear you're a prohibition rabble-rouser."

"Oh." She mentally shook herself. A grin broke loose and shattered her reserve. "It was nothing. We just busted up a saloon and almost got thrown into prison. All fifty of us, all women."

"Way I heard it, there were axes flying and whips and over a hundred yelling and screaming womenfolk, driving the poor men of Willowford right out into the cold of night."

Rebekka threw back her head and laughed, a contagious sound

that invited everyone to join in. "So that's how the story has grown." She looked to the two widows who were chuckling along with her. But when her gaze returned to Jude, her breath stopped.

He was smiling. A real smile that banished the sadness from his eyes and crinkled the corners. "You women are some piece of work." Even his teeth showed.

It was all she could do not to fling herself across the space. He smiled! Jude, the sad, not only spoke a longer piece than she'd heard from him yet, but his smile...

"Supper's on the table soons you wash up." Mrs. Sampson plunked a pitcher of hot water in front of Jude. "Your room's been closed up, so it'll be a mite chilly, but leave the door and the register open and it'll be warm in no time."

"Thanks." Jude walked back out into the back entry, picked up his saddlebags and then the pitcher on his way back through the kitchen. "You musta known I was coming." He nodded at the cake on the counter.

"If I'da knowed you was coming, I'da baked you an apple pie." Mrs. Sampson turned to finish the gravy she was stirring on the stove.

Rebekka heard a ghost of a chuckle float back from the dining room. A smile and a chuckle all on the same day? Would wonders never cease?

That night after filling Jude in on all that had gone on in his absence, they broke out the instruments and played all the tunes they could think of.

"How 'bout another piece of cake with our coffee?" Mrs. Sampson asked as she put away her gutbucket. "This sure has been mighty pleasurable."

Rebekka closed the cover on the keyboard. "I'd love some." She spun around on the stool and caught herself falling into the deepest blue eyes she'd ever seen. Clear, warm, like a lake on a summer's day.

"Me, too." Jude reached for her hand and pulled her to her feet. "Rebekka, we need to talk."

"Cake's on." Mrs. Knutson stopped in the doorway arch.

"Oh, excuse me…I mean..."

"We're coming." The mood lay in tatters at their feet.

As Christmas drew nearer, the days seemed to move in double time. Rebekka, like many others, ordered many of her Christmas gifts from the Sears catalog, at least those she didn't make herself. As the packages arrived on the train, she wrapped them and placed those for her family in a trunk. She'd take them with her when she boarded the train for Minneapolis the day after the pageant.

At school, preparations for the pageant progressed on schedule. One night Rebekka asked Jude if he would help make the sets for the Christmas play.

"Of course. When would you like the help?"

"Would tomorrow be all right? John and two of the other boys need some carpentering help and then the painters can go to work."

"Sounds like a major production."

"Oh, it is, and the children wrote most of it themselves. They even composed two songs to use." She sat down at the piano and played through both tunes, singing the words along with the melody. "See, aren't they wonderful?"

Jude nodded. *Yes, you are,* he thought. *Wonderful and beautiful and. . .* He closed his thoughts off like shutting the damper on a stove. And not for him. When he told her what he'd done, she'd close down that wonderful smile and turn away, afraid to be with a man who had killed his wife.

The day before the pageant, the blizzard struck. It howled across the plains and the Missouri for three days, burying everything in drifts ten feet tall and twice as wide. Then it shoveled up the drifts and tossed them in the air, blowing with a fury unstopped by humans or their flimsy houses.

No one ventured out. The trains stopped in the nearest town. Only the furious wind, driving the snow before it, lived on the prairie.

On Christmas day, the world awoke to silence. Silence so deep it hurt the ears to hear it. While bitter cold captured the drifted snow and froze it into mountains and ridges, the sun reflected off the glittering expanses to blind anyone who ventured forth.

"Are you sorry you couldn't visit your grandmother?" Jude asked as he and Rebekka stood at the kitchen window. They could see the rope connecting house and barn that lay partially buried beneath the frozen crust. Jude had followed it to go out and feed Prince during the storm.

"I'm more sorry about the pageant. The children worked so hard and, for some of them, the presents at school might have been the only ones they received."

"You can always put it on in January."

"We will. It's just that they were so excited. You lose some of that with delaying," Rebekka sighed and turned from the window. She couldn't tell him she'd been glad to see the blizzard that stopped the trains. She wouldn't want to be guilty of wishing anything as awful as that storm on the farmers and townsfolk alike, let alone all of God's other creatures.

After dinner, they gathered in the sitting room around the piano to sing all the carols they knew and then some over again. Mrs. Knutson brought out her Bible and read the Christmas story from the Gospel of Luke.

Rebekka heard herself saying the so-familiar words along with the reader. "And in those days..." Into the hush of the afternoon, the story carried the same message as it has all through the ages. A Babe was born, the shepherds and angels rejoiced. When Mrs. Knutson closed her Bible, they all sat in silence for a time.

"I love the part where 'Mary kept all these things, and pondered them in her heart.' " Rebekka leaned her head against the high back of the wing chair.

"I wonder about the innkeeper. Here I have a boardinghouse. What would I have done if I was full up and a young couple came, asking for a room?" Mrs. Sampson rubbed under one eye. "It's so easy to sit here and say 'Shame,' but what would I have done?"

"Knowing you, you'd have moved them right into the sitting room and helped deliver the baby yourself," Mrs. Knutson said, smiling at her dear friend. "You've never been able to turn anyone away."

"Thank you. I always said God gave me this big house for a reason."

Jude listened to the exchange, agreeing wholeheartedly. She could have turned him away but she didn't. "I think about the shepherds who believed what the angels said and right away went looking for the Baby. Shepherds are a mighty tough audience. But then, I guess if the whole sky starts singing and you see a multitude of angels, that oughta about you convince anyone."

What about you? Rebekka thought, trying to listen to what he was saying between the lines. *Will it take the entire heavenly choir to convince you that God loves you no matter what?* Love, what a wonderful word. She turned it around in her mind, looking at it from all angles. She loved her teaching and her students, playing the piano, singing. She loved the sun on her face and the breeze in her hair. She loved Jude. Wait a minute! Sure, she loved Jude like a friend and brother in Christ.

But Mr. Larson was a brother in that way also and walking with him didn't set her toes to tingling. Her toes and all other parts inside and out. Sheriff Jordan's smile didn't make her go mushy in her middle.

She used the conversation flowing around her to watch the man who set her heart afire. While he rarely smiled, she knew what it did for his face now. And his voice, that deep, melodic way he had of talking, as if he thought out each word in advance so as to use the best one. She hadn't planned to feel this way about any man. Was this her Christmas gift from the Lord of Hosts?

"I have something for each of you." Mrs. Sampson rose to her feet. "It's not much but, well, what would Christmas be without presents?"

Each of them went to their rooms and returned with wrapped gifts. Rebekka handed hers around and sat back in the wing chair to open her presents. A lace collar made by Mrs. Knutson, a warm muffler with matching hat and mittens in a warm rust color that set the roses blooming in her cheeks from Mrs. Sampson, and the third box, she hesitated to open. She looked up to catch Jude watching her, the smile lurking at the corners of his mouth.

She unwrapped the parcel. Inside knelt a hand-carved wooden angel, her arms spread as if to welcome the world. The feathers on her wings, carved in intricate detail, invited the caress of a fingertip.

Rebekka struggled against the tears clogging her throat and burning her eyes. "She's…she's just beautiful." She looked up to see Jude watching her. Was that love she saw glowing in his eyes? Could she feel the way she did and not have him return the feelings?

"My, my, son, I didn't know you could carve like that." Mrs. Sampson shook her head. "You're a real artist."

"I didn't know, either. Out there at the Jamesons', old Grandpa spent his evenings whittlin' so I asked him to show me. That little angel was hiding in a hunk of cherrywood, just waiting to come out."

"Thank you. I've never had such a perfect present." Rebekka traced the grain of the draped gown. "She's so beautiful."

Like you, Jude thought but didn't say. He had no right to say such things, but he couldn't stop thinking them.

Mrs. Sampson opened a set of eight napkin rings of rich walnut and Mrs. Knutson two spools for her lacemaking.

Jude opened his presents as if he couldn't believe anyone would give him something. The red muffler from Mrs. Knutson he wrapped around his neck, the gray wool socks from Mrs. Sampson he promised to wear the next day, and the final package he held in his lap. His fingers had a life of their own as they untied the silvery bow and carefully pulled apart the paper. The mouth organ lay in a bed of tissue, gleaming as the light hit the chrome-and-brass trim. He picked it out of the nest and put it to his mouth. Long, sweet notes hung on the air, each a part of another, as he played "Silent Night."

Rebekka could feel the shepherds quaking and the glories streaming down. The room, her heart, seemed full of the glories of Christmas.

"Thank you." His words blended with the notes hanging in the room as if loathe to part. Other words hung on the air between the two young people, unspoken words but feelings deep enough to withstand the not telling.

After the new year, Rebekka started reading *The Pilgrim's Progress,* since the storms continued unabated and everyone was virtually housebound. One night they remained in the sitting room after the reading when Mrs. Sampson asked what they thought the story meant.

"Nothing," Jude said, looking up from his carving. "It's just a fine story, that's all."

"No, it's an allegory." Rebekka kept her finger in the place. "And all allegories have a meaning." Jude just shook his head.

"This is the story of all of us who fail and fall," Mrs. Sampson said with certainty. "It shows how God always comes to meet us. He picks up his fallen children, dusts us off, and sets us on the right path again. We can never be so bad that He gives up on us." Jude snorted, the shake of his head nearly negligible.

"It's true." Mrs. Knutson joined the discussion. "All we have to do is ask for forgiveness and He gives it. That's why Jesus died, for our sins."

"Well, it's a good story." Jude held the piece of wood he worked with up to the light. "A real fine story."

"Remember that God even forgave Paul after he helped kill Christians, made him into a real leader in the church and for all of us." Mrs. Sampson laid her knitting in her lap. "I'm just grateful that He did it, that's all, or I wouldn't be here."

Jude looked up at her in surprise. Surely a woman such as she had done nothing serious enough to think about leaving life?

But when he climbed the stairs that night, he couldn't shake the thought. Would God really forgive all that he'd done wrong?

Chapter 12

School resumed in mid-February. Rebekka stood before her pupils. "Welcome back and let's pray that's the last of the bad weather."

"Whenth the pageant?" Emily raised her hand from the front row. Her feet could now touch the floor as she sat so straight in her new desk.

"How about the first of March? That will give us two weeks to prepare." The children cheered and fell to their lessons with a vengeance so they could have time to practice.

The pageant went off without a hitch. The curtain pulled back when it was supposed to, no one forgot their parts, and, at the end, the audience cheered for five minutes. But Jude's smile was the best accolade Rebekka could have wished for.

One morning Rebekka awoke to the music of dripping icicles. The chinook blew in during the night and was turning the snow to mush as rapidly as it could. The snow seemed to disappear almost overnight.

But when the rains came in torrents, the town began to worry. The Missouri was still frozen, there hadn't been time for the ice to melt, and now, with all the rain, there could be trouble.

Rebekka grumbled on her way to school one morning. First the prairie fire, then the blizzards and the terrible cold, now rains that seemed to be reenacting the forty days and forty nights of Genesis.

Bryde Creek rushed under the bridge but just barely. Another six inches and the bridge to the school would be impassible.

How was she supposed to prepare her students for the examinations when they hadn't been in school for half of the year?

Saturday, a watery sun peeped through the clouds. Sunday, Jude rode Prince out over the prairie rather than take up Rebekka's invitation to join them in church. When he rode past the church, he heard the congregation singing; he pulled Prince to a halt.

"Throw out the lifeline, throw out the lifeline, someone is drifting awa-a-y . . ." The words poured out of the cracks and crevices of the country church as if sung for his ears alone. He nudged his mount into a trot. Maybe next time the pastor was in town, he'd go with Rebekka. Couldn't hurt.

Monday, the rains returned, drenching the land and running off the ground still frozen under the mud.

Some of her students had stayed home and, by one o'clock, Rebekka toyed with the idea of sending everyone home. But she hated to make them walk in the downpour. Perhaps it would stop by the time school was to let out.

She could feel the tension in the room, the children sneaking peeks at the windows just like she was. "All right, that's enough." She rose to her feet and headed for the piano that had been donated at Christmastime. "We can take an hour out and call this getting ready for the last day of school's concert."

The children cheered and gathered around her, the little ones in front and the taller in the back. They ran through some drills with Rebekka striking chords up a half each time. The "la, la, la, la, la, la, las" rang clear to the rafters. When she swung into "She'll Be Comin' 'Round the Mountain When She Comes," everyone laughed and joined in all the funny sounds.

Their "toot toot" stopped in midsound. Rebekka listened. Who was hollering? What was that roar? It sounded like three freight trains bearing down on them.

She leaped to her feet and ran to the windows facing south. In horror she saw gray water surging between them and the town. Waves rolled before chunks of ice, tearing at the banks and already climbing up to the schoolhouse steps. Out in the main channel of the Missouri, trees ripped past, tumbling in the flash flood that rose by inches each minute.

How would she get the children out?

"Everyone, over here. John, you get the jump ropes from the cloakroom. Everyone, grab your coats. And let us pray. "Father God, please help us. Amen."

She checked the windows on the north. A rise just beyond them was their only chance. Could the big ones help get the little ones there?

"Rebekka, Rebekka!" A male voice sounded from outside. "Help me open the door." Water that had begun seeping under the door, gushed in when it opened.

"Jude!" Rebekka had never been so glad to see anyone in her life.

"Okay, children, follow the instructions exactly!" Rebekka lined them up, little ones held by the bigger.

"Okay, kids, we have ropes out here and men to help you. Come on out. John, you stay there to help Miss Stenesrude." He grabbed Emily around the waist and handed her off to the next in line, the water lapping at his hips.

Rebekka kept her voice calm, even though she was screaming inside. "That's right. Next." One by one, the children were passed the long distance between the school and the rise.

The water covered the floor. Rebekka could feel a rocking motion, as if she were standing on the deck of a ship. The men stood in waist-deep water.

Rebekka didn't dare look at Jude for fear he'd see the panic in her eyes. "Thank You, God. Okay, John, you go now."

"You, too. Here, take my hand."

"Get out of here!" Jude yelled this time.

Rebekka felt the building shift again. Like a grand ship on her maiden voyage, the school slipped from its pilings and tipped forward.

"Jude!" Rebekka couldn't tell if she screamed or just thought it.

"Rebekka!" Jude pulled himself up into the cloakroom. "I have the rope. We have to swim for it." He grabbed her around the waist and flung them both into the swirling river.

Rebekka clung to his neck, trying to keep her head above the freezing water.

Jude's face had the gray cast of one who was cold beyond endurance.

She found the rope with one hand and kept her other around his rib cage.

"Hang on, my dearest," Jude said. "We're almost there."

Three men waded out in the water and pulled the two ashore.

Rebekka had never been so cold in her life. Her teeth chattered like castanets and she fell into the arms that held out blankets. "Jude, where's Jude?"

"Over there," someone answered. "We're trying to get him warmed. He's been in that freezing water longer than anyone."

"The children?" She could hardly force the words past her clacking teeth.

"Cold, but all right."

"Willowford?" She felt herself slipping into a gray place where she would sleep the pain in her feet away. She thought she heard a voice but could no longer answer. Peace and oblivion.

When she woke up, the lamp reminded her of sunrise. She opened her eyes and looked around. She lay in her room at the boarding-house. Had the flood been a dream?

"Here, drink this," Mrs. Sampson ordered as she held a cup to Rebekka's lips.

Rebekka sipped, then pushed herself to a sitting position. "I'm fine. Where's Jude?"

"Sleeping in his room. He has some frostbite on his feet, but he'll be okay."

"What about the flood?"

"Like all flash floods, as soon as they crest, they're gone. The Missouri is plenty high and still flooding, but the town is safe again." Mrs. Sampson turned at the sound of another voice. "There's that man again. He'da been in here hours ago if I'da let him."

"Jude?" Rebekka felt her cheeks widen. She could no longer keep the grin from busting forth. "How's the school?"

"Fine, or so they tell me." Jude stood in the door. "Just off its pinnings and downstream about two hundred yards. We built it good and sturdy. Should last a hundred years or so." He stared at the woman propped against the pillows. He'd come close to losing her and he'd never told her how much he loved her.

He gave the two widows a look that sent them laughing from the room. When he sat down on the bed, he took Rebekka's hand in his. "I asked God to save us."

"And He did."

"I can't ask you to marry me until I go home and make things right with my family."

"Marry you?"

"And I need to explain what happened in my life." He stroked the tender skin on the back of her hand.

"Jude."

"I know God forgives me now. I—"

"Jude." She placed her fingers gently against his lips.

He raised his gaze from her hand to her face.

"I have one question." She studied the lines of his beloved face.

"What?"

"Do you love me?" She could feel the lump threatening to cut off her breathing.

"What kind of a question is that? Of course, I love you. What do you think I've been saying? But you have to know everything—"

"Then, yes." She reached for his strength, that formidable strength that had saved her and the children from the flood's waters. "I already know all the important things. What happened before has nothing to do with us." When he wrapped his arms around her, she snuggled into his chest. As she raised her face to look up at him, she caught a sheen in his eyes.

"That hymn you sang a while ago—'Throw out the lifeline...' "

Rebekka nodded.

"Well, seems we needed one right bad and there it was." He kissed her eyes. "But I'm home now." He found her lips. "I almost lost you," he muttered into the side of her neck.

"I'm glad I found you," Rebekka answered.

The kiss they shared was all she'd dreamed of and feared never to experience. Together, they looked out the window to watch the sun sink into the horizon. Dusk settled into the room, bringing the peace of evening. But Rebekka knew. And now Jude knew, too. For every dusk there is a sunrise, and together they would face anything that came their way. They and the Savior who promised a bright new morning after the end of a long hard day.

Dakota December

Chapter 1

"T'ain't a night fit for man nor beast." Sheriff Caleb Stenesrude peered out the window at a world blinded by swirling snow. Sam, a mottled brown and gray cow dog and faithful follower, whined at his master's knee. "What's the matter, old boy, you need to go out?" The dog whined again, his tail brushing the floor in feathery sweeps, then let out a yip as if to agree. "Wouldn't wish that on anyone." The sheriff bent his six-foot-plus frame and fondled the dog's caramel-colored ears. "Well, if you have to go, you have to go. I'll let you out the back so the wind don't sweep you right out to nowhere."

The man whose friends called him Caleb, and everyone else called Sheriff, padded in his carpet slippers through the pantry to the back entry. Once he had been referred to as a tree walking, and even in slippers the description seemed apt. When he cracked open the door, the wind tried to tear it from his hands, "You hurry now, you hear?" He anchored the inside door with one hand and shoved the isinglass-covered screen open just far enough for the dog to scoot out.

"Some way to spend Christmas Eve," he muttered, closing the door. He thought about all the preparations that had gone into the Christmas pageant at the church tonight, all the gifts gathered under the tree, the costumes made and the music practiced. He shook his head. Here he was, all alone, as usual.

Some nights he had fights to break up at the saloon or someone in his jail needed tending. He'd let old Max out this morning since he'd sobered up—again. Dag had given the old sot his job back at the blacksmith's and the room that went along with it. Good thing. If they'd found Max sleeping in his usual corner north of the saloon, he'd been dead by morning from this cold.

Caleb ran a hand through dark hair now sprinkled here and there with threads of silver. That and a face carved deeply by sun and sorrow made him look older than his thirty-five years. He scrubbed a leathery hand across his square jaw. He guessed he'd hit the sack, soon's that mutt got done with his business.

The wind changed from a whine to a howl, seeking entry and protesting the barriers. The man shivered in spite of his long Johns and heavy shirt and pants. He never had liked blizzard weather. Too many living things died.

He cracked open the door again and whistled but the wind blew the sound back down his throat. "Sam, where are you?" He heard a yip and shut the door in disgust. "Can't ya remember which door you went out?" Crossing the room, he could feel the temperature rise the closer he got to the great iron cookstove. He looked longingly at the pot of coffee simmering on the back. Should be strong enough to melt lead by now.

The dog barked again, louder this time. "Hold your horses. You're the one who changed doors." A series of barks pleaded with him to hurry.

Caleb jerked open the door. "Well, get your worthless hide in here." Sam backed off, barking all the while. "This ain't no time for games, git in here." The dog darted off the porch, lost immediately in the swirling blackness. But when Caleb started to close the door, Sam bounded back, his bark demanding now.

"All right, I'm coming." Caleb pushed the door shut but he couldn't silence the wails of the bansheelike wind. He stepped out of his slippers and into his boots, hooking his wool jacket off the coat rack in the same instant. He'd learned years earlier that when Sam insisted on his master following, he always had a reason and a good one at that.

Pulling his hat down tight on his head and wrapping a long woolen scarf around his face, Caleb stepped out into the swirling world. Sam hugged his master's knee, and then moved a little bit forward, leading the way.

They slogged through a hip-deep drift and finally bumped into the fence. Caleb looked back over his shoulder. He could barely see the light from his window. A shape loomed before him.

"Well, I'll be."

Sam yipped and pushed forward. A horse waited patiently, head down, nose almost buried in the snow.

"Help." A weak voice moaned from the horse's back.

Caleb climbed over the gate and reached up in time to catch the woman as she fell. To his astonishment, a small child, hanging on for dear life, fell with her.

"That wind'd do anyone in. Let's get you inside. Can you walk a'tall?"

The woman sagged against him. "Please, take care of my boy."

"Now don't you go frettin', ma'am. I ain't one to leave nobody out in a storm like this, let alone a child." As he talked gently into her ear, he scooped the child under one arm, like he was carrying a sack of wheat, and wrapped the other arm around the woman's waist, half carrying her too. "You stay there, horse, I'll be back."

If he could have figured a way, Caleb would have thrown them both over his shoulders. That would have been much easier as he fought his way through the snowdrifts back toward the light he could barely see. What a night for travelers to be out. Under his breath he thanked the good Lord for bringing them this far and for a dog with a nose and ears to beat all. This wasn't the first time Sam had dragged an injured critter home for tending.

Even the oxlike sheriff was out of breath by the time they all sagged against his front door. While the woman whimpered once in a while, he wasn't sure she even knew she was off the horse.

Afraid to let go of her in case she fell, he finally asked, "Ma'am, can you reach out there and open the door 'fore we all freeze to death?" He tightened his grip on the boy. While he could feel the lad breathing, the poor mite hadn't yet spoken a word.

When Caleb tried ushering the woman in ahead of him, she stumbled and nearly fell. She groaned as her cloak billowed out around her.

Caleb clamped his arm around her again and half-carried her across the room to the rocking chair in front of the cast-iron stove. While she slumped into the chair, he sat the boy down on the rug. Sam licked the child's face and, tail wagging, looked up at Caleb as if asking what to do next.

Caleb knelt in front of the rocker. The woman hadn't even started to untie her cloak. "Please, ma'am, make yourself to home. I'll pour you a cup of coffee and..."

At that moment, the woman bit off another moan and slumped forward, hands clasped around her knees. She rocked in place.

"Are you hurt? Do we need a doctor? I—I'm the sheriff here and I learned some about doctoring and that'll just have to do us since we can't go for the real thing in this blizzard." He caught himself. Blathering like an idiot he was.

He sat back on his haunches and stared at the rocking form in front of him. She looked mighty large for such a small woman. *Caleb Stenesrude, you idjit, she's breedin', that's what.* He swallowed—hard. "You—you ain't havin' the baby right—right here and now?" He shook his head again. "You ain't—" His voice squeaked. "Not really."

Her soft moan that rose on the end answered him.

"Oh, my. My, oh, my." Caleb rose to his feet, looked at the woman, then looked to the door and back again. The wind took that moment to try to blow the house down. No, he wouldn't be going for the doctor.

"How soon, ma'am, how soon?" His insistent voice seemed to penetrate her stupor.

"S—some time yet. Please—my horse. Can't let it die." He had to lean forward to hear her. The child stirred behind him. Jumpin' Josephine, he about forgot the boy.

Sam darted toward the door and yipped. He returned and looked up at his master.

"I know, we have to get that horse under cover before the drift covers the poor critter." He pulled on his ear, hoping the action would provide inspiration. Sam yipped again, as if congratulating the boss on understanding dog talk. He headed for the door and looked over his shoulder. "In a minute, in a minute." Sam sat, momentarily appeased.

Caleb looked down at the boy huddled by the stove. Eyes the color of a summer prairie sky looked up at him, then fear passed through like clouds over the sun. The child's chin quivered and a lone tear slipped down a ruddy cheek.

Caleb felt the stab of the boy's misery clear to his rawhide-calloused sheriff's heart. He knelt next to the child and with slow gentle hands began to unwrap the boy's tattered red muffler.

"Now, then, let's get you undressed so the heat of that stove can begin to warm you up." He used the same tone of voice to calm a fractious horse or a bawling calf. It worked on all living things and even some that weren't.

The woman arched in the chair above him, her fingers digging into the rocker arms.

Caleb shot her a glance full of compassion, but at her head shake, he turned back to the boy. "Good, there, son, don't you worry none, your ma is going to be just fine." But when Caleb reached out to check if the flush on the boy's cheeks was from the storm or a fever, the child flinched away. *Someone's been beating the poor little tyke.* The thought made Caleb move even more slowly and carefully. Right away he wished he could meet the low-down rat. Give him a taste or two of his own medicine.

One look at the woman, who was keeping all her misery inside so as not to upset the boy, made him willing to stake his life on the knowledge that it wasn't her. Where was the father? And what were these two doing out on a night like tonight?

"Okay, son, you just keep your things on until I come back from caring for your horse. Do you think you can watch over your ma for those few minutes I'll be gone?" By this time Caleb was beginning to wonder if maybe the boy couldn't hear. Perhaps he was deaf and dumb?

That idea was dashed immediately when the boy slowly nodded, his gaze darting between the woman in the chair and the man in front of him. The eyes looked like they'd seen far too much misery for one so young.

Caleb smiled his most comforting smile and slowly rose to his feet. "Now, you're not to worry, I'll be right back." His promise brought a ghost of a smile to the woman's face but it died under the onslaught of another birthing pang.

Caleb called for Sam and only took time to get his jacket securely buttoned and hat tied down before he and the dog were out the front door. I'm counting on you, Sam. You gotta get us back into that house." Sam whined and darted out to where the horse still stood as if frozen.

As the drifted snow had erased all chances of opening the gate, Caleb took the reins and slogged his way around the east side of the house, keeping one hand on the fence when he could locate it. At his side, Sam pushed him back toward the house when the man started to veer too far away.

"I ain't never knowed a northerner bad as this one," Caleb muttered into his muffler. The wind tore the sound away and sent the words to the four corners of the earth almost before the dog could hear them.

Sam yipped and stopped. Caleb brushed the building snow off the brim of his hat and peered through the driving ice pellets. "Good dog." He'd have gone right by the barn, if it weren't for Sam. No wonder people lost their way from the house to the barn in blizzards like this. He leaned his shoulder into the door, rocking it to break loose the ice and snow. When the door finally gave a screech that signaled it was back on its track, he nearly fell into the dark cavern.

The cow lowed from her stall and his horse stamped and nickered a welcome. The sound and fury were muted here in the snug barn where peace reigned supreme. *God knew more than many folks thought when He chose a stable as the birthing place for His Son,* Caleb thought, leading the weary horse into the spare stall and stripping off the harness. This poor woman, whoever she was, didn't even have a saddle. Wonder where she left the wagon? He brushed the snow off the poor beast and felt its ribs in the process. Shaking his head, he dug an old blanket out of the stack of feed sacks and threw it over the horse's back. He poured a scoopful of oats in the feed box, tossed in a forkful of hay, and snagged the water bucket out of his riding horse's manger.

"He needs it worse 'n you," he said, giving the rangy gray gelding an extra stroke and a slap on the rump.

Knowing he'd rather stay in the peaceful barn than face the ordeal ahead in the house, nevertheless, when all was done to his satisfaction, he pulled the door closed against the still howling wind. He grabbed the rope he had strung from the barn to the house for instances such as this and pulled the muffler up clear to his eyes. A drift had even buried one of the posts that held the rope up. Sam stayed right beside him through the accidental detour and got his master back on track.

After what seemed like hours of fighting the elements, Caleb stopped on the porch and filled his arms with wood for the fire. Good thing he'd spent a few days splitting and stacking firewood. Thank the good Lord for His blessings of a warm house, snug barn, and food to last out the blizzard. Not much chance anyone would be calling for the sheriff tonight. He had enough problems in front of him. "Lord above, give us a special helping of Your Grace this night as I help this poor woman bring her baby into the world." He paused long enough to brush some of the snow off and let himself into the kitchen.

Sam shook all over and trotted over to the stove where the boy still sat huddled in his coal. The dog nosed the child's face as if making sure he was all right, then curled up right next to him.

Caleb dumped the wood in the woodbox and turned to study the woman. She lay back in the chair, eyes closed. Her lashes seemed to him like dark feathers on skin so clear the blue veins under her eyes were unnaturally pronounced. He didn't want to think about it but the blueness could be traced to another source. Another spasm caused her to bite her lower lip and dig her fingers into the chair arms. When it passed, she looked up at him. She tried to smile but the effort proved too much and her eyelids drifted closed.

Caleb shifted his attention to the boy. He lay sound asleep, his head now pillowed on Sam. The dog wagged the tip of his tail, careful not to disturb his precious charge.

"Good dog." The big man removed his coat and hat, hung them on the rack by the door, and pulled off his boots at the jack. Even without the storm, this promised to be a long night.

Since there was no heat in the bedroom, Caleb made a pallet out of quilts and lay it by the stove. He put a pot of extra water on to boil, knowing there was plenty of hot water in the reservoir too. Tenaciously, he kept his mind on each task. He didn't want his thoughts to race ahead to the birth itself and throw him into sheer panic. No different than with a cow, he reminded himself. Nature knew what to do about birthing whether people did or not. His hands shook when he tore an old sheet into wide strips, and then proceeded to fashion a baby blanket and diaper-sized squares from the remnants.

When he tried to whistle "Away in a Manger" his pucker wouldn't cooperate. He licked dry lips and hummed under his breath instead.

"Now, ma'am." He scrubbed a weathered hand over his chin. "I can't keep calling you ma'am like this. I know you got a name. I am Caleb Stenesrude, sheriff of this little spot in the road called Soldahl, North Dakota."

He waited.

Her eyes darted from side to side, like a mouse caught in a feed barrel searching for an escape. She started to say something and grunted instead as the pain rolled over her, squeezing her entire being. When it passed she panted and forced out her reply through clamped lips. "I—I am Johanna—Carlson—and this is my son Henry. I—we thank you for taking us in like this." She closed her eyes and wet her dry lips. "I am sorry to be such a burden and on Christmas Eve, no less."

He immediately wished she'd open her eyes again. Looking into them had been like Finding a deep pool in a clear stream, the kind of pool where trout hid, waiting for a unsuspecting fly to dimple the surface. He'd seen pools like that, clear and full of promise, back in Wisconsin before he came west.

He gave himself a mental shaking and went back to gathering the supplies he thought he might need before this night was over. All the while his hands kept busy, and his mind continued pounding on heaven's door for protection for all of them in the hours ahead.

"You think I could put Henry in my bed to sleep? Poor lad is all tuckered out."

Johanna answered on a sigh. "Yes, if we can hear him if he calls. He suffers some from nightmares."

"We can and I'll tell Sam here to stay right beside him. A good dog lyin' alongside a body makes the dark easier to bear."

"Thank you, Sheriff."

Caleb started to correct her. He didn't much care for the title when it came from her lips.

He wondered how Caleb Andrew Stenesrude would sound with her soft—was it just a hint of Norsk?—accent. What was the matter with him, thinking things like that? For all he knew, she was married and her husband…No, he felt sure there was no husband in the vicinity. No man would leave his wife and son out in weather like this. Especially not in her condition.

He picked up the sleeping Henry and, nodding for Sam to come along, walked into the bedroom back of the parlor. He peeled back the covers with one hand as he lay the child gently on the bed. The boy stirred but instead of waking lay limply against the pillow. While Caleb removed the boy's boots worn so thoroughly the leather was split clean through, Sam leaped up on the bed and, after a glance to his master for permission, curled himself into the boy's side. Caleb tucked in the covers and laid a hand, surprisingly gentle for one so large, on the boy's forehead to check for fever.

"You take good care of him, dog, you hear me?" Sam thumped his tail and laid his muzzle on the child's chest.

Back by the stove matters had taken a turn for the worse. Johanna clung to the arms of the chair, trying to regain her feet.

Caleb leaped to her assistance. "Please, you could fall and hurt yourself."

"Have to lie down," she panted. "The baby is ready to come—n—o—w." The final word turned into a wail. She collapsed on the pallet and continued to pant, the contractions seeming to roll over and through her body with ruthless intensity.

When Caleb checked to see how she was progressing, he literally caught the baby as it slithered onto her soaked petticoats.

"Oh, dear God above, now what?"

The infant let out a yell fit to scare the wind howling in the chimney.

"Well, will you listen to that." Caleb cradled the squalling red baby in his cupped hands and stared at her as if he couldn't believe his eyes. He looked up to see Johanna watching him.

"You have a baby girl, ma'am, Miz Carlson. And she sure does have a hearty pair of lungs. All the rest of her appears intact, too."

"You—you need to cut the cord."

"All right." He looked around for a place to lay this now quiet mite.

"Put her here, on my chest." The woman patted the spot.

"But you'll get all—I mean—well, she's a bit messy, you know."

"If'n you got a clean towel, lay that down first since my dress ain't the cleanest." Was that a twinkle he saw in her eye?

The sheriff felt his confidence return. "'Course. That's what I was thinking to do."

Laying the baby face down on the woman's belly, he took the bit of rag he had torn and tied the cord off and severed the membrane. Now the little one was on her own. As if unhappy with that situation, she squalled again, already turning her head in search of sustenance.

Johanna groaned again as another spasm racked her body and expelled the afterbirth.

"Good. There, there, ma'am. You are doing just fine." Caleb cleaned up the mess as he spoke, doing all in his power to help his patient and yet not embarrass her. There should have been another woman present in this intimate task, or at least the doctor.

Poor lady would probably never be able to look him in the eye again. At the thought, his heart clenched as if caught in a huge hand. Must be he was mighty lonely this Christmas night to be worrying about whether this poor woman would want to see him again or not.

Calling himself all sorts of names, he brought out the strips of old sheet he'd torn up, folded a square patch to put over the baby's umbilical cord, and tied it in place. Next he folded a larger square around the infant to keep her warm and laid her in the crook of her mother's arm.

"How about if I clean her up later?"

Johanna nodded. "Sheriff, that would be just fine. You've done far more than you'll ever know." In spite of the weariness that pulled at her eyelids, she smiled up at the man kneeling beside her.

"She's so beautiful." Caleb touched the tiny fingers curled into a fist. The baby opened her hand and wrapped her fingers right around the end of his. At that moment Caleb lost his heart, giving it over to that bit of humanity whether he wanted to or not.

"I believe we should call her Angel," he whispered as if anything louder would break the spell. "That is, if'n you want to."

"I believe that would be right fine."

"Angel what? Shc nceds more of a name than that."

But the woman and child had both fallen asleep, breathng peacefully in the lamplight.

"Well, I'll be." It was some time before Caleb Stenesrude could tear himself away from the picture on the pallet. As he wrapped his tired body into a quilt, he whispered into the night, "Dear God, please let me hear if one of them needs me."

Chapter 2

He awoke with a start.

The room had turned chilly, no doubt fueled by the draft that sneaked across the floor and worked its way in through the quilt he'd wrapped around himself. The kerosene lamp he'd left with the wick on low now flickered feebly, the wick burned down too far.

What had awakened him?

Caleb threw back the covers and, after getting to his feet, made his way to the table, first to wind the wick higher and then to the stove to add more wood. The harder he tried to be quiet, the more the stove lids rattled and the wood banged against the sides of the fire box before flaring in the remaining coals. As the wood caught, he set the round lids back in place and dusted off his hands.

He listened and nodded. That's what it was, the quiet. The wind no longer moaned and whistled at the eaves, demanding entry like a frothing beast. He looked over at the pallet of quilts where mother and babe slept. Rubbing a calloused hand across his forehead, he thought back to the birthing. Gratitude for the ease of it made him clamp his jaw. What if the baby had been a breach birth or born dead? He shook off such morbid thoughts. That was over and done with. Now he only had to deal with a newborn baby, a woman who looked like she needed more than one night's sleep and a month of good feeding, and a little boy who wouldn't—or couldn't—talk.

Might be easier to take on a bunch of cowboys at the end of a long trail ride. The thought made him rub his forehead again. What was he gonna do with them? They couldn't stay here, in the house of a widower, without chaperones. Why, if Mrs. Jacobson down at the Mercantile got wind of this tidbit, she'd hang them out to dry in every home in Soldahl. He wouldn't be able to walk down the street without people whispering behind their hands. And what would this do to Mrs. Carlson? No, this wouldn't be the way to introduce her to the community.

Besides, he had no time for a boy and a baby.

At that thought the baby mewled, a tiny sound that called forth every caring instinct he never knew he had. The utterly helpless cry flew straight across the room and, like an arrow, sank into his heart.

Angel, that's what he'd named her. If the little family moved on he would probably never see her again. He wouldn't watch her grow and laugh and play.

He cleared his throat.

"I am awake, Sheriff, there is no need for you to try so hard to be quiet." The soft voice came through the dimness.

"Yes, ma'am. Is there anything I can get for you?"

The mewling changed to whimpers.

"No, thank you. I will nurse this one here and…"

"Does she need dry diapers?"

"Yes, I'm sure she does. Have you some here?"

"Just pieces of that sheet. She's wearing part of it now." Caleb left his place by the stove and fetched the folded pieces of cloth. He handed them down to the woman who had rolled on her side. "You need some help?"

"Yes."

He could tell the admission cost her dearly. He knelt beside the pallet and, unwrapping the sheet turned blanket, removed the soiled article. Then, after refolding a small square, he tucked it between the twiglike legs and wrapped the baby tightly in another piece of sheet.

"You do that like you've done it before." She shifted her gaze from the bundled baby to the man who now sat back on his haunches. "Not much different than wrapping a package in brown paper." He resisted the urge to touch the questing rosebud mouth with the tip of his finger. "I'll let you be now." He got to his feet. "You need-anything now, you just call out. Hear?"

"Yes, Sheriff."

Caleb crawled back into his quilt to give her the privacy he sensed she needed. The rustling of moving bodies and fabric, punctuated with Angel's demand for food, painted pictures on the backs of his eyes. Pictures of Harriet and the times she'd nursed their sons. Pictures of warmth and love. Even at only a few hours old, Angel nursed with determination. He could both hear and feel it. Caleb folded a hand under his head and kept a sigh to himself.

What a Christmas Eve this had been. Christmas morning was only a few hours away. Surely he had something in the house that might be given as a present to the little boy. He wracked his brain.

No toys. No child-sized clothing. All the gifts still lay under the tree at the church so he hadn't even an orange or a candy cane. He turned to his other side. Some of the townsfolk had dropped off presents of food—a ham, chocolate cake, julekake—to thank him for helping them at one time or another. He catalogued the things he had set in the pie safe. All well and good but no gift for a small boy who looked as if he hadn't had much in his young life.

Father, Caleb prayed, *You sent me these wanderers so now I have an extra request. Since they are here, could You provide a gift for the little fellow? You know I can't come up with an idea. And while I'm at it, thank You again for keeping that little Angel and her mother safe. Please keep Your angels guard over us. You seem to like babies born at this time of year. Amen.*

He lay snug in his quilt, one of those that his wife Harriet had made so lovingly. Strange how something she made could still bring him such comfort, let alone warmth.

As soon as first light turned the blackness outside to dark gray, he rose and added wood to the fire. After pulling on his boots and bundling up, he then headed for the barn to do his chores. He always thought better in the barn anyway.

With his head butted up against the cow's warm flank and milk streaming into the pail, he mulled over what to do next. By the time he'd poured milk in the pan for the barn cats, fed the chickens, tossed hay into the horse and cow mangers, and refilled the animals' drinking buckets from the barrel of water, he knew what he had to do. What time would Gudrun Norgaard be ready to offer him coffee and advice? Even if it were Christmas morning, she always knew what to do with angels and strays. This wouldn't be the first time he'd conferred with her and, knowing the way of the world, it probably wouldn't be the last.

He caught himself whistling on his way back to the house. The rooster finally got himself awake enough to greet the dawn that still struggled to be seen through the lowering clouds. The temperature had dropped along with the wind but at least the blizzard was over for now. He could still smell snow on the breeze along with wood and coal smoke as the people of Soldahl fueled up their fires for breakfast.

He had someone to cook breakfast for too. That thought lent a spring to his step that seemed positively un-Caleb-like had anyone been watching.

Sam met him at the door and scooted outside as soon as he opened it. By the time Caleb put the milk pail on the table, the dog yipped to come in. "Taking your duties with that little fellow mighty serious, aren't you?" The man only had to hold the door a second before the dog was through and, with a quick tail wag and a whine over his shoulder, Sam headed for the bedroom.

Caleb nodded in approval. Sam was smarter than he gave the critter credit for, and that was saying something. He left the pantry along with his boots and coat and padded into the kitchen. The coffeepot gurgled on the back burner. The floor where the pallets had been laid was swept clean. And there wasn't a human in sight.

They're gone! The thought caught him like an unexpected blow from a barroom brawler. But the sight of the boy's ragged muffler strewn across the horsehair sofa's arm eased his anxiety. She must be taking care of the boy.

Should she be out of bed? What did all this effort cost her?

On the wall by the front door, the carved walnut clock, his only legacy from his grandfather, chimed seven times. He'd go talk with Gudrun as soon as he fed his guests. Maybe she had some flannel or something that could be turned into diapers for Angel. Maybe Mrs. Hanson would know where some necessary things would be. Between Gudrun Norgaard, the grand dame of Soldahl, and Mrs. Hanson, her dedicated housekeeper, they knew about everything that went on in these parts.

His mind played with the words as, under his breath, he whistled the opening bars of 'Away in the Manger.' "

"You sound in a joyful mood." Her soft voice startled him so he clattered the black-iron skillet on the top of the stove.

"Oh, I am at that. Merry Christmas and good morning." He looked at her more closely. "Are you sure you shouldn't be lying down? I mean, like, you had that baby not very many hours ago." His fluster had attacked his tongue. Why should an itty-bitty woman like this make him stutter? When he faced a gang of drunken field hands he felt like he could conquer the world!

"I—I thank you for your concern, but me and mine, we must be on our way as soon as possible."

"On your way!. Woman, you just had a baby, we just had a blizzard. Looks to me like another is right on its heels and it's cold enough out there to freeze spit before it leaves your mouth." Caleb rattled the pan and shoved it off to the side. "Sides, I'm just readying up some breakfast for us. You do think you could stay long enough for a meal?" He could hear the sarcasm but seemed unable to stem it. What in thunder was so all-fired important she had to run off like this?

He took a slab of bacon out of the pie safe and eggs from the pantry and assembled his fixings on the table. He started to cut the bacon and instead turned to the stove. Fetching two mugs off the warming shelf, he poured coffee into both and pointed at the rocking chair. "Sit."

She sat.

He handed her a mug and, wrapping both of his hands around his own, stood by the stove, lightly resting his haunches on the edge of the reservoir. "Thank you for making the coffee."

"You are welcome." Her voice came, as wooden and stiff as long woolen underwear off a winter clothesline.

"Now the way I see it. . ."

"What makes you think you see it at all?"

"Excuse me for sayin' this, but you show up on my doorstep in the middle of a blizzard, have a baby on my floor..."

"It wasn't exactly on your floor." She threw back her shoulders almost indignantly.

You are handling this like a hard-headed Swede. Caleb could hear his father's voice as if he were right in the room.

Caleb figured he'd better listen. "Now, I meant no offense, ma'am, but please, let me help you. The Good Book says to welcome strangers, might well be angels unaware."

"An angel I'm not." A spring thaw might be setting in.

"No, but that little one is and you'd sure be risking her life if you set out now." He spoke gently, like he did to all wounded and desperate creatures. Man, she sure could manage to rile him up. He studied the conflicting emotions as they drew maps on her face. When she lifted her chin and met his gaze, he knew she'd made a decision. He sure as heaven hoped it was the right one.

Chapter 3

"I will stay."

Caleb felt his breath leave in a whoosh. He hadn't been aware he was holding it. To cover his flash of jubilation, he raised the mug to his mouth and took a swig. Even after being out of the pot this long, the rich coffee scalded the back of his tongue. He could feel the heat clear to his gullet.

"Are you sure this—my being here with my family—will not cause you hardship?"

"No, not at all." A vision of Mrs. Jacobson in full sail flashed across his mind. Dear Lord, forgive this slight untruth. "Not at all." He returned to his bacon slicing and carefully laid the slabs in the pan, making sure the slices were evenly spaced. As if that mattered. When the bacon sizzled to his satisfaction, he sliced the bread and proceeded to set the table.

Finally, when he looked over at Mrs. Carlson, she was resting peacefully in the chair, eyes closed, her cheeks two red circles on an otherwise pale face. Mayhap he should stop by and see the doctor on his way back from Gudrun's. Wouldn't hurt to have him check her and the baby out.

Where was her husband? If she'd been a widow, wouldn't she have said so? Where had she come from and how long had they been on the road? The thoughts sizzled through his mind, like the grease that danced in the frying pan.

The click of Sam's toenails alerted him. Caleb looked up to see Henry stop in the doorway. A wet path down one cheek gave mute testimony to the tears shed, but not a sound had come from him. Caleb knew he would have heard the child crying. Sam whimpered.

Mrs. Carlson jerked alert in her chair. "Oh, Henry, come here." She reached her arms out to him. Giving the man standing at the stove a wide berth, the slender child rushed into her arms.

"I ain't goin' ta bite you, son." Caleb kept his voice easy. That wasn't just shyness he recognized in the look the boy threw him. That was out and out fear. Nigh on to terror. "There's a slop bucket out on the back porch so's he don't need to use the privy. I ain't shoveled a pathway out there yet."

"Thank you, I found it earlier." She kept her arm wrapped around the boy, as if to shield him.

"There now, you can come up to the table to eat or I can bring it to you there." Caleb took a plate off the warming ledge and slid two fried eggs onto it. He added bacon, wished he'd thought of frying the leftover potatoes, and looked up at his guests.

Henry was glued to his mother's shoulder, staring at the plate of food as if he'd never seen such bounty.

"Can you manage the chair? I can put a pillow on it." He put the plate down and did as Caleb suggested without waiting for his mother's approval.

When they were both seated at the table, the boy now on her lap, Caleb fetched butter and jam from the pantry, along with forks and knives. Somewhere he knew he had napkins but for the life of him, he had no idea where.

When they looked up at him, as if asking permission, he waved them on. "Go ahead, eat up whilst it's hot."

"Do you not say grace?"

'Course. But mine ain't done yet—oh all right." He slid into his chair. "E Jesu navn, gor ve til brod..." He intoned the Norwegian words his mother had drilled into his soul when he was but a young sprout at the table. At the "Amen" he rose and returned to the stove. Good thing he'd shoved the pan back or it would surely be smoking them out of house and home.

Sam took his place at the boy's feet.

Caleb looked over just in time to see a small hand sneak a bit of bacon to the dog. The boy looked up in time to see Caleb watching him and his face went deathly white. He hid his face and as much of the rest of him as possible in his mother's shoulder and shook his head when she offered him another bite of bread.

Caleb finished dishing up his own food and took his plate, along with the coffee pot, to the round oak table. "Can I warm yours up?" At her nod, he poured the dark liquid into both of their cups and eased into his seat. He felt the way he did when out hunting deer, as if the slightest sound would send the game leaping away, to vanish in the woods. Struggling to find words to say, he decided instead to satisfy his stomach. He felt like he hadn't eaten for a week. All the while he called himself every name in the book and a few new ones he'd just come up with. What was the matter with him? Only that he had let a woman like this and her shy-unto-tears son make him uncomfortable in his own house.

"Thank you, Sheriff. That was very good." Mrs. Carlson neatly placed her knife and fork across the plate. "And now if I can prevail upon you just one more time." He nodded at the question in her eyes. "Could you please bring my horse around? We must be on our way."

"Lady, if that don't beat all." Caleb started to slam his hands on the table but one look at the terror-stricken child and he toned his voice down. He shoved his hands in his waistband and tilted back in the chair.

He started again, forcing his voice to sound calm and soothing. "I have to tell you, I cain't do that. You and these children would freeze to death before you got five miles out of town, what with the drifts and all. That north wind would blow right through you and I know you love your children more than to submit them to that." *What are you running from?* He ached to ask the question, but while he had grilled many a suspect, he couldn't get the questions from his mind to his tongue.

"But we cannot stay here." She looked at him, across the child's head, one of her hands stroking the boy's hair. "You have been more than kind, you have saved our lives, but I know what life is like in a town. People talk."

"Not about this sheriff they don't." He knew she was right, that's why he'd been planning on discussing this with Gudrun.

"Sheriff, I'm surprised someone hasn't been at your door already,"

As if on cue, Sam let out a yip and rose from the floor at the boy's feet. A growl and then a bark announced the visitor before the knock on the door.

"Good dog." Caleb sent the woman a look promising further discussion, then made his way to the door.

"Merry Christmas, Elmer." But at the look on the man's face, Caleb went no further. "What's wrong?"

"There's a man been shot, Sheriff. You gotta come quick."

"Well, I'll be, can't people forget their squabbles on Christmas?" Caleb muttered as he rammed his feet in his boots and thrust his arms in the sleeves of his coat. Just before grabbing his hat, he turned to the woman by the stove. "You wait here."

Immediately chagrined at the way he snapped an order at her, nevertheless he followed his deputy out to the gate, plowing through the drifted snow and walking right over the fence on a frozen drift. Soon the entire town would know there was a strange woman over to the sheriff's house. Elmer Hanson was a good man with a loose lip and nothing Caleb did seemed to make a difference. And Lord knew, he'd tried.

Caleb settled his Stetson farther down on his head, wishing he had grabbed the woolen-billed one with ear flaps. A day like today was no time for a Stetson. "Any idea what happened?"

"Nope, none. He was laying by the livery, half-covered by drifted snow. Looks to been there quite some time."

"How you know he was shot?"

Elmer turned and cocked one eyebrow at his boss. "Has a hole in his chest. Tried to stop the bleeding with a rag. Didn't look to do much good."

"You s'pose he got lost in the blizzard?" His breath blew out in a cloud of steam. While the sun was trying to separate the clouds, it hadn't succeeded as yet.

"Maybe he was looking for the doc and just didn't get that far." Elmer slapped his hands together to improve the circulation. "Man, it's cold still. He wouldn't a laid there long without freezing to death, if the bullet didn't get him."

They stepped up onto the boardwalk, making faster time when they didn't have to plow through snow. Smoke rose from the hotel chimneys but the Mercantile, the drug store, and Swenson's barber shop all wore their Sunday sleepiness. Even the saloon was closed in honor of the holiday. No on else had ventured out, leaving the street blanketed in pure white.

"You want me to get the doc?" Elmer sniffed, then hawked and spit.

"No. Why bother him if the man's dead for sure? We can put him on the wagon and take him to Sorensons. Even undertakers have to work on Christmas. Terrible." They left the boardwalk, turned the corner at the feed store, and stopped just outside the doors to the livery.

Caleb could hear Will Dunfey, Dag Weinlander's apprentice, caring for the livery animals. The boy lived in a snug room in the barn off the blacksmith shop.

"You talk to Will?"

Elmer shook his head. "I told you, I came straight to your house." He pointed to the body lying on the other side of a drift. "There he be."

Caleb dropped down to his haunches. Everything Elmer had said looked to be true. "You ever seen him before?"

"Nope, never."

Caleb studied the face frozen in death. Swarthy, black beard, big nose. Caleb thought he looked like the gypsies he'd once chased out of town. But long dead, that was for certain. "No trace of a horse or wagon?"

Elmer looked pained. "Sheriff, that blizzard wiped out anything and everything. You know that."

"You think he was dumped here?"

Elmer shrugged. "Whyn't we just haul him over to Sorensons and go on home. I shoulda done that without bothering you." He gave the sheriff an appraising look. "Who's that woman at your house? I din't know you had company."

"Just a stranger who got caught in the storm." Caleb strode off around the corner of the building. "I'll get Will to harness us a horse and wagon."

An hour had passed by the time they got the body delivered and Will dropped the sheriff and Elmer back at the sheriff's office tucked into a corner of the county courthouse, one street off Main. Elmer clanked the glowing cinders in the potbellied stove and added more coal.

"What you goin' to do about him—the body I mean?"

"Guess we'll just ask around if anybody knows of him. Maybe put it out on the wire, a description and all. Wait and see if anyone inquires about him. Can't bury him 'til the spring thaw, that's for sure." Caleb took the proffered cup of rotgut that in Elmer's mind passed for coffee and added two spoonfuls of sugar. When he was on duty the coffee was drinkable, black the way he liked it, but his deputy made a pot and boiled the life out of it, then set the pot to simmer. The only good thing about the drink this morning was its heat. Even the steam felt good when he reaised the doctored brew to his lips.

A picture of Mrs. Carlson sipping from her breakfast cup flashed through his mind. What if she took it in her mind to leave?

"Think you can hold down the fort today? Shouldn't be too much going on." Caleb forced himself to stand when all he wanted to do was head for home.

"Can't think why not. You don't mind if I go to church though?" Privately, Caleb thought his deputy's devotion to the Lord had more to do with the younger sister of Mrs. Jacobson, who was visiting for a time. Mrs. Jacobson and her husband ran the Mercantile, or rather she ran the store and him too. But Mary Louise had caught the eyes of most of the town's bachelors. Not only was she pretty but she was of marrying age and not spoken for.

Caleb had been forced to point her in another direction when she set her bonnet for him. Why, he was old enough to be her father. And he told her so.

"You go on to church and have a Merry Christmas, Elmer." Caleb nodded and left before the young man could ask the question buzzing behind his eyes. Asking him to keep his mouth shut about the sheriff's guest would have just made matters worse.

When Caleb reached Main Street again, he debated whether to stop at Gudrun's, the doctor's, or just head on home. He looked up the street to see smoke coming from the Lutheran church's chimney. Mighten be he should talk to Pastor Moen instead of Gudrun. He kept abreast of the town events nearly as well. So often people in trouble called on the Lutheran pastor, and with good cause. John Moen took exemplary care of his flock, including any strangers, strongly believing and preaching the joy of hosting angels unawares.

Like the Angel sleeping at his house. Caleb started home, but turned off the street to Doc's anyway. Mrs. Carlson had looked a mite feverish. As he firmly believed, better safe than sorry.

Dr. Harmon himself answered the door. When Caleb explained the situation, Doc nodded, his mouth full of Christmas bread, and shoved his arms into the coat sleeves.

"I'll be back in a few minutes," he hollered over his shoulder. Grabbing the black leather bag he kept by the door, he followed in Caleb's footsteps. "Shoulda gotten out here earlier and shoveled this, but Mrs. Abramson had a bad attack last night. Thought I'd never get home. When I finally staggered in the door, all I wanted was my bed."

Caleb nodded. "You went out in that blizzard?"

"No, they came for me just about the time it quit." Doc looked up at his anxious friend. "What's the rush? You said she seemed fine."

"Just a feeling I have. First that fellow dead by the livery and now..." Caleb shook his head. Long ago he'd learned to trust his feelings that something wasn't quite right. They kicked the snow off their boots against the front porch post.

Tail wagging, Sam met him at the door.

But the house was empty.

Chapter 4

Leave it to a woman not to obey orders.

"Maybe she's in the other room." Doc pointed in the direction of the bedroom.

Caleb strode through the parlor, knowing that his search was in vain. The house had that empty smell, even though she couldn't have been gone long. And Sam hadn't left that boy's side since they arrived. Sam took his charges seriously.

"No, nothing."

"You sure you didn't dream this woman up?" Doc grinned at his friend but quickly snuffed out the humor. The sheriff's face made it clear what he thought of the joke.

"How'd she get away so fast?" Caleb rubbed his upper lip. "Sorry to have brought you out. Think I'll saddle up and follow her. With no one else out on the streets, she'd leave an easy trail."

"Bring her to my house when you find her. Be better for her there, and for you too. You know those jokers'll be all over your hide and the women too. Martha and I'll take care of her 'til we figure what else to do."

Why did that suggestion make him want to grit his teeth? Caleb leaned down to scratch the top of Sam's head. The dog whined and, after a quick finger lick, headed for the back door.

"That's the way all this started " Caleb muttered. "You and your need to find a tree." He turned on his way and waved at the doctor.

"See you soon, I hope."

As soon as he opened the back door, the dog lit out over the snow as if wolves were on his heels. Over the fence and the drifts, straight on a beeline for the barn.

Caleb knew enough to follow, although the knee-high snow slowed him somewhat. Sam had his gray nose pressed to the crack in the barn door, his tail whipping from side to side. A whine suggested in no uncertain terms that his master ought to pick up his feet a whole lot faster.

"I'm coming. I'm coming." Sam darted through the crack before Caleb, his shoulder against the door, pushed it full open. In the same moment, he realized there were no horse tracks leaving the barn door. The snow was so packed against the door, it had only been opened enough to let one person in. Just as if he'd left it after milking and caring for the animals. Tracks went in, but no tracks came out.

"Doc! Doc Harmon!" He yelled as loud as he could.

"Coming."

With that Caleb entered the barn, fear and anger waging a war in his soul. Whatever possessed her to start out like this? She hadn't appeared daft but now he was beginning to wonder. He blinked in the dimness but didn't let that slow him down.

"What do you think you're doing?" He leaped forward to catch her as she fell.

"Take care of Henry, please." Her voice quavered and her eyelids fluttered. "I—I'm sorry."

"You should be." Caleb felt like shaking her. How could she be so stubborn as to put herself and her children in such danger? She'd gotten the bridle on her horse and an old saddle blanket in place. A saddle, not his good one, stood on its horn beside the stall post. Was she going to steal it? He shook his head. But of course, she couldn't reharness the beast.

"How bad is she?" Doc Harmon knelt beside them.

"I don't know." Caleb looked around again. Henry huddled in the corner of the stall, clutching the quilt-wrapped baby in his thin arms.

The two were almost invisible in the darkness of the stall. Sam scooted past his master and, after a quick swipe of the boy's nose, wriggled into the straw beside him. Caleb's horse snorted and stamped his feet. The cow grunted as she lay down again. Here in the barn all seemed so peaceful, so normal. Except for the woman with the bright spots of fever on skin so pale you'd think you could see right through it.

She moaned softly and turned her head from side to side.

"We better get her to my house where my wife can nurse her. I'd guess she's ended up with an infection and, traipsing out here to the barn with two young'uns, well, I don't know. Sometimes you just wonder." He took her wrist between his thumb and fingers and counted her pulse. "You suppose something frightened her?"

"She was pretty determined to get on the road. Either she is running from something or has someplace pretty important to get to."

Both of the men spoke in the hushed tones of a sick room.

The baby whimpered.

Caleb glanced up in time to see Henry clutch the bundle to his chest. "We're not going to hurt you or your mother, son. You know that."

"You want I should go get the buggy?" Doc asked directly in Caleb's ear.

"No, since the horse is bridled, why don't you mount up? I'll hand her up to you and I think Henry here can ride behind. I'll carry Angel."

"Angel?"

"Well, she was born on Christmas Eve and all. I thought it fittin'." When Doc didn't answer, Caleb added. "She said I could name the baby since I helped birth it." How come he sounded so defensive? Caleb shook his head. "Let's get a move on, okay?"

Doc answered with a snort and, getting to his feet, threw the saddle over the horse's back and cinched it in place. By the time he was mounted and the woman secured in his arms, both men were puffing. Even though she didn't look bigger than a minute, as dead weight she was as cumbersome as a sack of grain.

"Come on now, son. You get up behind here."

Henry shrank farther into the corner, if that were possible.

"Henry." At the sharp command, the boy disappeared into the wood.

Caleb rolled his eyes heavenward. Would nothing go right this day?

He sank down on his haunches, one hand on the manger side. "Now, son." He softened his voice and moved with the slow patience he used when stalking game. "We're trying to take good care of you and your mother. I won't hurt you but you have to mind me. Now give Angel to me and I'll give you a boost up behind Doc Harmon."

Henry wrapped one arm around the now sitting dog.

"Okay, Sam can go with you."

"Caleb." Doc Harmon groaned.

Too late, Caleb remembered Mrs. Harmon didn't cotton to critters in her house. Oh well, what else? He leaned forward and gently unlocked the grip the boy had on the baby. When she whimpered again, Henry started to draw back but after a sigh that came clear from his boots, he scrambled out into the open.

"Now, I'm going to put you up on the horse behind Doc here. Can you hang on by yourself?" Henry nodded.

The saying was easier than the doing. With the bundled baby in one arm, he picked up Henry with the other and hoisted him up. At that moment Angel let out a yell that made her mother moan and raise her head.

"Where? What?" She started to push away. "My baby?"

"You shoulda thought more of her when you started this hare-brained scheme," Caleb muttered.

"Hush, now." Doc spoke firmly using his practiced doctor voice. He explained what they were doing as Caleb took the reins and led the horse over to the door. With a mighty shove, he pushed it open wide enough for the loaded animal to make its way through and turned and closed it when the horse snorted at the wind that had kicked up while they sojourned in the barn. The gray-bellied clouds hung low again, ready to dump another stormy helping.

By the time they reached the doctor's house, snowflakes no longer drifted down but slanted on the wind. Ice crystals from the earlier storm blew off the drifts and stung Caleb's face. He had known a second storm would follow on the heels of the first. Something in his bones told him.

Caleb and the doctor looked at each other, their burdens and back to each other.

"I'll…" "You…" They spoke at once.

Caleb shook his head and, dropping the horse's reins with the hope the animal knew about ground tying, strode up the snow-covered walk and knocked on the door. When Mrs. Harmon answered it, he handed her the baby with a quick explanation and spun back to get the others. He swung Henry to the ground and reached back up for his mother.

"I'm sorry to be such a burden," Mrs. Carlson whispered when Caleb lifted her down.

"You ain't no burden at all." Caleb hefted her up in both arms, chest high and tight against him. He followed his former footsteps to the open door and, swinging sideways to keep from bumping her, made his way down the hall beside a twittering Mrs. Harmon.

"I'll explain it all later, Martha," Doc growled. "Let's just get her to bed quick as possible. You get some of that willow bark tea seeping and this young pup here might like a cookie."

Sam's toenails clicked on the wooden floor behind them.

"Caleb Stenesrude, you get that dog outta my house. You know I..."

"Leave it be, Martha." The doctor's tone brooked no argument. He set the boy down and immediately Sam glued himself to Henry's leg. Tail sweeping the floor, Sam reached up to swipe Henry's cheek, once and then again for good measure.

Henry appeared to be trying to fade into the dog's hide. He kept his gaze down so the adults could only see the top of his head.

"Where do you want me to put her?" Caleb called from the hallway.

"Oh, my goodness, in the front bedroom." Martha clucked her way down the hall.

Doc Harmon stooped down and lifted Henry's chin with one finger. "Not to worry, son. Your ma will be all right and Mrs. Harmon just don't like dogs too much. She likes little boys just fine and she'll get used to Sam here." He laid one hand on the boy's shoulder and the other on the dog's head. "You two go on back to the kitchen and wait there. You might take off your wraps and leave them here on the chair."

Like a mouse trapped in a feed barrel, Henry's gaze darted up and down the hall, up to the doctor's face and down to the dog's. Doc Harmon waited.

As if of their own accord, Henry's hands pulled off one mitten and then the other. When they dangled on their crocheted cord, the fingers eased one button out of the hole and then the other. All the time Henry kept his gaze on Doc Harmon.

"There now. I'm going back to take care of your mother. You two will be right fine here." He paused, gave the boy's head a pat, and headed down the hall.

Mrs. Carlson, now divested of her outer garments, lay under the patchwork quilt in the four poster bed. Her fingers clutched the edge of the quilt as if a windstorm might steal it from her. Her eyes, fever-bright and frantic, appeared huge in her wan face.

"Where's my baby?" Her whisper carried to the man standing with his back to the room, looking out the window.

"Mrs. Harmon has her."

"Caleb, why don't you go see about that poor horse?" Doc entered the room and crossed immediately to his patient. He dug his stethoscope out of his vest pocket and warmed the metal end in the palm of his hand.

"I'm going to take it home and put it up in the barn." Caleb pulled a gold watch out of his pocket. "Then I intend to go join in the Christmas service at church."

"It's almost half over." Doc looked at his friend over the edge of his glasses.

"Not if Reverend Moen tries to make up for no sermon last night." Caleb paused at the door. "Good day to you, ma'am. I surely do hope you feel better soon." He made his way to the kitchen where he could hear Mrs. Harmon talking to Henry.

"Will he be all right here?"

"Landsakes, a'course he will." She set a plate of molasses cookies next to the glass of milk that was already half gone.

A white mustache edged Henry's upper lip. He reached for one of the sugar-topped treats and nibbled on the edge. One hand never left the dog's ruff.

"And the dog?"

Mrs. Harmon looked from the dog up to the quivering boy and back to the dog. Sam wagged his tail and leaned closer to the child, as if he understood he was on trial. "Oh, pshaw, of course he can stay. I'll fix him a nice bed out on the back porch and..."

The boy flinched as if she had just struck him. A tear started at the corner of his eye.

Mrs. Harmon threw her hands in the air. "All right, he can sleep by the bed."

A sigh of relief escaped from around another bite of cookie.

"That'll be all then." Caleb crossed the linoleum-covered floor to stand by the breakfast nook. "I will be back later this afternoon. You mind Mrs. Harmon and remember to let Sam out for a run when he asks." The boy nodded.

"You want to come for supper, Sheriff?" Mrs. Harmon asked as he turned to leave.

"Thank you, but I've been invited to Gudrun's. I'll check back though, like I said."

The horse stood where they'd left it, snow clinging to its sorry hide and dusting the saddle. "Poor beast." Caleb brushed the snow off the saddle seat and, gathering the reins, swung aboard. He neck-reined in a circle and started back up the street at a trot.

But Caleb's thoughts were not so measured. What could have frightened her so much she chose to run—in the face of a blizzard—instead of stay where she and her family were warm and dry?

Chapter 5

W*ho was the woman with the baby? Who was the dead man they'd found by the livery?*

As the choir broke into "Angels We Have Heard on High," Caleb was jerked back to the present. He joined in the hymn but even when he was mouthing the words, his mind remained back at Doc's house. While he hadn't planned on entertaining strangers on Christmas Eve, it had happened. Caleb was of the school of thought that nothing happened without a reason. An angel had come into his life. He knew that for sure, he'd named her. But what about that angel's mother?

He swallowed a gasp. What if she were running from the law? She'd been in such an all-fired hurry to get going again.

When Reverend Moen smiled across his congregation from the pulpit, Caleb had to smile back. Wait 'til the pastor heard about these goings-on, if he hadn't already. The sheriff had worked hand in glove with the Lutheran pastor to help some unfortunates, usually without anyone outside being the wiser, in spite of Mrs. Jacobson and her nose for gossip.

The reverend had reminded his congregation of the perils of that deadly sin more than once but it hadn't seemed to make a difference to certain members of the community.

Caleb looked down the row to the woman in question. Her nose could ferret out the wispiest rumor and she always managed to put her own twist on it before passing the morsel on. She sang on, looking the good Christian praising her Lord on this most holy of days.

"Rejoice for the Savior has come." Reverend Moen could always be counted on for a real uplifting sermon. "Christ is born, and through Him we are reborn every day." As the sermon continued, Caleb tried to keep his mind on the pastor's words. Every time it floated on over to Doc Harmon's house, Caleb jerked it back. He heard phrases like "entertained angels unawares." That sent him thinking about the baby he helped bring into the world. No matter what happened with Mrs. Carlson, he would never regret helping Angel take her first breath. That tiny body that fit into his hands had such a strong pair of lungs, he was amazed. He could feel a smile coming on just at the thought of her.

"Jesus came to bring us love. He is love."

Love all right. He'd felt it burst like a firecracker in his heart when she kicked her tiny feet and flailed those minute hands. Tiny fingers that still managed to wrap themselves around his. Each part of her so perfectly formed. Had Mary felt like this when she held God's Son for the first time? And what about Joseph? Did he have doubts since he knew the baby in Mary's arms wasn't his?

"And now, the blessings of the Almighty God be on and with you all."

Caleb came back to the hard wooden pew with a start. He rose with the rest of the congregation and bowed his head. While the pastor prayed, Caleb added his own. *Please keep them safe and bring health to the mother. Help Doc help her. And thank You for sending them to my house on Christmas Eve. I'll never forget it.* He added his "Amen" to that of the others.

Caleb greeted his friends and neighbors, trying to make his way toward Gudrun without seeming to have any goal in mind. Everyone commented on the blizzard and how abruptly it struck.

"Snuck up on us like a hunting cat," one man said. "And then screamed like a banshee. I told my missus right then there wouldn't be no Christmas program. You shoulda heard my young'uns. Moaned worse 'an the wind."

"Heard there was some poor cuss who didn't make it through the night," someone said. "You figured out who he is yet?"

Caleb shook his head. The speed of the community grapevine always caught him by surprise. "Anyone heard of someone missing? All I know, he ain't from around here." At their headshakes, he excused himself and caught up with Gudrun and Dag Weinlander and his wife Clara at the door. After the usual greetings, he took Gudrun's hand and tucked it under his arm.

"Just to make sure you don't slip on the ice out here." He smiled down at the fashionably dressed woman beside him. A black felt hat with a curled brim and jaunty red feather hid much of her silver hair worn in its usual bun at the nape of her neck. The mink collar of the black wool coat fit snug up to her ear lobes where pearl earrings nestled. With one gloved hand, she grasped the collar more closely to her slender neck. She straightened shoulders already ramrod stiff and returned stare for stare out of faded blue eyes.

"You're looking well today."

"Now, Caleb, you know sweet talking won't cut the ice with me, but thank you, anyway. What is it that's on your mind?"

"Can't I just be neighborly?"

She raised one eyebrow. "Mrs. Hanson baked cinnamon rolls this morning."

Caleb sighed. "After all the other things she's been baking? That woman is a treasure."

"So you'll come for coffee?"

"As if I needed a bribe."

Dag Weinlander, owner of the livery and the blacksmith, stopped at her other side. After the greetings, he continued, "Glad you'll be joining us. I hear we have a bit of news to discuss."

Keeping a noncommittal look on his face took effort. Why had he immediately thought of Mrs. Carlson? Surely Dag was referring to the dead man. Caleb just nodded. "I will see you shortly then." He handed Gudrun up into the carriage, tipped his broad-brimmed hat, and headed back up the steps of the church.

The crowd had cleared out faster than normal and there was only one person left talking with Reverend Moen. Caleb waited until the woman moved on, then stepped forward to shake the minister's hand. "Good sermon, Reverend, as usual."

"Thank you, Sheriff." The twinkle in the man's eyes acknowledged his use of titles. "So, how can I help you?"

Caleb checked around to make sure no one else was in earshot. Even at that, he led the pastor back inside the vestibule. "Get you out of that wind." He took in a deep breath. "I have the most amazing story. You talk about entertaining angels. Well, I got me one last night."

At the interest on Moen's face, Caleb told his story. "I'm going to ask Gudrun if they have a place for her, the little family I mean. You s'pose in that big house they have room for a brand-new baby and a little boy who doesn't talk much? Fact is, I haven't heard him say a word so far. And the mother? I think she's mighty afraid of something." Caleb rubbed his nose and cleared his throat. For a man of few words, he'd kinda been runnin' off at the mouth lately.

Pastor Moen appeared to be giving the matter some thought. He nodded slowly, his eyes glued on Caleb's. "Who else knows about your visitors?"

"Well, Elmer noticed 'em when he came to tell me about the dead body."

Moen flinched.

"I know, I know. But he kinda caught me by surprise. And the baby, Angel, chose that moment to make her presence known."

"Angel?"

"Well, Mrs. Carlson said I could name her and I thought that was about the most perfect name, considering the circumstances and all."

"So what is it you want me to do?"

"Nothing much, I guess. Just wanted you to know the truth of it all, right from the beginning. And people seem to tell you things, so if you hear something I might need to know you could kind of pass it on."

"You want me to go to Gudrun's with you?"

"You want some of those cinnamon rolls too?"

"Mrs. Hanson baked cinnamon rolls on top of all the other?" The reverend shook his head. "That woman is indeed a wonder." He paused. "So, are your visitors all right at your house for a while yet?"

Caleb shook his head. "I didn't finish my story. She tried to take off this morning and I found her in a heap in my barn. Doc was with me and we took her directly to his house. She was burning up with fever."

Moen groaned.

"I know, I shoulda got the doctor last night but that blizzard was so bad, I just didn't dare chance it. And now if she..."

Reverend Moen held up a hand, along with an emphatic shake of his head. "No, don't you start in again, Caleb. There was nothing more you could have done for your wife and family those years ago and I know you did the best you could here and now. How many times do I have to tell you that Jesus came so you wouldn't have to carry that burden of guilt around any longer? And you don't need to add to it, neither. You hear me?"

Caleb kept his feet from shuffling through an act of will. He knew the pastor was right but the knowing and the doing weren't always the same. He didn't want to count the times they'd had this discussion. Most of the time he was able to agree with the pastor but then something happened like today and he fell back right back in the same old pit. Pastor Moen had worked mighty hard to pull him out of it back those five years ago.

"I'll let you get on to home then, I know your missus is waiting."

Caleb reached out and shook Moen's hand. "Merry Christmas. And thank you."

"Merry Christmas, Caleb, and you let me know what happens."

"I will."

After a brisk walk back to his house, Caleb saddled his horse and headed toward Main Street. All the while his hands did as required, his mind gnawed at the twin bones he'd been given in the last twenty-four hours. Two strangers in his town, one bringing death, the other life. Two mysteries to solve. Sheriff Stenesrude had never liked loose ends.

Something made him turn down the street to Doc Harmon's before seeing Gudrun.

After a brief greeting, Doc looked up at his guest and shook his head. "I'm afraid it's milk fever, Caleb, much as I hate to tell you."

Chapter 6

The dead man couldn't be her husband, could it?

Johanna Carlson took a deep breath to still her pounding heart. The baby in her arms squirmed, making the mother realize she'd clenched the newborn to her chest in a ferocious grip. Immediately she relaxed and set the rocker into motion.

She made herself smile at the boy staring up at her, terror rounding his eyes to saucer size.

She had to remind herself that even if this son of hers didn't speak, she could read his reactions better than anyone. He didn't need someone to draw him a map when he could hear what the deputy said as well as she. No child should have to live with more fear in his belly than bread. Hers had for far too long, and it looked to be continuing.

She listened closely to the sheriff's conversation, even though he had dropped his voice. When he turned and asked, or rather ordered, her to stay, she nodded. What else could she do? Only with an effort did she keep from squirming at the discomfort of sitting in the chair. How could she possibly ride the horse after just birthing Angel? And where would they go?

"You just take it easy now." Caleb had turned to her and said. I'll be back as soon as I can, shouldn't be long."

She nodded, more to say she heard him than that she agreed. How far back down the road do you suppose the wagon is? Is it buried in the snow, not to be found until the spring thaw? If only she had started earlier in the season. But she hadn't dared.

The dead man—who was he?

The thought that it might be—she couldn't even say his name—Henry's father caused her to grip the rocker furiously with one hand until the room stopped spinning.

"Come, Henry, get your things together. We must be on our way."

The boy wrapped both arms around Sam's neck, all the longing in the world evident in the gesture.

"Henry, son, I'm sorry but you'll have to leave Sam behind. When we get to our new home, we will have a dog again. One that belongs just to you." Memory of another dog put a catch in her voice. "Come now. Mabel is waiting for us out in the barn. Sheriff Stenesrude took good care of our horse last night, just like he took such good care of us." She glanced down at the baby sleeping in her arms. "Such good care."

She wished she could unbutton the bodice of her dress, it was so hot in the room. Perhaps she had lost more blood last night than she thought, she felt so weak. And hot. She wiped a hand across her forehead and rubbed her eyes with her fingers. Maybe a glass of water would help.

Carrying the baby in one arm and using the other to brace herself on the backs of the chairs arranged around the kitchen table, she carefully made her way to the sink and dipped water out of the bucket. After drinking, she wet a cloth that lay on the edge of the dry sink and wiped her forehead. She didn't remember feeling so weak after Henry was born. In fact, she'd gotten up and made supper.

She stared across the room to the coat rack by the front door. It seemed better than a mile across the linoleum-covered floor.

"Henry, can you be a big boy and bring Mama her coat?

If you pull a chair over there, you can get both mine and yours down."

Henry buried his face in the dog's ruff.

"Henry!" Much as she hated to, she put a strong dollop of sternness into her voice.

Henry leaped to his feet, eyes wide again and searching the room as if for a place to hide. Sam followed suit, hackles raised, trying to see what was bothering the child.

"Henry, you needn't be afraid, but I need your help. Get our coats now, like a good boy."

Henry shot her a look full of hurt and hustled to do her bidding. By the time he'd retrieved the coats, scarves, mittens, and finally their boots, his lower lip quivered and a fat tear threatened to spill over and run down his pale cheek.

"That's my good son," she said with a smile. Since when did smiling and helping her boy take so much energy? She helped him with one hand, then finally put the baby down on the table to have two hands to dress both herself and Henry. When they were bundled up, she wrapped the quilt snugly around the sleeping infant and, one step at a time, made their way to the back door. Sam acted as if he were tied to Henry's side with baling twine.

Shutting the door firmly on the dog took all her strength. She leaned against the isinglass door to catch her breath. The sun had turned the backyard into a patch of diamonds. Squinting against the fierce beauty of it all through her tears, she followed the trail through the snow to the gable-roofed barn. With each step the barn seemed farther away.

She had to lean against the wooden corner to catch her breath and let some strength return to her knees. Henry sniffed beside her. She looked down to see the tears frozen on his eyelashes.

She looked longingly back at the house. Why had she left there anyway? Was she out of her mind? The accusations rang in her brain as she struggled to shove open the heavy barn door. She rocked it back and forth, biting back the tears that threatened to run down her cheeks.

Hurry! Hurry! He won't let you go if he comes back. The door finally gave and opened with a shriek of metal on ice. She clung to it as she struggled to get her breath back. "Go on, Henry, get inside where it is warmer." She could hear Sam barking from in the house, so many leagues behind them. Blinking to focus her eyes in the dimness, she ordered her trembfing legs to go forward. Spots continued to dance before her. She shook her head, then caught hold of the upright post when a wave of dizziness made her stagger.

Why didn't you stay in the house? Think, woman, think. Like voices in an argument, the words rang in her head. She tried to reason it out. If the dead man were her husband, then he wouldn't be after them. If he weren't, he didn't matter. But then, Raymond might still be on their trail. They had to get away!

"You sit in the hay and hold on to Angel while I bridle the horse." She tried to smile reassuringly but the look on Henry's face told her how miserably she had failed. "Henry, son, you have to help me. Now sit there." She motioned to a mound of hay by the horse's stall. When he did, she laid the quilt-wrapped bundle in his arms. "Just hold her and you'll both be warmer." The words came slowly, in sympathy with her trembling actions.

She looked around the barn and spied a shabby saddle on braces on the wall, beside the one the sheriff obviously used. Without the baby, walking was easier. How could it be so hot in the barn? Was she running a fever? So far to the saddle. She tried lifting it. And tried again. With a mighty heave, she jerked it loose and fell with it to the floor. A wrenching deep inside and a telltale gush told her she was in trouble.

Staggering to her feet, she dragged the saddle to the stall, grabbed the bridle off the nail, and stumbled into the horse's stall.

"Easy, easy." The words came between pants. She leaned against the warm body, trying to absorb what strength she could. When she could stand upright, she stared at the horse's back. She'd forgotten a blanket. Turning, she looked at the saddle blanket covering the other saddle. So far away. Too far. They'd have to do without. She reached down to grab the saddle. The world went black as she collapsed across the leather gear.

Chapter 7

She's going to live ... isn't she?" Caleb heard his voice break. What was the matter with him? After all, as sheriff he'd seen all manner of life and death. He hardly knew this woman.

But the other side of him, the heart side, chided him gently. *No one could go through a birthing with a woman like you did and not care about her. Maybe there is more to this than you know.*

Caleb ignored that soft prompting as he had the other. "I mean, she has two small children to take care of. They need her."

"Now, Caleb, you think I don't know that?" Doc Harmon rubbed the top of his bald head. "But helping her live at this point is more in the good Lord's department than mine. I'll do what I can and the best you can do is get down on your knees and pray." He picked up the woman's wrist and counted her pulse. "We do the best we can and then leave it in God's hands. That's all."

The sheriff winced. He'd rather go break up a fight in the saloon.

"You'll keep me posted?"

"Of course. You going over to Gudrun's?"

Caleb nodded. "They'll have an idea what to do for her, and the young'uns."

"Ask her if she knows any of the women with extra breast milk. We need to keep that Angel girl alive 'til her mother gets better. Shame I haven't delivered any babies for some time."

Comforted that the doc spoke in terms of Mrs. Carlson getting better, Caleb left him to his ministrations and walked back to the kitchen. Mrs. Harmon had Henry sitting on her lap, albeit a mite stiffly. Sam sat as close to her knee as possible.

"I'll be back later."

Henry's eyes filled with tears. He squirmed to get down.

"No, you stay there. Sam'll be right with you. I need to talk to a friend of mine and then I'll be back. Your mother is in the bedroom back there if'n you want to go see her." He shifted his gaze to Mrs. Harmon. "How's the little one?"

"Sound asleep, the little lamb." The soft and fluffy woman shook her head. "But when she wakes, we better have something here to feed her. Her tummy needs mother's milk, not cow's milk."

"Uh-huh." The sheriff could feel a burning about his ears. All this talk about milk and such, you'd think he'd never had a child of his own. He clapped the Stetson on his head and departed by the front door. Right into another driving blizzard. "Weather'tain't fit for man nor beast. Leastways, this one ain't as bad as the first." He swung aboard the horse waiting by the gate. As far as horseflesh, went, this one lacked some. He dug his heels into the bony ribs and the horse struck off at a teeth-cracking trot until it had to slog through a drift. When if stopped in the middle, the sheriff groaned and dismounted. Muttering all the while, he plowed his way to the front of the horse and broke the trail.

"Come on, horse, pick up your feet."

By the time he reached the big house with gingerbread trim now hidden behind whirling snow, he wasn't sure who was more tired, him or the horse.

He tied the animal inside the carriage house and followed the path that had been shoveled once this day up to the back door of the mansion.

"Landsakes, Sheriff, I thought sure you gived up like any sane man would on a day like this." Mrs. Hanson, queen of the kitchen and confidante of the aging Mrs. Norgaard, brushed a trailing tendril back into the bun that seemed to loosen even more. Her always rosy cheeks bloomed brighter from the heat of the stove. "Come in, come in." When he stopped to kick snow off his boots, she took his arm and pulled him past the door to the back porch. "If there ain't been snow on my floor before today, I'd be after ye but right now get over here by the fire and warm yourself. I'll tell herself that you're here."

"What's all the commotion?" Dag Weinlander strode into the room, hand outstretched. "Caleb, good to see you again." He was a man who made most men feel short, but Dag's heart outreached his handshake. Hair the color of summer mink lay close to his head and framed his square jaw with a rich, well-trimmed brush. His blue eyes crinkled at the edges in lines familiar with laughter.

Caleb knew that laughter had not always been Dag's wont. Clara, his wife and a fairly recent import from Norway, made certain he experienced the joys he'd so long done without. "I need to talk with Gudrun and Mrs. Hanson, no secrets against you or nothing."

"Well, since this is Christmas and a time for surprises, I'll let you get by with such, this time." He clapped a hand on Caleb's shoulder, pointed to the coffeepot Mrs. Hanson had set at the table, and left. "I'll find my womenfolk," he said over his shoulder.

"Now there's a happy man." Mrs. Hanson nodded and finished pouring the coffee. "You start with this and I'll get the cinnamon rolls out. I know that's what you really come for." She bustled about the room, setting things out on a tray and glancing over her shoulder, question marks all over her face.

"It's not a secret," he finally said, the cup warming his hands. "Just thought I'd only have to say it once."

"Have anything to do with that woman birthing her baby at your house last night?"

"Now how did. . . ?" Caleb shook his head. "I mighta knowed you'd a heard already. Ain't nothing in this town sacred?"

"Come on in." Dag motioned from the door. "They're waiting

for you."

Caleb picked up the coffee-laden tray and followed his host, leaving a spluttering Mrs. Hanson to bring up the rear.

As soon as they were all served to Mrs. Hanson's satisfaction, Mrs. Norgaard, in her usual manner, drove right to the point. "You're here about that woman and babe, correct?"

Caleb nodded, still amazed at the efficiency of the town grapevine even in the midst of a snowstorm. He told them the entire story from Sam's first bark. "She's mighty sick and Doc says she may get worse before she gets better." He forced himself to sit still on the horsehair sofa. "I promised the boy his mother would get better, didn't know what else to do." The boy's eyes still haunted him.

"Doc believes she will pull through then?" Gudrun sat in her normal position, back ramrod straight, not even the buttons of her dress touching the back of the chair. Black pointed-toe slippers peeked from the hem of the matching watered silk dress.

"I—he. . ." Caleb sucked in a deep breath. Leave it to Gudrun to cut right to the heart of the matter. "He didn't say that."

"I see."

"What about the children?" Clara Weinlander asked after passing the china plate stacked with cinnamon rolls. Dag took one and passed the plate to Caleb. When the sheriff shook his head, Dag proferred the plate again.

Caleb smiled his thanks and bit into the still warm pastry. Mrs. Hanson could open a bake shop of her own and he would be her first customer—every morning. He finally looked up at the younger woman. "That's a good question." Should he tell them his suspicion that Mrs. Johanna Carlson was running from something—or someone?

"You might as well tell me the whole story."

How could such a diminutive and elderly woman make him feel as if he'd just got caught with his hand in the cookie jar? And with such few words too. He should take lessons from her. He shook his head. "I wish I knew the whole story. There's been no mention of a mister and none to say she's a widow. To be honest, we ain't had much time for talking, we was busy with other things if you get my drift."

"The children, Caleb, who will feed that baby if her mother has milk fever?" Clara leaned forward.

"I don't rightly know. Doc, he was hoping you'd a heard of someone. Not everyone calls the doctor."

"You could bring the children here, we have room for a wet nurse. Surely there is a woman who would like to earn some extra money."

"Well, now, far as I know, there ain't no moncy available."

"Now, Caleb, you know there's always money here for those who really need it," Gudrun stated, looking at him over the tops of her gold-framed glasses.

"'Poor but proud' was no doubt quoted with this woman in mind. I can't see her accepting help gracefully.' "

"Graceful or not, she's in no position to argue. We'll deal with her sensibilities in due time." Gudrun raised the bell on the round table beside her chair. "Mrs. Hanson will have rooms ready in an hour or so. We'll expect you back with the children before supper which you will eat with us."

Caleb looked over at Dag for support but the man just smiled and shrugged his massive shoulders. After all, what could one do when Gudrun got on her high horse—but set the spurs to your own mount and do your best to keep up?

As Gudrun decreed, by suppertime all had fallen into place. A young woman from the German community just south of Soldahl and her baby were made comfortable in an upstairs room. Her already merry eyes twinkled even more at the sight of two cradles beside a grand four poster bed. In short order she ensconced her month-old son in one and put Angel, after a long overdue feast, to sleep in the other. Henry, with Sam stuck to his side, hadn't left the kitchen, cowering in the warm alcove behind the black and chrome cook stove. He'd managed to put away a couple of sour cream cookies, making sure that Sam got his share, and a glass of milk. Sam licked away the milk mustache which

Mrs. Hanson ignored for the time being.

She tisk-tisked her way about, preparing the evening meal. "I sure do hope you like chicken and dumplings. 'Course you prob'ly don't have no room left after them cookies but I reckon Sam there will eat what you don't."

"We don't think he is hard of hearing, you know. He just don't talk," Caleb said softly when he entered the room.

"Oh." She lowered her voice.

Caleb nodded and went to squat in front of the boy's hideout. "Henry, I just checked and your ma is doing about as well as can be expected. You come now with me and we'll join the family in the dining room."

Henry shook his head. Sam whined at the stranglehold around his neck.

"Well, now, I sure do think that would be the polite thing to do and all. Your ma would want you to be polite."

The boy looked from the sheriff to the dog and back.

"Mrs. Norgaard, she don't take to dogs in her dining room, I don't believe. Sam will stay here waiting for you."

The boy's hold tightened. Sam gazed at Caleb with imploring eyes.

"Easy there, son, you're about cutting off his wind." The boy released his hold enough to get a quick lick on the cheek.

"You coming, Caleb?" Dag opened the kitchen door. "Oh." He nodded and tongue firmly in his cheek, left. A minute later, he returned. "Bring the dog."

Caleb rose to his feet. "Come on, Sam."

Sam wriggled and stared after his retreating master. He whined.

Caleb slapped his knee. "Come on, Sam."

Toenails tapped on the linoleum floor. The dog whimpered.

"Henry, you can see Sam wants to come. Why don't you do him a favor and let him mind me?" He waited for what seemed like an hour, especially since he was holding his breath. He released it when the boy shifted to his knees and then rose to his feet. Fist still tangled in the fur of the dog's neck, he stopped at Caleb's side.

Caleb's heart turned over at the fear swimming in the boy's eyes. Someone had hurt this child right bad. If only he could get his hands on the swine, he wouldn't hurt any more children, that was for certain. "Not to worry, son. They like little boys here."

Henry took in a deep breath and let it out in a ragged sigh. When Caleb extended his hand, the boy put his in the sheriff's. In fact, that worthless polecat of a man wouldn't get a chance to hurt anyone else ever again.

Caleb lifted Henry up on the stack of books and a pillow set atop a chair, then took the seat beside the boy. Sam thumped his tail, when Henry looked down at him, and licked the boy's hand. Then he stretched out, muzzle on his paws, enjoying a respite from child care.

"Henry, my name is Mrs. Weinlander and I'll help you with your supper if you need it." She looked up to catch Caleb's gaze when the boy flinched away. She smiled reassuringly at the child. "You just nod when the serving things come by."

Dag asked them all to bow their heads for grace and asked the blessing on the meal, including a petition for the healing of Mrs. Johanna Carlson.

Caleb heard the small sniff from beside him at the mention of the sick woman's name. He added a request of his own for the small family facing such trials.

As each dish made the rounds of the table, Henry looked first to see what Caleb took and then nodded at Clara. She put small servings of chicken and dumplings, green beans cooked with bacon, a sweet pickle, and butered one of Mrs. Hanson's homemade rolls.

Conversation flowed along with the good food as each of the adults cast surreptitous glances at the boy eating so carefully but cleaning up every morsel on his plate. Clara refilled his plate when he looked up at her and then toward the platters and bowls.

His mother taught him good manners, Caleb thought, feeling proud as if he'd had something to do with it. He didn't let on that he'd seen the bits that made their way to the dog on the floor. When Gudrun caught his eye, he knew she'd seen too. With the wisdom of years, and the heart of a woman of God, she said nothing.

"Mrs. Hanson, you could come cook for me any day." Caleb wiped his mouth with a napkin and watched Henry do the same.

"You know you're welcome here any time." Gudrun made as if to rise. Caleb leaped to his feet and pulled her chair back. "We will have our coffee in the parlor."

Henry's eyes turned dinner-plate size when he saw the evergreen tree nearly hidden by all the decorations in front of the bay window. He stopped in the arched dorway.

Caleb watched as the child stared up and down the tree and then over to the mantel where fat candles nested in pine boughs and cones, finished off with big red bows at either end. The swags on the windows and the garlands that framed every door also received his full attention. Caleb knew what was going through the child's mind. Until he came to Gudrun's house, he had never seen such magnificence either.

Clara came and knelt in front of the boy. "Would you like to come see the tree with me? I like looking at things up close so I can really see them. I'll even show you my favorite ornament."

Henry looked up at Caleb, his eyes asking for permission.

The sheriff nodded. Henry shifted his free hand from the man to the woman. Sum, of course, was a permanent extension of his other.

Caleb watched as Dag's diminutive blond wife, her wine-red velvet dress pooling about her, knelt in front of the tree and began taking an ornament at a time off the branches and showing it to the child. If adoration had a face, it was Henry's. That Dag was a lucky man. The thought of eyes like precious gems flashed through his mind. He'd only really seen them once. She'd kept her head bowed or her eyes closed much of the time.

Would he ever see them flash again? *Please Lord, let it be so.*

Later Caleb led Henry to the room prepared for him, with Sam in tow. "Now, you'll be just fine right here. Angel is with her nursemaid right down the hall and this here's the bed your ma will be sleeping in, soon as she gets better. You might want to warm it up for her."

Henry hung back, his eyes taking up most of his face.

"I'll wait here 'til you fall asleep."

The boy sighed and began to unbutton his shirt. Tucked up warm and cozy a few minutes later, he clutched the edge of the blankets until his knuckles turned white.

Caleb leaned against the bedpost and wrapped his hands around his knee. The boy looked lost in a sea of white sheets and pillows. Much against his better judgment, the man looked down at the dog sitting by his feet and thumped the bed covers. With a leap that hardly touched the bed, Sam wriggled under his charge's arm and flicked his tongue over the pale cheek.

Caleb swallowed the rock that swelled in his throat at the look on Henry's face.

Sam twitched the tip of his feathery tail when Caleb whispered goodbye some time later. Henry never stirred. Caleb stopped off at the room where Angel slept in the cradle. He tiptoed in at the beckoning of the young woman rocking her own child by the window. After a smile at her, he leaned over the cradle. Angel lay on her side, tightly wrapped in her infant blankets. She'd managed to free one walnut-sized fist and it lay beside her baby-red cheek. He touched the tiny fingers and instinctively they clasped his.

Caleb beat a hasty retreat. She sure packed a wallop for such a tiny mite.

Back at Doc Harmon's another picture greeted him, this one, too, flushed but restless. Mrs. Carlson moaned and rolled her head from side to side.

"Man, are you trying to freeze her to death?" Caleb whispered. He shot a look of horror at the half-open window.

"Got to get her cooled down somehow and cold clothes alone weren't working. Now I got some snow packed beside her and with the room cold, she's cooling off. You sit here for a while and just talk to her. Tell her about Henry. We got to make her want to live worse'n the easy way out by dying."

"You don't think she's going to give up, do you?" Caleb ignored the pang that shot through his heart.

"That's your job, keep her wanting to live to see her young'uns. I just do the doctoring and I done all I can.

Chapter 8

Angel needs you."

The wind whistled in the gap of the now barely open window, snow powdering the sill.

The woman stirred, her hands plucking at the sheet covering her.

Caleb wanted to cover her with the quilt but he could still feel the fever when he laid the back of his hand to her forehead. But her color was better and he had to grant Doc the benefit of the doubt. After all, he didn't like anyone telling him how to run his job as sheriff.

"Henry, you'da been right proud of him over there at Gudrun's. He is one brave youngster. Now I know he's scared, the fear shouts from his eyes, but he does what he has to do. He and Angel, they're waiting for you to come to them. I thought that in the morning, if you're up to it, I'd bring Henry over for a quick visit. He's pretty worried about you."

Caleb thought a moment. *Now how do I know that for a fact? The boy never said a word.* Could she hear him? *Dear Lord, You can hear me and I know You are listening. All I see is two babes who need their mother desperatelike. So, please, for mercy's sake, let this woman get back on her feet again.* He heard the clock chiming in another part of the house. Doc said he'd be back to spell him about three.

Caleb removed the cloth from the woman's forehead, wrung it out in the pan of water, and replaced it. If only there were something he could really do. He got to his feet and crossed to the window. Fewer flakes were falling and the wind seemed to have let up some. He stuck his hands in his back pockets and hunched his shoulders in an effort to work out the kinks.

Back in his chair he tried to think of something to say. He'd about used up his store of words for the entire week when he noticed a Bible on the bedstand. Flipping to the Psalms, Caleb began to read. "He that dwelleth in the secret place of the most High shall abide under the shadow of the Almighty. I will say of the Lord, He is my refuge and my fortress: in him will I trust."

When the doctor tiptoed in some time later, he checked his patient and nodded. "I think we might have turned the corner, she's sleeping restful now."

"I'll mosey on home then. Thanks, Doc."

"Thank you, Caleb. Any time you get tired of sheriffing, you can sign on as a nurse."

"Yeah, well, think I'll stick with what I know." He snagged his Stetson off the chair back and, gathering up his sheepskin coat, nodded once again. "Night."

The moon peeked out from behind a cloud, then hid again. The temperature was dropping, Caleb could tell, even as the snow clouds hurried to the south. Still he left the Carlson horse in the doc's barn and plowed through some new drifts on the walk to his house. After hanging up his coat, he stoked the stove again and made his way to the bedroom. Across the foot of his bed lay the red scarf that had been wrapped so carefully around Henry's throat when the little family arrived in the blizzard.

Caleb picked it up and ran it through his fingers. She'd made this special for her boy, he could tell, each stitch perfect and of the softest wool, dyed red to please a boy's heart. "Dear God, don't let up now. Please keep on with Your healing work," he whispered out loud. The house seemed even emptier than usual without Sam.

Caleb fell asleep wondering about the man found dead by the blacksmith shop. Who was he? Maybe the morning would bring some answers.

"She's asking for her babes," Doc said with nary a greeting.

"Thanks be to God," Caleb muttered under his breath as if not quite used to saying such things but needing to do so now. "Should I bring Henry over?"

"Yep, and Angel too. Wrap her up in a quilt. Your horse should be able to manage the drifts, though I wouldn't say the same for the sorry piece of horseflesh you left in my barn."

"I know, that's why it's there. Makes me wonder how long they were on the road. May be there hadn't been money for horse feed. Sure does make one wonder."

"You want to put out a notice on the teletype? Mayhap someone's looking for her."

Caleb rubbed the side of his nose. "I think we'll wait. Sent one out already this morning on that man in the morgue." He hoped Mrs. Carlson would tell him about her history herself, soon as she felt up to it. In the meantime, he'd fetch the children. Shame they couldn't use a carriage but none of the streets had been plowed out yet. He knew Clara and Gudrun would make a visit to the sick woman as soon as they could get through.

After the prescribed greeting at the big house, along with fresh coffee and warmed cinnamon rolls, Clara brought the children to him, already bundled up for the trek across town.

"Thank you, ma'am." Caleb drew the red muffler from his pocket and wrapped it around Henry's neck. "So your ma can recognize you. I think you been eating so much good food here, you grew a foot."

Henry flashed Caleb a look of doubt and ducked his head again. One hand still clutched the fur around Sam's neck.

"How about if I take one and you the other?" Dag entered the warm kitchen, all dressed for the elements. "Won't take me but a minute to saddle my horse."

Clara rocked the bundled baby back and forth. "You're going to bring her back, aren't you?"

"You mean Angel or her mother?"

"Both, if you could." She looked down at the sleeping infant in her arms. "I put a couple of diapers in, just in case. She ate about an hour ago." Clara looked up at the sheriff. "You be careful with her now."

Caleb could feel Henry at his side. Perhaps it was a good thing Dag had offered to help. And to think that woman had tried to leave on a rickety horse with both young'uns and sick to boot. He'd have to have a serious talk with her when she had some strength back.

"I know, Caleb, God does work in mysterious ways, His wonders to perform." Clara swayed in the age-old rhythm of women comforting their babes. Caleb didn't pretend to understand the female of the human species. One thing he knew for certain: If anything happened to these two little ones while in his care, the wrath of Clara and Gudrun united would be worse than anything a mere man could dream up.

He handed the mounted Dag the infant after Clara had seen to the quilt flap being tucked over the baby's head just so. Then he tossed Henry up into the saddle and swung aboard, whistling for Sam who'd gone to sniff a bush or two. Together they trotted down the drive that Dag had already shoveled free of drifts and toward the doctor's house.

"Well, Henry, your ma's been asking about you." Mrs. Harmon unwrapped the boy and hung his things on the coat tree by the door. "And how is our Angel this morning?"

"Now let's forget all that howdy stuff and just bring them back to their ma while she's still awake." Doc Harmon entered the room in a rush. "I got a woman out to the south of town who's set on having her baby a bit early. Martha, you better prepare that other room, just in case."

Caleb and Dag, their charges in hand, followed the blustering doctor down the walnut-paneled hall.

Henry broke away from Caleb's grip and threw himself against the woman lying, eyes closed, in the bed.

"Ah, Henry." She smoothed his hair with her hand. Her voice quavered, shaking like her hand. "I heard you have been a good boy for these kind people." She looked up, a smile almost making it to her face. "Thank you for bringing them."

Dag freed the infant from the quilt and laid her in her mother's arms. "She has been well fed, in fact the wet nurse we found says she eats like a little pig. She will stay until you are able to care for your daughter yourself."

"Thank you." Mrs. Carlson kissed the baby's brow and snuggled her close. "I—I'm sorry to be so much trouble."

"Landsakes, child," Mrs. Harmon said, bustling into the room immediately after her husband left. "Not every town gets its own personal Christmas Angel. You be more a gift than a trouble."

"I'll repay..."

Mrs. Harmon threw her hands in the air. "Talk of payment already. You quit worrying about paying and think about getting better. Now, Henry, I got a cup of cocoa out there with your name on it, along with those cookies you liked so well. Sam near to busted down the back door 'til I let him in. He's waiting for you too." She held out her hand and, after checking for a reassurance from his mother, the boy placed his in her ample grip.

Caleb could hear Mrs. Harmon's running commentary as they made their way toward the kitchen.

"I'll be back in an hour or so to help you with the return trip." Dag said. "I need to check on things at the shop. Will's been taking care of chores over Christmas and I'm sure no one's come in today to have their horses shod." He nodded to the woman in the bed. "Later, ma'am," and left the room.

Caleb took his place in the chair where he'd spent so many hours the night before.

"You were here before, weren't you?" Her voice seemed stronger but not by much.

"Yes."

"I remember your voice." The baby whimpered and stretched her tiny arms. "I—I can't thank you enough."

"The best thanks you can give me is to do what the doc tells you and don't go trying anything stupid again." He could see her crumpled on the floor in his barn. The thought made his throat tighten.

"I won't."

Why was it he could hear a "for now" at the end of her sentence? Stubborn woman. He knew he'd have to watch her. But then, was watching her such a penalty? He shook his head at the silly thought. If he got this poor woman tucked under Gudrun's wing, she'd be safe enough. And considering the verses he'd read the night before about living in the shadow of the Almighty's wings, this small family had plenty of protection.

She was sleeping when Dag reentered the room and the two men made the return trek to the mansion. Angel was letting them know in no uncertain terms that it was feeding time. Henry almost laughed once at Sam's antics playing snowplow with his nose. All in all, it had been a successful morning.

He repeated the process the next morning, this time to find Mrs. Carlson sitting up in the bed. The smile she bestowed on him for bringing her children flew like an arrow straight to his heart. He'd not known she could smile like that, but he did know he'd do anything within his power to bring that smile to her face again.

"The doctor says I can get out of bed soon as I have the strength."

"Now that's right good news." Caleb took his place in the chair.

"He also said that Mrs. Norgaard is planning on taking us in?" A shadow flickered on her brow. She sighed.

"I know, you hate to be a burden. For such a bitty woman you got a powerful sense of burdening." Caleb leaned forward, elbows on his knees. "If'n that is bothering you so much, I got an ideal way you can pay her back." He raised a hand, palm out. "Now give me a minute before you go spluttering at me. We was to have a Christmas pageant on Christmas Eve. The town had been preparing for weeks but the blizzard wiped it right out. Now Pastor says we will have it on Sunday, New Year's Day. There's only been one real problem all along and that's that we've had no baby Jesus. All the babies born around here were just too big for Mary Moen to handle in the manger and all. Now, if you would be willing for little Angel there to star in her first performance, we would all be mighty grateful. Just didn't seem right having a doll play the part, even though Ingeborg Moen made a right fine rag doll of the appropriate size."

Mrs. Carlson breathed a kiss on the brow of her sleeping infant and raised her sapphire gaze to the sheriff's face.

"We'd be right proud to do that. But I have a favor of you. Please would you make sure I get to the service too. If'n I can't walk well enough, perhaps you could carry me."

Caleb knew what the doctor would say. And it would be in no uncertain terms. He also knew what it cost this woman to ask for help. Besides, he'd carried her before and she was some slimmer now. He nodded. "What Doc Harmon don't know can't hurt him. But know this. If you get sicker because of it, he will have my head."

"Thank you, Sheriff." She smiled again and her eyes drifted closed. "Now if I could only stay awake for more'n a couple of minutes."

"I'll be back later with the carriage to take you to Gudrun's house. She thinks you'll get well faster when you can be with your children. And when Mrs. Norgaard says something, not too many of us argue with her." But when he took Angel back in his arms, he realized the mother hadn't heard a word he said. Her soft, even breathing told more of her improving state than her worries about staying awake—and being beholden.

The move was accomplished with a minimum of fuss with the doctor promising to call on his way back from checking on the other new mother.

Clara returned to the kitchen after looking in again on the small family. "They're all sound asleep, Henry curled up next to his mother and Sam on the rug—for a change."

Mrs. Hanson shook her head. "Dogs ain't to be in the house, let alone the bedroom." She rolled her eyes heavenward. "But if it helps that little fellow, I guess we'll all put up with it."

"You try to sound so stern, but we all know you have a cream puff for a heart." Clara helped herself to a cup of coffee. "Any word on where they might have come from?"

Caleb shook his head. "I didn't ask but nothing has come through. It's like they appeared out of nowhere. That man that we found dead, though, his family claims he got shot in a fight at the local saloon over in Drayton and hightailed it before the sheriff come. They'll be over for the body tomorrow."

"Such goings-on." Gudrun thumped her cane for emphasis. "So, what's this I hear about our baby playing the part of baby Jesus?"

"I just thought it might help Johanna, er, Mrs. Carlson..." He made the change at the raised eyebrow of the town matriarch. "To feel not quite so beholden." He knew better than to call the woman by her first name but it seemed they'd been friends for a lot longer than four days, after what all they went through together. But since when had she become Johanna in his mind?

"That was good thinking on your part." Gudrun tipped her chin so she looked over the tops of her gold wire glasses. "You'd best be careful, though, Caleb. I wouldn't want you to get hurt in all this."

What was she, a mind reader as well? Could she sense what Caleb was already beginning to feel? Caleb took a sip of his coffee. He knew how to keep a close rein on his feelings…After all, he'd been doing that for years.

Chapter 9

W*hat am I going to do?*

Johanna planted another kiss on the soft fuzz of her baby's head. Never had she felt sheets so fine or slept in such a bed with carved posts at all the corners, until she came to this house. Surely she had died and gone to heaven. But the pain in her chest let her know this was still earth. When oh when would she be able to feed her daughter as she ought?

The doctor reminded her to be patient, that the hardness would disappear in a day or two if they kept up the hot packs and let Angel nurse as long as the mother could tolerate. Thank God for that young woman in the other room who had milk aplenty for both babies. So many things she had to be thankful for! She would spend the rest of her life praising God for His boundless kindness.

A soft knock at the door turned her attention away from her worries. "Come in."

Clara pushed the carved door open and stuck her head around it. "I wondered if you felt up to a bit of company?"

"Oh, yes, of course." Johanna tried to push herself up against the pillows. "We might as well send Angel back for a feeding, she got none from her mother."

"Here, let me take her." Clara bent over and picked up the whimpering child. "Oh, Mrs. Carlson, she is so lovely."

"Can't you please call me Johanna? I would be much obliged if you would."

"Of course, and as you know, I'm Clara." She disappeared into the other room where Johanna heard murmurings as the baby was given back to the wet nurse. Patience, the doctor counseled, patience. But lying here with nothing to do...

Johanna threw back the covers. Lying in bed wasn't natural no matter what the doctor said. "Would you please help me to that chair?" she asked when Clara returned to the sick room.

"Uff da, I had a feeling we wouldn't be able to keep you down much longer." Clara wrapped an arm about Johanna's middle. "Just lean on me."

"Goodness." Johanna sank into the rocking chair and breathed a sigh. "I'm so weak. Why, I got up the day Henry was born and cooked supper that night. Whatever is the matter with me?"

"You've been mighty sick, near as I can tell. Fever always takes some out of a person, let alone birthing a baby." Clara took the opposite chair. "Doc says you should stay in bed."

"Well, the doctor isn't here and if I lie there one more hour, I shall go out of what little mind I have left."

"You could read." At the arched look of her visitor's brow, Clara smiled. "Write letters?"

Johanna dropped her gaze to her hands clasped in her lap. *Oh my, if you only knew.* But she didn't dare share her secret with anyone.

"What is it you like to do?"

"Like to do?" Johanna thought of the breathlessness crossing the room had caused. "I can knit, or mend, or do hand sewing." Her hands fluttered, as if needing an anchor. "I need to be doing something."

"All right. We had hoped you would be content to just rest and get well but if this bothers you so much, I will talk to Gudrun and we will come up with something. In the meantime, are you comfortable? Is there anything I can get you?"

Johanna shook her head. "Please, I don't mean to be ungrateful. You have all been so good to me and mine, strangers that providence dropped into your laps."

"No, I understand, I would be the same." Clara rose to her feet. "How about if I help you back to bed for a while and when I return we can take a turn around the room? And you will eat something to make you stronger." She raised a hand to forestall Johanna's objections. "And, yes, I will find something for you to do."

By Friday Johanna could navigate the upstairs but she hadn't yet tried going down the spiraled staircase. With each dawn she indeed felt stronger. The pile of mending had disappeared under her nimble fingers and she itched to use the treadle sewing machine she found in a room down the hall. Never in her entire life had she had so much time on her hands.

Saturday evening the entire town bundled up and strolled down Main Street to the Lutheran church for the pageant. All the participants arrived an hour early to get into their costumes, except for the stand-in for baby Jesus. She was home being fed in an attempt to help her sleep through the performance.

"Are you sure you are strong enough to go?" Caleb had an arm around Mrs. Carlson's waist as they negotiated the stairs.

"Yes, I am. I wouldn't miss this for the world."

Clara followed behind them, babe in arms. "I should be there now to help my class get ready but I know Ingeborg has everything under control. It's not often one gets to carry the star of the show. Makes me wonder how Mary felt."

"She tucked all the things away in her heart, Scripture says. I'm sure she took them all out many times for rumination later." Mrs. Norgaard took Dag's arm. "To think that at one time, Jesus was no bigger than our little Angel here. Astounding, isn't it?"

Johanna kept a tight hold on Caleb's arm. Walking around upstairs was different from coming down stairs wearing a coat and all. She tried to hide her shakiness with a smile but when Caleb put his arm around her waist again, she knew he could see through her.

"I can carry you, you know." His whisper was meant for her ears alone.

She shook her head. What would the townspeople have to say about something like that?

The church Christmas tree stood in the corner ready to have its candles lit, colorful packages stacked beneath its branches. Silver icicles twinkled in the light from the gas lamps and crocheted crosses shimmered white against the green branches.

Caleb looked down at Henry who had the sheriff's pant leg clenched in one hand. Somehow they'd convinced him that Sam didn't go to church. In the faithful dog's place, Caleb had become the safety blanket to which the boy clung. As soon as they were all seated in the front pew, Clara nodded to Mrs. Moen who peeked out from behind the sheets turned curtains strung across the front of the church.

People continued to file in until every pew and chair was occupied and the walls became props for those left standing. When the organ wheezed to life, a hush fell on the room. The lights were dimmed but for the ones in front. Only a tiny giggle from behind the curtains told of those waiting to begin.

Clara took the sleeping Angel back from her mother and sneaked behind the curtain, to return empty-handed. "They promised to take good care of her," she whispered after she sat back down between Johanna and Dag.

Johanna lifted Henry onto her lap so he could see better.

A man's voice, deep and musical, began reading from the Gospel of Luke. "And it came to pass in those days, that there went out a decree from Caesar Augustus…"

A draft skittered across the floor and up everyone's legs. The congregation turned as one to see a young woman on a donkey, led by a boy with an obviously fake beard. The tap-tap of the donkey's hooves provided a counterpoint to the reading. Part of the curtain pulled back to show the Sunday school chorus, singing a song of Mary and Joseph, their eyes shining.

"And so it was, that, while they were there, the days were

accomplished that she should be delivered. And she brought forth her firstborn son. . . ." The curtain opened to young Mary Moen, who played Mary, and Will, the blacksmith apprentice, as Joseph, laying an infant in a rough manger. The cow beside them chewed her cud and two sheep knelt in the straw on the floor.

Johanna blinked back tears. Like the family before her, she'd had her baby in a stranger's house and had been surrounded by love and care. As the story and songs continued, thoughts of home intruded. How was he? Was he after her? She quickly joined in the hymn and closed the door on her memories. Here, for now, she and her children were warm and safe.

At the first sign of whimpering young Mary took the baby in her arms and, laying Angel against her shoulder, patted and rocked the infant like mothers the world over. Joseph knelt beside her. The donkey stomped his hoof and twitched his ear. The white-clad children had donned their angel wings to sing again as the shepherds made their way down the aisle. Finally the wise men joined the tableau, in spite of the star that stuck on its wire and refused to hang over the stable. Reverend Moen finished his reading, the organ broke into "Silent Night," and everyone rose to sing the carol.

Johanna could feel her voice quivering. Never had she seen such a pageant. Never had the age-old story found such a welcoming heart, never had God's Word been made so real. She looked up to see Henry in Caleb's arms and when she swayed, felt Clara's arm go around her waist. She rested between the two strong bodies as the curtain opened again and the actors took their much deserved bow. Angel, wide awake now, managed to free her arm from the confines of the swaddling wraps and wave as if she knew what part she'd played.

The applause finally dimmed, swelled, and dimmed again. Mary Moen left the stage and brought Angel back to her mother.

"Thank you for letting her be in our pageant. What a good baby she is."

"Thank you." Johanna cuddled her daughter close. She looked up to catch a sheen of what? Tears in Caleb's eyes.

He sniffed once and nodded. "She sure is. Not often a pageant gets an Angel to play the part of baby Jesus." His whisper made those around him chuckle.

Back in her mother's arms, Angel fell fast asleep and slept right through the passing out of the gifts from the base of the Christmas tree. When the child still dressed in a white angel costume, with one wing slightly askew, handed a wrapped package to Henry and another one handed him an orange, the stars in his eyes shone brighter than those twinkling in the heavens.

Sitting on Caleb's lap, he looked first to his mother and then up at the sheriff. At Caleb's nod, Henry slid to the floor and, turning, laid his treasures in Caleb's lap so he could open the box. Carefully he untied the string and folded back the red paper. Inside the box was a pair of red mittens and under that a tablet and two sharpened pencils with an eraser.

The smile on the boy's face nearly split the sheriff's heart in two. So much more he had wanted to put in that box but he knew he dared not since that would be showing favoritism. Sure as shooting, one of the more vocal of the church women would comment and make Mrs. Carlson feel bad.

He'd already figured out that staying on the right side of her pride took some real doing.

On their way out of the church some time later, he took care to let Dag shepherd the two younger women and he, with Henry on one arm, extended the other to Gudrun. He caught the flash of humor in her eyes and the slight nod of commendation. As usual, they were in cahoots to keep the gossip mill on a starvation diet.

"I want to thank you all for such a wonderful evening," Johanna said when they had gathered in the parlor after the children were put to bed. Henry had headed for the kitchen and latched on to Sam as soon as Clara removed his winter gear. In spite of Mrs. Hanson's tsking, the dog accompanied the child to bed, along with the tablet that he clutched to his narrow chest.

"You are more than welcome." Gudrun smiled at her guest. "I've never seen a more perfect Jesus in a manger. And can you believe how motherly Mary acted?"

"With all the help she's been to her mother in raising the younger ones, I'm not surprised. She is one capable young woman." Clara looked up from her embroidery hoop.

"She's just a little girl." Dag turned from his study of the fire.

"She's ten years old and tall for her age. Can you believe that we had a Mary playing Mary?" Caleb shook his head. "And an Angel playing the best part of all."

"Do they always use real live animals for the pageant here?" Johanna asked. "I've never seen that done before." Of course how could she tell them, she hadn't seen a pageant in years. Not that she hadn't wanted to, but...

"Mostly. It gives the children something to worry about besides their lines. That old cow of Doc's knows the program so well by now, it could tell the kids what to do. One year the sheep got loose and took off around the schoolroom, but that was before we had finished the church. No one who saw that one ever forgot it. Mr. Norgaard, bless his soul, was reading the lesson that year. He could hardly continue he was laughing so hard. Mrs. Adamson, she's long gone to her reward too, never forgave him for such hilarity with the holy Scripture."

"I'm surprised they let the animals come again."

"Took a few years but when the Moens came to Soldahl, Ingeborg kind of insisted. To keep from offending the new pastor, the animals returned to the Christmas pageant." Gudrun shook her head with another chuckle. "Oh, the stories I could tell about Soldahl."

"Well, I better head on home," Caleb said with a sigh. "This has been right nice tonight." He got to his feet. "Good night, all."

Mrs. Carlson stood too. "One thing before you go, Sheriff."

He stopped, waiting for her to continue.

"Is there any chance, I mean, I hate to ask but. . ." She twisted her hands and continued on a rush. "Have you been able to find my wagon yet? I need to get on the road again soon as I can."

Caleb felt his breath go out in a rush. A quick glance around the room told him his feelings were shared. What was driving Johanna Carlson that she would risk her life, again?

Chapter 10

"For cryin' out loud, woman . . ."

Johanna flinched as if he'd struck her.

Caleb lowered his voice. "I—I'm sorry for shouting like that. Please, please forgive me." Speaking softly and slowly took all his effort. Why did this woman get under his skin like this? He looked up in time to catch a half-smile on Gudrun's face before she had a chance to banish it. Did she know something he didn't? Well, it wouldn't be the first time, that was for sure.

Johanna lifted her chin and seemed to grow a foot taller in the process. "I'm sorry I asked. I will go look for it myself."

"Now, let's take a moment to think on this," Dag said from his place leaning against the mantel. "Mrs. Carlson, there is no way we will allow you to take that sorry horse of yours and go looking for a wagon all by yourself. You have no more idea where it might be than we do since you got caught in a blizzard."

"I agree," Gudrun added with an emphatic thump of her cane. "Your children come first."

At the sound of Gudrun's voice, the starch went out of Johanna's spine and she dropped her head forward. "I'm sorry, you are right. But I don't want to put you out any further. You have all done so much to care for me and mine . . ." She raised her chin again, to half-mast. "How will I ever repay you?"

"Not by running off, or at least trying to—again." Caleb tried to snatch back the final word but it sneaked out.

"You are correct, Sheriff, there is no need to belabor the point. But as soon as the roads are passable, I must be on my way. I must." She dropped her gaze again when she felt all eyes on her. *What have I done, will they think me mad? Or worse yet, ungrateful?*

"Well, I'll be getting on then. 'Night all." Caleb started for the door and Dag accompanied him.

"Good night." Johanna looked up to see sympathy swimming in Clara's eyes. "If you'll excuse me, I think I hear Angel beginning to fuss. It must be time for a feeding." Lying wasn't usually her way of dealing with such kindness but she knew if she didn't get out of there, she would break down. And there was no way that would happen. She didn't want these people to have to lie for her, if and when he came.

"I have a suggestion," Gudrun said the next morning at the breakfast table.

Johanna looked up from buttering Henry's pancakes.

Clara paused in the act of pouring a second cup of coffee.

Mrs. Hanson nodded. "I figured you would sleep on it and come up with something."

Gudrun dipped her head in acknowledgment. "Near as I can tell, nothing in our home has a rip or tear remaining. There is no hem not sewn back in or lace neatly stitched back in place. Am I correct?" She looked toward Mrs. Hanson first and then Clara.

"We do have the upstairs linen closet yet to go through but those things are so rarely used." Clara looked to Mrs. Hanson.

"I went through them myself when you were doing so poorly, they are in fine shape."

"That means you have nothing more to do, here, correct?" She eyed Johanna.

"I feel that way."

"I have an idea your fancy work is as meticulous as your mending."

"I try to make it so."

"Have you ever done altar cloths?"

"No, but I've made tablecloths, runners for buffets and dressers, handkerchiefs. I—I used to make them for the local store to sell. There was a shop in town that catered to those with extra money for the finer things. The things I made all sold right away."

"And you can also be a dressmaker?" Gudrun looked over the tops of her glasses.

"Yes, but I haven't as much experience there. You see, I . . ." She clapped her mouth shut. She'd almost said too much.

Gudrun waited. When nothing further was forthcoming, she cleared her throat. "Let us go back to the altar cloths. I would like to donate a set to the church before I die. This has been a long-time dream of mine, but. . ." She shot a glance at Mrs. Hanson. "I am not as adept with a needle as I'd have to be, and Mrs. Hanson, bless her heart, just hasn't the time."

Clara covered her mouth with her napkin, then excused herself.

"I—I could do that for you? If you tell what pattern you want and all."

"Now, isn't that a fine idea. I'm sure Clara would love to help you and perhaps the two of you could work in some baby clothes too. I keep praying we will have little ones running around here sometime soon." She raised her cup for Mrs. Hanson to refill. "If the word gets out that we have such a treasure here, there will be others coming to the door, asking to hire our seamstress."

"Do you think the local general store would be interested in showing some of my things?" Johanna wished she'd kept her mouth closed. If he came looking for her, he'd recognize her handiwork. But he would never spend the money on the train and, as the sheriff had said, the roads weren't passable yet. She should have a couple of months to work on the altar cloths. Not that she'd really need that long. Besides being precise, she had a quick hand.

"Good. Then I will order the linen fabric, I know we have nothing so fine in town. Should be here in a week or two. In the meantime, I know there is some flannel in the sewing room and plenty of fine cotton for baby dresses. You could start with those. Also we could see what is available at Miss Sharon's."

"Miss Sharon's?"

"She's the local dressmaker. I'd have suggested you talk with her but I know she recently hired a young woman to assist her. Right after Christmas is a slow time for all the shopkeepers."

Johanna sat at the table, wondering if this were what being run over by a train felt like. Had she really agreed to do the altar cloths? And told so much about herself? She looked at the satisfied appearance of Mrs. Norgaard and knew she had.

"I think I will send a message to Mrs. Moen to come talk with us. She might even have a pattern or two we could use. I want to keep this quiet. If the Ladies Aid gets wind of it, they'll want to put it all to vote and it would be two years from now before we could begin." She sipped her coffee. "But then I've been known as eccentric so something like this won't surprise anyone."

Clara came back into the room. "We should go over and measure before we order the fabric, don't you think?" She patted Henry's shoulder. "You want to go with me to do that? It's so bright and shiny out, you'd think summer is nearly here."

Henry looked to his mother first and, at her nod, to the young woman behind his chair. If she hadn't been watching, she'd have missed the brief ducking of his chin.

"Good, maybe we'll make snow angels on the way." She took his hand and headed for the coat rack by the front door. "We'll be back later. I know we need some lace and more embroidery thread so I'll go by the Mercantile."

"And Miss Sharon's?" Gudrun asked.

"Of course. Hurry, Henry, before they find more for us to do."

Within the hour Johanna found herself before the sewing maching, hemming flannel into diaper squares. While she'd never used such a fine machine before, she followed Mrs. Hanson's instructions and soon had the treadle flying.

"Dinner is ready," Caleb announced from the doorway.

"Oh! You...ow!" Blood welled from where the needle stitched right into her finger.

Caleb crossed the room in three strides. He took her hand in his. "Here, let me see that."

Bright red dotted the white flannel and now dripped into his hand. He covered the wound with his thumb and pressed. "This should stop that."

"You startled me."

She looked up into hazel eyes with gold dots around the iris, eyes filled with concern and something else. She'd heard that eyes were the windows to one's soul and if that were the case, this man's soul was as fine and strong as the hand holding hers. That soul reached out to her with love and compassion.

Love! She snatched her hand from his and looked wildly around the room, anywhere but at his handsome face. When he stepped back, she leaped to her feet and, fleeing to the other side of the table, began folding the stack of squares she'd hemmed. The space between them gave her a chance to recover her breath.

"Mrs. Hanson asked me to tell you that dinner is served."

"I—I'll be right down. Y—you go ahead." She glanced down to see a bloodstain on another diaper. "Oh, no."

"You could let me bind that up for you." She could feel his mellow voice clear to the marrow of her bones. What was the matter with her? This had to stop. What if he felt the same way?

The thought brought a lump to the back of her throat. There was no future for anyone in loving Mrs. Johanna Carlson. There was only heartache and possibly even danger.

Chapter 11

Such eyes she had. Deep, fit to drown in.

"Sheriff, you going to Millie's for dinner?"

Caleb thumped the front legs of his chair back on the floor, along with his booted feet. "How many times have I told you not to sneak up on me like that?"

"I—I thought you heard me. I wasn't being extra quiet or nothing." Elmer slouched, like a dog that had just been kicked. "I thought you'd want to know that a teletype just came in, about some missing woman. Since you been looking for something about that Mrs. Carlson, thought you'd be interested is all." He held out a teletype form.

"Well, why didn't you say so in the first place?" Caleb tried to retrieve his heart from down around his boot tops. He laid the paper carefully in front of him. But as he read, his heart settled back in its proper place. This was about some young woman who'd never had kids, just up and disappeared from her home in Fargo. Caleb breathed a sigh of relief. "Send back that we ain't seen hide nor hair of this person. She probably headed to St. Paul or Chicago."

"Sure, boss. By the way, how's that Angel baby and her mother doing? Sure did look mighty purty up there in that manger. Just think, she hadn't come to town, the pageant wouldn't a been near so special. Why I said…"

"The reply, man, just send the reply." The sheriff shook his head.

Let Elmer get going, and he wouldn't stop jawing for a week. As the man left the office, Caleb almost wished he'd let him talk on. When he wanted to learn the town gossip, all he had to do was get Elmer talking and act the least bit interested.

He propped his boots back up and let his mind wander again. Only now he had more questions than thoughts. Who was she—Mrs. Johanna Carlson? Was that even her real name? Was she a widow? Or was she on the run? The latter seemed the most plausible. She had that running look about her and she had tried to take off right after having the baby. He should know about running. But it had been a long time since he'd felt the need.

He'd even thought of sending out a teletype of his own but something kept him from it. She'd been careful to reveal nothing of her past and that would possibly have been an invasion of her privacy. He thumped his boots back down, rattled the coal in the stove, threw in a big chunk, and shut die damper down. After shoving his arms into his jacket sleeves, he turned the sign on the door to "Closed" and left the office.

A few minutes later he knocked on the door of the mansion.

"Why, Sheriff, how good to see you." When Mrs. Hanson opened the door, the fragrance of cinnamon and apple drifted out. "How'd you know I was baking apple pies?"

"Just a sixth sense, I guess. Sure does smell mighty good. You know if you'd open a place down on Main Street, I wouldn't have to come so far for my coffee."

"Don't you go giving her any ideas, we'd be lost without her," Clara admonished with a wide smile as she descended the curved walnut staircase. "Come with me and we'll fix up a tray. I know Johanna is due for some refreshment too."

"Seems to me we see the sheriff more since she moved here," Mrs. Hanson murmured just loud enough to be heard by the two in front of her.

"But we'll never tell, will we?" Clara whispered back.

Caleb could feel his ears heat up like someone held a candle right beside them. "Where's Gudrun?"

"Working on her accounts. She will join us."

Caleb leaned over to sniff the perfume rising from the slits in a golden pie crust. "Ah, if I were the marrying kind, I'd ask you to hitch up with me in a minute." He closed his eyes, the better to savor the fragrance.

"If'n I were twenty years younger, I'd take you up on it." Mrs. Hanson swatted his hand away from the knife on the table. "Leave off, I'll make sure you get an extra large piece. Here, I thought this was for after dinner."

"There's plenty for that too. Dag over at the shop?"

"Ja, he don't take off midmorning like some we know."

Clara giggled from pouring coffee into the silver server. "I'd be willing to bet money that he'll show up too." Just then the sound of snow being kicked off boots at the back door made them all laugh.

"Right on time," Caleb called to the man removing his coat on the porch.

"I smell apple pie." Dag hung his coat on the tree by the door. "Something told me I was needed at home." His grin set his blue eyes to twinkling. He crossed to the sink and began scrubbing his hands.

Clara sniffed. "You've been at the forge."

"Ja, that I have. Two teams needed shoeing and Anselm brought in his plowshares at the same time. That is one man that plans ahead. If all the farmers thought like he does, we'd have more steady work and less of a rush at plowing time." He dried his hands just in time to take the tray from his wife and lead the way to the parlor.

Clara flew up the stairs to the sewing room, her voice calling Johanna as she ascended.

Gudrun came out of her study, leaning slightly on her cane. "I thought I heard a party in the making. Now, where did that Henry take off to?"

Caleb remained at the door to the parlor so he could watch the stairs. Clara came first, Henry's hand in hers. Sam looked down at his master, up at the small boy, and back down as if to say, you told me to take care of him, I'm just doing my job. Caleb nodded his approval and Sam wagged his tail.

"Johanna will be right down, she's just changing the baby."

Good, Caleb thought, *then I get to see Angel too.* He followed the others into the room that now seemed bare without the Christmas tree in the bay window, and took the chair with a view of the stairs. When she came down, the smile she bestowed on the infant in her arms made him catch his breath. Her smile radiated pure love like the sun radiated warmth. The pallor was gone from her face, along with the lines of worry she'd tried to disguise. Instead of the dark skirt and much-worn waister, a gown of green serge, trimmed in black at the collar and cuffs, set her eyes, those incomparable eyes, to sparkling.

He only got a glimpse of that sparkle but it went right to his chest. Would she ever look at him like that? The thought made him choke on his coffee.

"Are you all right, Sheriff?" Even her voice sounded different, more assured, not so tentative.

"I—I'm fine." He swallowed and coughed again. "Just went down the wrong way." He looked up in time to catch a knowing glance shared between Mrs. Hanson and Gudrun. Was he so transparent?

Johanna bent over and held Angel out for him to see. "She's started smiling already."

Caleb touched the tiny fist with a gentle finger. Immediately Angel wrapped her fingers around it and turned her head at the sound of his voice.

"Angel, baby Angel, how you doing?" The grasp of her tiny fingers felt like a gift from above.

The tiny, perfectly formed lips twitched and spread in a smile. If he'd delighted in the grasp of her fingers, the smile did him in. She studied him and he her. He touched her cheek with the knuckle of the finger she held and the smile came again.

"She likes you."

"She better. She and me, we had quite a discussion that night she came into the world." He looked up at Johanna. "You don't suppose she remembers me—my voice, do you?"

"Why not? We have no idea how much babies remember. You want to finish your coffee and you can hold her?"

Caleb put his coffee cup back in its saucer on the table beside his chair, beside the plate of pie with only one bite taken. "I'll take her now. You go enjoy your pie."

Angel snuggled into his arms with a big burp. Johanna quickly laid a cloth over Caleb's shoulder and arm. "Just in case."

"Yes, it wouldn't do for our sheriff to patrol the town with baby spit on his shirt." Gudrun lifted her cup to lips that twitched to keep from smiling.

Caleb ignored the chuckles and, in a low voice, kept up a running commentary to the baby in his arms. So long since he'd done this with his own two small ones, he'd have thought he'd forgotten how. But it all came back with a rush. The sweet smell that only came from a baby, the tiny weight of her, the eyes that wouldn't let him go. He knew they said that babies couldn't focus this soon, but he'd bet his badge that Angel was looking right at and through him. She stretched, her arms reaching from the blanket wrapped so tightly around her. Tiny fists waved in the air and she scrunched her face at the same time. She burped again, this time a stream of milk coming out the side of her mouth.

Caleb used the cloth and wiped it away. When Johanna motioned that she'd come get her daughter, he waved her away. "She's fine here."

"But your coffee is getting cold."

"No, never mind." Caleb rocked a bit in the chair. Henry and Sam came to stand beside him. The two might well have been lashed together for the tight fit they were. Henry's hand looked to be permanently embedded in Sam's neck ruff.

"So, you think she's okay? For a three-week-old baby, that is? I know you can't play with her much yet but one day you will." Henry looked up at the sheriff and back at the baby. He leaned slightly against the man's knee, his weight barely felt. As Caleb carried on his one-sided conversation, he continued to rock Angel until her eyelids drifted closed. She yawned, her lips forming a perfect *O,* her eyes wide. After one more relaxing sigh, her eyes jerked open along with her hands and then closed again.

"She's asleep." Caleb whispered and Henry, bless his heart, nodded. Between the two, Caleb felt he'd been given a medal.

"You want me to take her?" Johanna started to rise.

"No, we're fine." He'd transferred one hand to Henry's shoulder and commenced to stroke the boy's back, just as he would a high-strung horse. The boy could hear, he was smart as any ten-year-old if not more, and, wonder of all wonders, he was leaning into the stroking like he couldn't get enough. Quite a fine piece of work for one morning.

Johanna watched the three from across the room. How could she keep them all from becoming too attached? She would be leaving as soon as the weather allowed. Poor Henry, to be offering his trust only to have it rudely taken away again. But wasn't it better to have love in your life, even if you would lose it again, than to have no love at all?

She sighed. To whose heart was she speaking after all?

"I need to get back to those altar cloths, if they are to be finished this winter." She refolded her napkin and laid it on the tray.

"That gold thread tangles something awful," Clara added. "I'm wondering if there is something we can substitute." She got to her feet along with Johanna. "I follow my slave driver back to work."

"You needn't. . ."

"Johanna, I'm only teasing." She put her cup and saucer on the tray. "Thank you, Mrs. Hanson, for your usual delicious delicacies. If you need me, you know where I am."

In a flurry of skirts, the two took the children and headed back up the stairs.

Johanna looked back down once to see Caleb watching her. She started to smile, nodded instead, and continued after Clara. The picture of him with her children refused to leave her mind.

The days fell into a pattern with caring for the children, working on the altar cloths, and visiting with Gudrun, Clara, and Mrs. Hanson, who always found ways to entertain Henry. He could usually be found in the kitchen, helping with the baking. She was never sure how much of his dough went into the rolls or cookies and how much went into him. If he weren't kneading dough he might be reading in the library with Clara, or in the study, intent on following the lines Gudrun drew on the paper that became his letters. He could now write his name without coaching.

When company came, which was often, Henry fled upstairs to play quietly beside his mother.

Johanna enjoyed working with the fine material and lovely threads for the altar cloths. They were doing green, purple, and white for the major liturgical seasons, of which she'd had no inkling until now, attending the Lutheran church with her mentors. The stack of baby things grew too, far more than Angel needed.

Clara wanted a baby. Dag wanted a son. Gudrun wanted children running through the house and even sliding down the banister. But so far, it hadn't happened, since their first baby had died right after his birth.

How will I ever repay them for all their kindnesses? The thought ran through Johanna's mind often and with never an answer. She'd never had life so easy. No housecleaning, or at least very little. She insisted on keeping up her own rooms, including the sewing room, but Mrs. Hanson and a woman they had come just to clean, kept up the rest of the house. A woman collected the laundry each week and brought the clothes back folded or ironed and ready to put away. All but the diapers, which Johanna insisted on doing, and even for that, she had to struggle to keep ahead of Mrs. Hanson.

"Why, I can do a boiler of those while the soup's cooking," she'd say. “You just keep on with those lovely things you’re working on. What a surprise that will be to the folks at the church.”

But somehow the news got out that there was a new seamstress in town and since Miss Sharon only did dressmaking for women and older girls, soon customers were beating a steady path to the mansion door.

“I can’t turn your home into a sewing shop,” Johanna said one day in mid-February. She stood before Gudrun’s desk in the walnut-paneled office. Walnut file cabinets took up the space between the two tall windows and lawyer’s bookshelves with glass fronts lined another wall. Johanna forced herself to stand straight and not squirm. The formal room made her feel like whispering.

“Have I complained about all our visitors?” Gudrun clasped her hands on the green felt blotter.

“No, but...”

“But?” Gudrun nodded to the chair in an invitation for Johanna to sit.

“But it just isn’t seemly. Yours is such a fine house, better than the likes of I could ever dream of.” Johanna sat on the edge of the seat, her back as straight as that of her mentor.

“This is no longer my house, as you well know. I too live here on sufferance and when Dag and Clara are happy with the arrangement, so am I. And so should you be.”

“Oh, please, do not think I am not happy. I have never lived in such splendid surroundings and when we leave here, it will be difficult to adjust again. That is part of my concern.” Johanna leaned forward. “You know, I cannot stay here forever.”

A smile touched the corners of Gudrun’s mouth. “Why not? There is plenty of room and you have certainly made yourself useful. I can see you helping Mrs. Hanson more as she suffers from the lumbago at times. And I believe I know of a man here in town who will come courting as soon as you give the word.”

Johanna could feel the blood leave her face. Suddenly she felt lightheaded. “That can never be.” Even she could hear the stark despair in the simple words. She shook her head and studied the recent needle prick on the side of her thumb. "Johanna, I know there are things from your past you want, you need, to keep to yourself. Once I heard Reverend Moen say that a sorrow shared is cut in half. Let me help you with your burden."

"I can't." Johanna shook her head again, slowly as if it were too heavy to move. "I simply cannot."

Chapter 12

They're finished." Johanna set the last of the flatirons back on the stove.

Clara traced the cross embroidered in gold thread on the set of white cloths. "I was beginning to wonder if we'd make it before Easter. I know Gudrun hoped to present them in time for the Easter services." She looked over at Johanna. "What a lot of stitches." She raised a much-punctured finger in the air. "And I have the holes to prove it."

Johanna looked at her own hands. She'd taken to putting goose grease on them at night to keep them soft. But her hands this winter were a far cry from usual. Without cows to milk and floors to scrub, her hands had the look and softness of one no longer used to heavy labor. Hardening them up again would take some doing.

"Let's call Gudrun so she can see them before we pack them all up again. I'll put the coffeepot on and you go get her."

"What about Mrs. Hanson?"

"She went to the store and then planned to stop and visit with one of the church ladies." She glanced out the window. "I hope she gets back before the snow starts again. I was hoping this was the real thaw and not just a teaser."

"It's too early for that."

"I know, but I want to get out in the garden and bring cut flowers into the house. You should see that front entry when I have a big bouquet of lilacs or roses on the table, reflecting in the mirror. When I was in

Norway, I never dreamed of flowers like the ones that grow here. And when I don't have to do all the spading and weeding, it makes them even more pleasurable." She rattled the grate and added several pieces of split wood to the coals. "Wait until you see our garden out in the back. Dag said I could add more roses this year and I'm looking for a yellow one. I love roses, don't you?"

Johanna nodded. The only roses she'd ever had were the wild ones she cut by the road and they never lasted long in the house. Best they be left to grow into hips for making tea in the winter. "I'll go call Gudrun."

How do I tell her I will not be here to see the roses bloom, to smell the lilacs? Perhaps there will be lilacs where I am going? She took in a deep breath and let it all out on a puff. If only she knew where she was going. Probably as far west as the wagon and the horse would go. When they stopped, she would too, and hope to heaven there was a place for her to work or land to homestead. She'd heard there were still sections to homestead in parts of South Dakota or on the western edge of North Dakota.

She tapped on the office door.

"Come in."

Johanna pushed the door open to see Mrs. Norgaard down on the floor on her hands and knees, helping Henry build a tower out of the odd-shaped pieces of wood that Caleb had carefully cut and sanded. When he gave the boy the box, Henry's eyes lit up like the forge in full spate.

"Well, I never."

Gudrun leaned back against the chair and straightened her skirts. "You caught us in the act, didn't she, Henry?" Like everyone, she included Henry in her talking as if he carried on a conversation like all the others.

Henry's smile wreathed his face when he pointed to the intricate edifice they had constructed, including even the chair leg in their plans.

Johanna knelt down and peered inside. “That is a mighty fine building.”

“It is a church. We just ran out of lumber for the steeple, didn’t we, son?” Gudrun staggered to her feet with a groan and a dusting of hands. “Been too long since I’ve been down on the floor for anything.” She reached over to give Henry a hand. “Come along, I’m sure you and Sam will be able to put away a cookie or two.” The dog wagged his tail from his place in front of the crackling fireplace.

Barely able to contain her laughter Johanna followed behind the three as they marched out the door. No one outside this family would believe her if she announced Mrs. Norgaard had been building with blocks. But then, she’d never tell. This would be another of the memories she was storing up for the dry spell ahead.

“Wait until you hear the news.” Mrs. Hanson came through the back door like she’d been blown in by a blizzard. “Oh, my land.” Her voice softened when she caught sight of the paraments for the altar spread around her kitchen. “If that ain’t the puniest. Wait ‘til the reverend sees this.” She fingered the gold fringe tied so carefully on the ends of the pieces. “If that ain’t to beat all.” Dabbing at a tear that had gathered at the corner of her eye, she looked up to catch Gudrun’s smile. “This will do you proud, that’s for sure.”

Johanna and Clara opened the box they’d been saving for just such a time as this. With tissue paper between each piccc, thcy laid them all in the box, color by color, ending with the purple since that would be used first. When they closed the reinforced carton, Mrs. Hanson took a string and tied it around both ways several times.

“Just in case. Be a shame to get anything so fine, dirty, even by accident.” She clasped her hands over her heart. “I know God will be glad to see His house fancied up with these for Easter.”

“I think He’s more concerned about the state of our hearts, but we won’t argue the point.” Gudrun took a place at the table. “Now, I heard there were cookies for a starving boy and perhaps even his old friend. What do you say, Henry?”

They were sitting around the table enjoying the cookies and coffee when Mrs. Hanson slapped her hands on the table. "Oh, in all the excitement, I forgot to tell you my news. Miss Sharon is getting married and moving to Montana and wants to sell her shop. All I could think was what a perfect place that would be for you, Johanna."

"Me? But I have no money to buy a business." Johanna coughed on a cookie crumb that stuck in her throat. "What an outlandish idea."

"I think it is a fine idea." Gudrun set her cup back down precisely in the groove of the saucer. "I know this must be an answer to our prayers."

"Whose prayers?" Johanna's voice squeaked on the last word.

"Mine and Clara's. And I know you've been praying for help too but you haven't shared what you wish with the rest of us. Johanna, we only want what is best for you, but I must confess my selfishness in wanting you to remain in Soldahl."

"And mine." Mrs. Hanson beamed from one to the other. "I just knew this was the most perfect thing. Not that Miss Sharon won't be missed, but you will be able to stay here."

"I don't have any money to buy a business." *Even if I could stay here,* she thought desperately.

"That can be worked out, I'm sure." Gudrun turned back to Mrs. Hanson. "Did you find out when she is planning on leaving?"

"Of course. She hopes to be gone by Easter. If she hasn't found a buyer by then, she will just pack it up and take the merchandise with her. She said the bank owns the building anyway, but then I 'spect you know that already."

Gudrun nodded. "The bank holds the note. Ernest Hopstead gave her the loan on my say-so, what, seven years ago, and since then she's renewed the loan to buy more supplies. I hate to see her walk away from her investment like that without recompense."

"Well, she has stars in her eyes for sure. She thought she was long past marrying age and here that drummer just whisked her off her feet. She said he's saved up enough to start a horse and cattle ranch with his brother in Montana."

Johanna listened to the conversation eddying around her. Was this her chance? Had God really heard her prayers and was now answering?

She remembered the night of the blizzard that blew them to Sheriff Stenesrude's doorstep. Seemed she'd been praying nonstop since long before the wagon got caught in the drift. And once they mounted that old nag, she'd pounded the gates of heaven for sure. She hadn't dared take a better horse…She stopped the memories before her friends could read anything on her face.

"I would love to be able to stay in Soldahl but I just don't think it is possible." She watched Henry's shoulders slump. *I know, son, if there were only a way.*

Looking up, she caught Gudrun's stare over the tops of her glasses, a look that penetrated to the bone. The desire to tell the truth welled up and could only be capped with a supreme act of determination, the same determination that had kept them on the horse when the wind tried to blow them clear to Texas.

"Well, we will have to discuss this later." Gudrun laid a hand on Henry's shoulder and smiled down into his upturned face. "Henry, would you be so good as to fetch my shawl? I left it on the back of the chair in my office." When the boy slid from his chair and darted out of the room, she turned back to the others. "I believe this is better discussed without him present. Now, Johanna, I know how happy you are here, it is evident in your face and bearing, besides in the wonderful stitching you do. I believe your owning that business would make a fine addition to the life of Soldahl and you all know that is something near and dear to my heart. If you feel you can remain here, we will work out some kind of terms for you to purchase that business. Miss Sharon has a nice little home in the back of the shop and there is a fenced yard and pasture beyond that."

Henry appeared in the doorway without a shawl.

"Oh, I'm sorry, child, I must have left it on the end of my bed."

Henry darted away again and they could hear Sam's toenails clicking on the newly waxed floor.

"Wouldn't you at least like to go look at it?" Gudrun asked with a gentle smile.

Oh, if you only knew. The thought of having a shop like that of her own was a dream come true. Could it really happen? Was she safe here? Soldahl wasn't really on a road to anywhere. Would he look here? If he were looking. Had God answered another prayer and protected them from his wrath by sending him elsewhere? How long could she go on living this lie? Or was it a lie? She'd never told them she was a widow. *But you let them assume that,* she scolded herself silently. If only that gentle little voice would be quiet.

She drew herself up straight, as if pulling her feet out of mud. "I would indeed like to go look at the shop. If you think it possible for me to make our living there, then it is worth looking into."

"Thanks be to God." Mrs. Hanson breathed the prayer on a sigh.

Henry trotted into the room and handed Mrs. Norgaard her shawl of soft rose wool.

"Thank you, dear boy. Here, would you please help me put it on?" With his assistance, the shawl rested around her shoulders and somehow her arm found its way around his waist. He leaned against her, one hand smoothing the softness of the wool.

Johanna sighed. What a bundle of conflicting feelings she had stuffed in her heart. But she knew she'd made a wise decision. Henry needed the love and attention he received from these dear people like the spring soil needed rain and sun. Even if they were forced to flee again, he would always have this time to remember. As would she.

"When do you suppose we could go look at it, the shop, I mean?"

"The weather is somewhat inclement for me today." Gudrun glanced out the window. "But I see no reason why you and Clara could not go. Mrs. Hanson and I will keep the children here until you return. Please ask Miss Sharon to make an inventory of the supplies she has in stock and an estimation of what she would like for those materials. I will ask Ernest at the bank what he values the building at and the amount of the loan remaining."

A wail could be heard from the nursery upstairs.

"There is Angel. I will go feed her and then change into something warmer."

"I will be ready by then too." Clara leaped to her feet. "This is so wonderful."

"I will have a couple of notes written for you to deliver." Gudrun rose to her feet also. "Henry, I do believe Mrs. Hanson needs some wood carried in from the porch to her woodbox. What do you think?"

Johanna left the kitchen as Henry hit the door to the porch running. "You better put a coat on," she threw over her shoulder, knowing that Mrs. Hanson would never let the boy go outside without one. They all took such good care of him and made him feel important by asking him to help. How blessed they were.

A peaceful quiet filled the nursery as she settled Angel against her. The baby rooted around, making snorting noises that turned to the song of suckling. Her deep blue eyes fastened on those of her mother and a gently curled fist found its way to the curve of her mother's body.

Johanna felt the clutch in her throat that came so often in this moment. The rocking chair creaked its song, with the brush of her foot against the rug as a counterpoint. The creak and swish lulled both her and the babe.

The sound of the front door opening jerked her fully awake. If they were to call on Miss Sharon, she'd best hurry. Rising to her feet, she heard the sound of Caleb's voice teasing Mrs. Hanson.

Please don't tell him what we're thinking of doing. The thought caught her by surprise. "Why ever not?" she whispered to Angel as she laid the baby back in her cradle. But deep inside, she knew the answer. Perhaps she could live in Soldahl, but she could never allow her feelings for the sheriff to be known.

Chapter 13

Oh, my."

"What is it? Don't you like it?" Clara turned to the woman following her into Miss Sharon's dressmaking shop. A bell over the door announced their arrival.

"Oh, no, I mean, that's not it at all." Pausing at the first shelf of materials, Johanna stroked the bolt of emerald green velvet with just the tip of her finger, as if a firmer caress might make it disappear. Matching laces and ribbons vied for attention beside the velvet; to the right lay bolts of fine wool, both gabardine and worsted. Hat frames hung on pegs along the upper wall, while summer dimities, calicos, and ginghams invited her perusal on another wall. The jewel tones of the silks took her breath away.

"May I help you?" A woman brushed aside the curtain covering the door to what Johanna supposed was the workroom and the living quarters. With light brown hair coiled in a no-nonsense bun, lively brown eyes, and a slightly red nose that twitched mischievously, Miss Sharon reminded one of a friendly field mouse. "Why, Mrs. Weinlander, how nice to see you."

"Thank you, Miss Sharon. I'd like you to meet my friend, Mrs. Carlson."

The mouse twittered. "Oh, you're the mother of the darling baby who played Jesus at the pageant how is she and you I hear you are a wonder with a needle and thread we have so much in common won't you come sit down so we can visit or is there something that you need here in the shop?"

Johanna felt like she needed to gasp for air. Did the woman never stop to breathe? Which of those questions should she answer first?

"Oh, excuse me, I know I get a bit carried away at times. How is it I can help you?"

"We've come to talk with you about your shop." Clara included Johanna with a glance. "Mrs. Hanson said you are looking to sell."

Miss Sharon gestured for them to follow her. "That I am, so let's sit where we can talk comfortably, then I will show you around."

Johanna looked at Clara to get a wink in return.

"She takes a bit of getting used to," Clara whispered as she led the way behind the shop owner.

"Uff da." Johanna spoke for Clara's ears alone.

A broad cutting table and a sewing machine proclaimed the room they entered to be the workroom. Miss Sharon beckoned them through another curtained doorway, into a cheery kitchen and parlor all rolled into one. A red and white checked cloth covered the square oak table and matching cushions the seats of the ladder-backed chairs. Curtains of the same bright fabric at the windows made even this gray day bright. Braided rugs on the floor, a tabby cat snoozing in front of the cast-iron stove, and a teakettle whispering on the back burner all said "home" to Johanna.

"I've the teapot hot if you would like to join me for a cup of tea. I've been so busy I haven't taken time for a setdown all day."

"You have new orders then?" Clara took one of the chairs at the table.

"Landsakes, all of a sudden everyone wants new Easter dresses and they didn't say anything until I announced that I was leaving." Miss Sharon bustled about her kitchen, measuring tea leaves into a china pot and setting out cups. "I thought to make me a new dress for the wedding but George, have you met George Drummond, he's my fiance." She said the word with obvious delight. "He says he don't want me to spend more time here than necessary. He's ready to leave for Montana, the sooner the better. I thought to having a close-out sale but if I can sell the shop and my business together, someone else will be all set. I've made a good living here and the people of Soldahl much appreciate someone knowing style and fine sewing. Even though Mrs. Jacobson over at the Mercantile carries ready-made now and you can order from the Sears and Roebuck catalogue, when the women want something special, they come to me."

"I heard you had to hire a helper." Clara accepted the cup of tea with a smile. "Thank you, this is such a treat."

"I did, and I was hoping she might take over here but at the suggestion of that, she ran like a scared rabbit. Guess she was afraid I was going to head out at night and leave her with all the work or something." She lifted her cup and sniffed the aroma. "Nothing like a nice cup of tea on an afternoon, I always say. Coffee is for morning and tea for afternoon." She pushed ajar across the table. "Here's honey if you like a dollop of sweetness."

Johanna sipped her tea, wishing she could be in the other rooms, going through all the drawers from the smallest that might hold buttons to the large bins for fabric bolts. She wanted to touch each bolt of fabric and run her fingers over the feather boa draped over the dressmaker's form in the corner.

The bell tinkled out in the shop.

"I'll be right back. Probably someone to pick up their order." Miss Sharon bounced to her feet and out the door.

"Oh, the look on your face." Clara leaned forward so she could talk softly.

"Am I so obvious?" Johanna shook her head. "She is amazing."

"That she is and in a hurry to leave for Montana. You could finish all those dresses as well as she can."

Johanna sighed and shook her head. "Clara, I know you have a heart of gold but I cannot afford a place like this, all the lovely materials and such. And the banker here, he doesn't know me from

Eve to give me a loan and. . ."

"Just you leave those worries up to Gudrun. She still owns that bank and…"

"Gudrun owns the bank?"

"Ja, didn't you know? When her husband died, she kept the controlling ownership and the manager, Mr. Hopstead, owns the rest. She thought that way he would be more inclined to manage it well. Not that he wouldn't anyway, you understand, but he'd been Horace's second in command and it just seemed fitting."

Johanna sank against the back of the chair. "No wonder she knows so much of what goes on around here."

"She knows a lot more than she ever lets on or shares with the rest of us. When someone confides in Gudrun Norgaard, you know your secret is safe with her. Your business will never be discussed over the back fences like some others I know." Clara bobbed her head for emphasis.

"There now, where were we?" Miss Sharon set the curtains to flapping on her way back in.

"I think we would like you to show us around a bit more, there are bedrooms upstairs, is that right?"

"And a bit of a barn out back. I used to keep a horse but finally decided I didn't need one. Everyone comes to me if they need sewing done." She crossed to a door to the back. "Here, I'll show you the pantry first."

Dusk shadowed the land by the time the two women walked up the street to the Norgaard mansion. A gas lamp outside the front door welcomed them home and the smell of supper cooking greeted their entry. Henry threw himself against his mother's skirts.

"Here, let me take off my coat first." Johanna patted his shoulder and cupped his cheeks in her hands. "What's this I see, I think someone had a cup of cocoa." He tried to lick the evidence off, the tip of his tongue doing its best. Johanna took his hand after hanging up her outer things. "Come, let's go wash you up and then I think I hear Angel crying. Has she been good? Have you?"

He nodded and tugged on her hand. In the kitchen Mrs. Norgaard sat in the rocking chair by the newly blackened stove and held the baby flat on her back resting on her knees between the woman's two arms. Angel appeared to be hanging on every word the old woman whispered and sang.

Johanna stopped in the doorway to better appreciate the scene until Angel tightened her face and whimpered. Her mother knew that whimper would soon turn to a squall if not interrupted quickly. "Here, I will take her. Thank you for watching her."

"So long it has been since these old arms held such a beautiful infant as Angel." Gudrun handed up the baby with a sigh. "It seems like a lifetime ago since my Harold was that size, if he ever were."

Johanna paused. For some reason she'd thought Mrs. Norgaard had never had children.

"Yes, he died of the influenza the year he was three and the good Lord never saw fit to bless us with another." A shadow hovered in her faded blue eyes. "I still sometimes wonder why."

"That's so's you'd have time for all the other children you've helped and the families who bless you every night for one good thing or another. You treat the whole town of Soldahl as your family—and half the countryside." Mrs. Hanson leaned over to check the chicken she had roasting in the oven. Her face flamed red from the heat of the open door.

"Ja, that is true." Clara joined them, a sheaf of papers in one hand. "Here are the papers you wanted from Miss Sharon. She said she knew a buyer would want them so she had them all ready." Clara handed them to Gudrun with a smile. "I think you'll be pleased. I know we were quite taken with the shop, weren't we, Johanna?"

Angel's fussing was escalating with each passing minute. Though her mother tried soothing her, shifting her weight from one foot to the other, Angel would have none of it.

"I need to go feed her, then we can talk." She fled up the stairs to the nursery and settled into the rocking chair. Once the baby was happily nursing, she let her mind roam back to what she had seen. The well-stocked shop, the house just big enough for her and her children, a fenced backyard for them to play in, even a tree where she could hang a swing. There was a pasture for the horse and a cow, if she should want one. Miss Sharon had talked about the garden plot buried under the snow and the lilacs bordering the fence.

The desire to make a home in this place filled her, and her heart ached with longing. Never in her entire life had she felt such peace as within the walls of this house and she knew she could carry that feeling over to Miss Sharon's shop. Couldn't she? Could she leave her other life behind forever, could she close the door on the senseless brutality? To those who asked, couldn't she say she was a widow? Perhaps Mr. Carlson died in the blizzard or of an illness, an accident? So often she'd wished him dead.

Was it so wrong to want a new life? To provide a safe home for her children?

She stroked Angel's rounded cheek. "Oh, child, you have no idea what your life could have been. Do I dare stop here? Will we be safe? Can I—we—live a lie?"

She ignored the voice of her conscience whispering in her ear and, after rocking Angel to sleep, she lay the baby in the cradle and made her way back down the stairs. She could hear people talking in the parlor so she turned in through the double doors and paused.

Caleb and Dag were leaning against the fireplace mantel, deep in a discussion over something upon which they did not agree. They were enjoying every moment of the argument. Caleb pounded one fist in the palm of the other hand for emphasis. Dag threw back his head, laughing and shaking his head at the same time.

Sitting close together on the horsehair sofa, Mrs. Norgaard and Clara had their heads together over some papers in the lamplight.

Mrs. Hanson nodded to Johanna as she brought in a tray with cups of coffee. "Supper will be ready in a few minutes but I thought you might like these for starters." She set the tray down on the coffee table and picked up a plate of melted cheese on tiny squares of toasted bread and began passing it around.

Caleb saw Johanna when he turned to accept one of the appetizers. The smile that broke over his face made her heart leap in response. As he crossed the room to her, she had to smile back, it was only polite after all, and besides, her face refused to do anything else.

"How is our Angel today?" Such a simple question and he asked it every time they met.

"Sleeping now but she'll be awake again after supper." Perhaps he really did come only to see the children.

"Good, good."

When had he taken her hand? How could the warmth of one man's hand signify peace and another's spell only hate? Or rage. She shivered at the thought.

"Can I get you a shawl or something? Surely there is a draft here, come over by the fire."

When she tried to withdraw her hand, he tugged it instead and led her toward the fire. "No, no, I am fine."

Dag obligingly moved over. "Here, I am sorry for hogging the warmth. You'd think I'd get my fill of fire with the forge and all but on a cold night like tonight, nothing feels better than a crackling fireplace, even though the furnace heats the house."

Johanna took the place they offered her, right in the middle. The two tall and broad-shouldered men made her feel tiny—and safe. She took the coffee cup Caleb handed her and sipped, closing her eyes in bliss. With the fire warming her back and the coffee her insides, she still felt his undeniable warmth even though they were not close enough to be touching. At the mention of Miss Sharon, Johanna rejoined the conversation.

"The shop appears to be financially stable, with sufficient inventory and fairly low overhead," Mrs. Norgaard was saying. "I'd be sorry for Soldahl to lose a business such as this. Our women need nice things without having to go to Fargo or Grand Forks."

"What's wrong with the Sears and Roebuck Catalogue?" Caleb pointed to his shirt. "Seems good enough to me, I wear their clothes all the time."

"So do a lot of other people and not only clothes but household goods and even farm machinery. They are providing a fine service, but..." Gudrun looked over her glasses. "If we all bought from the catalogue, we wouldn't need any businesses in Soldahl. All we'd have would be a post office, a train station, and a grain elevator." Her tart reply made the men chuckle.

"And a bank?" Caleb winked at Johanna.

The teasing and laughter between these good friends still seemed strange to her. There had been so little levity in her life. She had yet to join in; she could never think of anything to say.

"Now the saloon, that is what really draws the farmers and the ranchers in. We couldn't do without a saloon."

"I suppose you'd like for Johanna to open one of those?" Eyes flashed behind the glasses.

"No, no, just stating a fact." Caleb raised his hands in mock surrender. "You are right, the dressmaking shop is important to the well-being of the residents of Soldahl and the surrounding countryside."

"Quit your funnin' and come and eat." Mrs. Hanson ordered from the doorway. "Henry and I be waiting for you."

Guilt that she'd left her son to the good graces of Mrs. Hanson made Johanna take a step forward. She should have been in the kitchen helping prepare the meal instead of lazing around in the parlor. What was the matter with her, getting ahead of her station like that? The thought plagued her, easily shattering the sense of peace she'd been harboring. She set her empty coffee cup on the tray, but before she could pick it up, Caleb beat her to it.

"I'll just take this back to the kitchen and join you in the dining room."

Once again he caught her off guard. Being taken care of like this could become a habit. Would it be possible for her and the sheriff to remain friends? She'd heard stories of men leaving their families behind and starting new lives in the West. Could she do it too?

But, Johanna, a voice seemed to whisper in her ear, *all your life you've told the truth. Can you live a lie now?*

I already am, she thought. *Surely one more won't make any difference.*

Chapter 14

So, do you think you would like to own the dressmaking shop?"

Johanna stared across the desk to the woman sitting erectly in the chair behind it. Gudrun clasped her hands on the blotter in front of her and looked over the rim of her glasses. The silence of the office felt as thick as before a thunderstorm, yet the twinkle in the faded eyes promised the freshness of spring rain.

"I—I..." Johanna blinked and started again. "You know I would like to, that isn't the problem. I have no, or rather, so little money." She'd earned a few dollars sewing for others. Shaking her head, she continued. "And I have nothing to barter."

"You have yourself and the skill of your mind and hands. I have watched you as you deal with others and you deal fairly, you understand how to set a price for your work. In my mind those are the attributes of a good businesswoman. The bank is willing to loan you the money based on those things. Those and the fact that the shop itself has made money in the past and is filling a need in the community."

"The bank—or you?"

"The bank, on my recommendation." Gudrun leaned forward. "You want a new life, why not here where you already have friends to help you get started?"

Johanna closed her eyes and sighed. *Is this what I am supposed to do? Dear God, I've been asking for an answer, is this it?* "Why not? You are right but I feel like I'm standing on a high cliff and about to jump off."

"Just so you don't feel like someone is pushing you off. I am so certain I am right that at times I get a bit heavy-handed, at least that's what some of my friends tell me." The twinkle brightened. "That is a failing of mine for which I've had to ask forgiveness more than once. But in your case, 1 feel so strongly this is the right move, that the shop will be good for you and you for it, that I can't help but push. Your buying it will make everyone happy, including Miss Sharon and her George. What a wedding gift we are giving them. They'll be able to leave sooner than they had hoped."

Johanna let the words roll over her. She heard them, but for the life of her, she couldn't respond. She, Mrs. Raymond Carlson, Johanna, would own a dressmaking shop in the town of Soldahl, North Dakota. She would live there in that lovely little house with her two children and people would come to her to order their dresses and fine linens. And hats too, she added as an afterthought. She'd never made a real hat, only those she knit. *But I can do it, I know 1 can.*

With each thought she could feel her spine straightening and her shoulders squaring. I *will sign the papers Mrs. Johanna Carlson and that will be the end of that.* The day she signed the papers would be the day for her new life to begin. Not that it hadn't already but that would make it official.

"When will we—what is the next step?"

"If you are in agreement, as soon as a contract is ready, we will meet with Hopstead so you can sign it. The wedding is on Saturday and Miss Sharon said she could be moved out by Sunday. You will have to get together with her so she can show you where everything is. I think she would like to leave much of her furniture so she doesn't have to pay to ship it to Montana but that is something you can discuss with her."

Johanna could feel her hands begin to shake so she clenched them into fists and buried them in her lap. Soon even her lips were shaking. Surely Mrs. Norgaard could hear her heels clicking on the floor. What in the world was she doing? Borrowing such an enormous amount of money from a bank and from a friend and thinking she could have a business of her own? What in the world possessed her to think she could do such a thing? What would Raymond say, that is, providing he ever found out? And her mother and father, why they would roll over in their graves.

You're afraid, a little voice whispered in her ear. *Scared spitless,* she wanted to scream back. And with just cause.

"You know, my dear, my husband, God rest his soul, used to say that when you had God as a partner, you didn't need to be afraid or worried because you had the best partner possible. I think that applies to all areas of our lives, both business and everyday living. It sure has helped me through many decisions. I always pray, knowing God will answer."

"Thank you, I'll remember that." Johanna got to her feet. "I think I better go check on Angel and I have some mending to do for a lady. Thank you for all you have done for us. God surely counts on you as one of His servants." She darted from the room before the moisture welling up overcame her parched throat and spilled out her eyes.

"We found your wagon," Caleb said a couple of nights later when he'd come for supper. "You'd gotten way off the road and down in a low spot. The drifts just covered it over until this bit of a thaw." He shook his head. "Thank God you had the presence of mind to get on the horse and let him bring you in."

Johanna nodded. She thanked God every day for the miracle of their rescue. 'Thank you, Sheriff." Henry tugged at her sleeve and pointed to Sam. The dog wagged his tail. "I know, we have Sam to thank too." She put both hands around the dog's face and looked directly into his eyes. "Sam, you are the best dog in the whole world." Stroking his soft head, she wondered what would happen to Henry when Sam returned to his own house. Surely the sheriff didn't intend to give up his dog forever. So many things to think about.

"Thought I'd take your horse out tomorrow and drag the wagon free and bring it in."

"You need some help?" Dag asked.

"Yup, could use some." He looked over at Johanna with a smile deepening the creases at the outside of his eyes. "We'll put it in the lean-to of the barn at your house. I already took some hay over there and a sack of grain for your horse. If you want you can buy milk from the Ericksons, on the next block and one house in. Their cow freshened so they have plenty, and they usually sell a few eggs too. I'd bring some in for you but my hens quit laying about the time that you arrived. They didn't like that blizzard any better'n the rest of us."

"Thank you." Johanna thoughts flew to the boxes of dishes and pans, sheets, and quilts Mrs. Hanson and Gudrun had been packing for her. They said it was all stuff no longer used in the big house but to Johanna it was riches unheard of.

Three more days and she could build a fire in her own cookstove, tuck Henry into what would be his own bed, and work as late into the evening as she desired. She would pay the mortgage off long before its time if there were any way humanly possible.

The whole town turned out for the wedding and to send the bride and groom on their way. After the service, they greeted everyone, cut the cake, and ran for the train.

"I'm so glad you came to take over for me," Miss Sharon, now Mrs. Drummond, called to Johanna from the steps of the train. "Thank you, thank you everyone." She waved again as the "All aboard" echoed down the track.

"So, would you like us to help you move in now?" Caleb stood at Johanna's shoulder, Henry between them.

"Really?" Johanna fingered the keys given her just before the bridal couple boarded the train. She'd never had keys to anything, let alone a house and shop.

"Why not? It isn't like you have a trainload of stuff to move. We'll hitch up your horse and bring him 'round to the mansion. I heard tell that there are a few others with items to help you get started, the Moens for sure." Caleb hefted Henry up on his shoulders. "Let's get to it." He waved to Dag who was just handing Gudrun into the sleigh. "I'm ready anytime you are."

Dag returned the wave. "I'll meet you at my house then."

"How about you and Henry stop at your new house? You can look around and decide where you want things while we load up."

Johanna felt caught up in the middle of a twister. "But..."

"No problem, Mrs. Hanson and Clara know what is to go, they'll probably beat us over there. Gudrun can watch Angel until we get things a mite more settled, then we're all invited back for supper. I think Mrs. Hanson had this all planned, she just likes to let the rest of us think we're in charge." He took her arm and, all the while he talked, they made their way up the now bare boardwalk to stop right in front of the picket fence surrounding the weathered building. He pushed open the gate and waved her through.

Johanna stopped halfway up the walk. An aged oak tree spread bare branches over the western side of the house, promising the cool rustle of leaves and shade during the hot summer. One branch cried for a rope swing. Under the snowbanks, Miss Sharon had said, slept hollyhock and pansies, daisies and daffodils. Johanna closed her eyes to imagine a pink climbing rose twining up the porch post and across the lintel. She'd have a rocker on the front porch and maybe a pot of flowers, bright and cheery. Miss Sharon's sign would come down to be replaced by…

Her eyes flew open. "What am I going to call my shop?"

"Johanna's sounds good to me, better than *Carlson's."* His voice came from right to the left of her ear. She could feel the heat of him, even through her wool coat. The temptation to lean back and let his strong body hold her up sent warmth flying into her face. She could feel it, like a windburn. Almost in desperation, she fumbled in her pocket for the set of keys. With them securely in her hand, she led the way up the steps, across the porch, and to the storm door. She took a deep breath before opening the door and sliding a shaking key into the hole. She turned it, heard the click, and, after shooting an imploring look, put her hand on the knob.

Please, Lord, let this be the best move ever. Please bless us and our new home. She took another deep breath, let it out, and turned the doorknob. The bell tinkled over the opening door, a welcome sound, and she stepped inside. Sure enough, all the fabrics were as she'd seen before. The room looked like Miss Sharon might be in back, working on a garment for a customer. Johanna fought down the urge to call "Is anyone home?" and took two more steps into the room.

"You'll be all right here?" Caleb's deep voice broke the stillness.

"Ja, we will." She whispered her answer, afraid if she spoke too loud, the spell would break. At that moment she slammed the door on that former life, one she would put out of her mind and heart forever to begin this life anew.

"I'll be going then. We should be back within an hour or so."

She turned and looked up to the man who had set her son down when they came through the door. The low ceiling didn't allow for a tall man with a boy on his shoulders. Thank you, Caleb. I cannot say it enough."

"You just look around and decide where you want things so's we can all help put them away when we get here."

"I will." She crossed the room again to let him out the door, her very own door, to her very own home and shop. "Good-bye." She turned to find Henry right behind her, his eyes huge in his face. His lower lip quivered.

"What is it, son?" How she wished he would talk. Life with him would be so much easier.

A tear trembled on his lashes.

"Did you want to go with the sheriff?" He nodded. A light burst in her mind. The dog, of course, the dog. "Sam will come back with him. He couldn't go to the church with us, you know." How she hoped Caleb would leave his dog with her son just a few more days. Enough time to get him settled in this new place. Come spring, perhaps someone would have a puppy to give away.

He brushed the tear away and heaved a sigh of obvious relief. Then, taking her hand, he joined her in her exploration of their home.

Together they opened cupboard doors and pulled out drawers. They located the door to the basement and decided not to go down there until they had a lamp. While the house was lit with gas lights, she wasn't even sure how to operate them, let alone find one in the dark. Up the narrow stairs to the second floor she threw open the door to a room under the eaves.

"This will be your room, Henry. See, your own bed, and look out the window. You'll be able to watch the horse and our cow, when we get one, out in the field." She plopped down on the bed. "What do you think?"

Henry stood at the window, then turned with a smile on his face. With a deep sigh, he ran and threw himself into her lap, burying his face in her skirts.

Johanna stroked his head. "I know, son, I know. We can both feel safe here." She lifted his chin and kissed his forehead. "Come, let's see the rest."

They'd only gotten as far as the workroom when the bell tinkled in the shop.

"Mrs. Carlson?" A woman's voice, one Johanna didn't recognize, called.

"Ja, I am here." She dusted off her hands and pushed the curtain aside to greet her guest. "Mrs. Moen, what a nice surprise."

"I was afraid you might not be here yet, but we brought a few things to help you set up housekeeping." She opened the door and called, "Come on in!"

Within minutes the room was full of Moens, each bearing a gift of some kind, a nine-patch quilt, some canned fruit, a loaf of bread, butter in a butter mold, a braided rug rolled under Mary's arm, and finally Reverend Moen entered carrying a rocking chair.

"Where's Angel?" Mary asked.

Johanna turned to the girl. "Mrs. Norgaard is keeping her."

"Oh." The girl's face fell. "I was hoping to hold her."

"Where do you want me to put this?" asked John Moen.

"In here by the fire," Ingeborg answered, motioning him into the kitchen. She found places for each of their offerings and kept on being the shepherd as the wagon pulled up from the mansion. The children helped bring in the boxes and, as soon as Clara made it through the door, she began putting food in the pie safe out on the back porch, dishes on the cupboard shelves, and handed Henry the broom.

"That goes out on the back porch, I imagine." When Dag brought in a rather large box, she showed him the stairway going up. "That's linens so we can make the beds."

Johanna had never felt so loved and useless in her life. Here were her friends doing all the things she should be doing and that would take hours. They were finished before sundown.

"Now, isn't this just the nicest?" Ingeborg Moen clasped her hands and gazed around the kitchen. A teakettle now steamed on the stove and the braided rug lay in front of the sink that sprouted a red pump on the left. A red geranium with a white eye graced the kitchen window sill and two dishtowels hung on the rack on the side of the cupboard. Henry sat in the rocker with Sam at his feet and one of the Moen children kept the chair moving.

"I'm sure Mrs. Hanson has supper ready so we best be going."

"And Angel is probably screaming her head off." Johanna grabbed her and Henry's coats off the pegs by the back door and bundled him into them. How could she have forgotten Angel in the midst of all this bounty? Poor baby certainly wouldn't accept such an excuse.

"We can all load in the wagon, then I'll take the Moen's home when I bring you back," Caleb said with a nod. He signaled them all to the door and, once outside, closed it behind him.

"Shouldn't I lock it?" Johanna fingered the key in her pocket.

"Whatever for?" Caleb stopped with one foot on the lower step. "No one around here locks doors."

"But it was locked when we came."

"That was only because Miss Sharon wasn't sure how long

before you'd move in." He took her arm. "Besides, it seemed more official this way. Come on, supper's waiting."

Feeling carried along by a rushing river, Johanna joined the others in the wagon. They really should have runners on it in this snow and ice but the horse pulled it forward anyway.

They could hear Angel crying as soon as their feet hit the front step.

Chapter 15

Bright and early Monday morning her first customer walked in the door.

Johanna laid Angel back in the cradle Gudrun had loaned her for downstairs and pushed back the curtains to the shop. "Good morning, how can I help you?"

"I would like a new outfit for Easter. Miss Sharon said she wasn't taking any orders and that I should come back to talk with you."

Johanna extended her hand. "I am Johanna Carlson and I will be glad to make you a new garment for Easter. Do you have an idea what you would like?"

The customer took Johanna's hand and shook it vigorously. "I am Mrs. Ernest Hopstead, wife of the bank manager. I believe you already have the beginnings of a fine reputation here in Soldahl. Miss Sharon usually let me look through the Godey's books until I found something I liked and then she talked me into what might look better." She gestured to her rounded figure. "But what she came up with was always stylish. I will need a hat to go with it."

Johanna could feel her heart hopping up and down like a frightened bunny. *Dear Lord, please give me wisdom.* "Have you looked around at the new spring materials? Miss Sharon had a goodly stock put in before she left for which I am exceedingly grateful." She studied the woman before her. A blue would like nice with her faded blond coloring. She crossed the room to a bolt of watered blue silk, not even daring to look at the price marked on it. "I think this would be lovely on you." Draping a length of fabric over the woman's shoulder, she moved her to stand in front of the full-length mirror.

"Oh, that *is* nice." Mrs. Hopstead slid gentle fingers over the sleek fabric. "And silk rustles so prettily too. Let's do it in that and now to find a dress I like."

Johanna sat her in front of a round table with a fringed cloth that swept the floor. The three latest fashion books already lay on the table. "I'll let you look and be right back." She no more got back to the kitchen to check on Angel, who was now sleeping, and Henry, who was playing with a horse and rider Caleb had given him, than the bell over the door tinkled again. By noon she had two dress orders for Easter and a set of monogrammed sheets for a wedding present.

By the end of the day she had her work cut out for her. Two more women had come in, one ordering three summer dresses for herself and two each for her two daughters.

"Make Abigail's, that's the one in blue, extra nice because it's time she caught a beau," the woman confided.

"Oh, I will," Johanna promised. "You'll all come by for a fitting the middle of next week?"

The other needed some alterations and wondered if Johanna could come to her house to fit them. With a smile on her face and panic in her heart, Johanna agreed.

She put the children down for their naps and began cutting the watered silk. She'd talked Mrs. Hopstead into tucks down the front of the bodice rather than gathered lace like the picture showed, knowing that lace would make the woman's bosom larger, which it certainly didn't need. She'd found the card file with Miss Sharon's comments on her customers as to what looked good, their measurements, and what they had purchased in the past. Carefully she had measured the woman to make sure the size hadn't changed. It had, making her grateful for her caution. Wisely she kept the numbers to herself, quickly realizing the woman had a vain streak about a foot wide.

The bell tinkled again and she left her cutting table to see who it was. "Clara, how nice of you to stop by." Relief poured through her at the sight of her friend. "Come in, let me put the coffeepot on."

"I hear you've been busy today." Clara pulled off her gloves and removed her coat.

"Ja, how did you know?"

"Oh, a little bird told me. I'm so happy for you, I could bust."

"Don't do that, Dag would get very upset with me." Johanna smiled in answer to the beam Clara sent her. "You are looking mighty happy today."

"I know, I have the most wonderful secret but I can't tell Dag yet until I am absolutely sure."

"You are with child."

Clara nodded. "I—we've been waiting so long and I was beginning to be afraid it wouldn't happen. Gudrun kept telling me all in God's time, but I never have been the most patient person." She looked over to the fine cottons. "You know all those baby things we made, I think that is what turned the trick."

Johanna chuckled along with her friend. "Come, we must have some of Mrs. Hanson's apple cake to celebrate."

Clara hung back, wandering over to the delicate cottons. "I was wondering if you would make us a baptismal gown for him or her. Of course Dag will say it is a him but we both know how important girls are too."

"I would love to sew that for you, and at least you don't have to have it done by Easter." Together they made their way to the kitchen, Clara admiring the silk on the cutting table on the way.

"I will need some things let out soon and I thought maybe you would make me some others with an expanding waist or no waist at all. I haven't even told Gudrun and Mrs. Hanson yet."

"Of course." Johanna rattled the coals and dropped in a couple of pieces of small wood to get the fire going faster. She pulled the coffeepot to the front. "This will only take a minute. You are the first one to drink coffee with me in my brand-new house." She took cups and saucers out of the cupboard, admiring the small stack of dishes as she did so. All of this was hers. For the first time in years she had things of her own, things no one would throw and break, pretty things that she didn't have to hide.

She'd just shown Clara to the door and gone back to cutting when Angel began to whimper. When Johanna finished cutting out the skirt panel, Angel was in full cry. Henry made his way down the stairs into the kitchen and stood at her knee as she settled Angel to nursing.

The bell over the door tinkled again. "Anybody home?" A man's voice called.

"Yes, Caleb, we're in the kitchen." She should have put the closed sign on the door if she wanted to nurse her baby in peace. She threw the baby quilt over her shoulder, already feeling the red climb up her neck. A man walking in on a woman nursing her baby just wasn't proper. "Henry, you go bring the sheriff back here, okay?"

The boy blinked sleepy eyes but nodded. When he heard a dog whine, he flew through the curtained door.

Johanna listened as the man and dog greeted the child. How good it would be to hear a childish voice responding. As a baby, he had made gurgling noises and answered her with coos and smiles. He'd begun to talk too so she knew he could. But ever since that night, he'd never spoken again, learning instead how to disappear into the woodwork so no one would notice him.

With Caleb he was a different child.

"Sam said he was getting mighty lonely for his friend here, so I thought maybe I would loan him to you for a couple of days, help you get settled and all, that is, if you want a dog under foot." Caleb had removed his coal and hat and hung them on the coat tree near the front door. He ran a hand back over his hair to smooth it down. The gesture tugged at her heart. Such a fine man he was, both in appearance and in heart.

"I don't mind at all. I know Henry missed him but I explained you needed him too."

"And that made it all right?"

She shook her head. "But he understood and endured."

"I think for such a small one, he's endured a great deal." Caleb pulled a chair out from the kitchen table and turned it so he could sit with his arms crossed on the back.

If you only knew. She hoped the thought didn't show on her face. It was hard to keep secrets from this man; he was too used to reading faces for the truth.

Angel finished her meal and let out a loud burp. Johanna rose to her feet and excused herself so she could put her dress back to rights. The baby waved her arms and smiled up at her mother, a milky bubble caught at the corner of her mouth. Johanna snuggled her close and kissed the downy hair, coming in darker than the baby fuzz.

When they returned to the kitchen, Caleb sat cross-legged on the floor, rolling a ball to Henry. "I just happened to see this at the Mercantile and thought that a boy needs a ball. I'm thinking that when spring comes, we'll have to put up a swing from that oak branch out there. God made it perfectly for such a thing."

"You've been reading my mind." Johanna spread a quilt on the floor and laid Angel on her tummy in the middle. She ignored the swipe of a tongue from Sam on the baby's cheek and went about warming the coffee again. "Would you like to stay for supper?"

"No, I better get on home, I have chores to do and. . ."

Johanna could almost finish his sentence: ". . .and it wouldn't be proper for the sheriff to be seen leaving the seamstress's home after dark."

"Another time then." She turned with the coffeepot in one hand and a cup and saucer in the other. "I'll serve this at the table." She poured two cups of coffee and a glass of milk for Henry, and then put a plate of cookies on the table, thanks to Mrs. Moen, and laid a couple of spoons in front of Angel.

Before she could sit down, Caleb had pulled her chair out for her. She took her seat, the heat rising up her face again. Why did this man have such an amazing effect on her? And what could she do about it? While her heart said one thing, her head overruled it. There was nothing she could do but ignore her emotions.

On Sunday he showed up to escort her to church. She'd spent the week sewing far into the night and rising early in the morning to continue her work. Every day she thanked the good Lord for the sewing machine that whirred away the hours. The fittings went well, in fact everything was going so well. How could life be so good to someone who was living a lie?

Reverend Moen's sermon verse," ...and the truth shall set you free," made her wince.

Caleb looked over at her, Henry sound asleep on his lap. Did he know? Did he suspect? The urge to tell someone her story ate at her for the rest of the week. Should she talk to Reverend Moen? She knew of his kind heart but he would have to abide by the Scriptures. Gudrun? Of any of her friends, she would be the one.

She finished the last stitch in the last Easter dress on Saturday morning, just after dawn lightened the eastern sky. While the sun was not yet up, she went to stand at her kitchen window to watch the band of soft silver deepen to gold and then flame into pinks and purples as the golden disc arched above the horizon." Perhaps they would have good weather for Easter. The thaw had been dripping off the icicles the last four days.

As on the other mornings, her prayer was the same. "Dear Lord, thank You for what You have given me and now, please show me what to do." The plea had nothing to do with her day's work. She set bread dough to rising, rolled out and baked a batch of sour cream cookies, and was well into scrubbing the kitchen floor when Sam and Henry snuck down the stairs.

"Breakfast will be ready as soon as I'm done here. Why don't you let Sam out in the meantime and then go get dressed?" At his nod, she went back to her bucket of soapy water. By the time she'd mopped up the last brush of water, she could hear Angel begin to fuss in the cradle she'd moved into the other room. Sam yipped at the back door, Henry meandered back down the stairs, and Angel passed from fussing to demanding. Like the time and tides, babies waited for no one.

Several people dropped by that day with gifts of food or small household items, welcoming her to the community and making her feel a part of Soldahl. Each time the bell tinkled, Sam and Henry would run to the door to see who was there. Johanna knew they were waiting for Caleb. By the time dusk fell, she could feel her spirits falling along with it. Though it was hard to admit, she'd been looking forward to his visit as much as the two who now had their noses plastered against the front window.

"Supper's ready," she called.

Just as they sat down and had said grace, the doorbell chimed again. Sam took off, his toenails making him skid on the freshly waxed floor. When Henry started to follow, Johanna shook her head. "You sit here and eat while the food is hot." She could tell from the dog's yips who it was. Henry's mouth turned down and he hung his head.

"Sorry I'm so late but the train didn't get here on time." While he spoke, he set a large square box down on the floor. Sam sniffed it and sat in front of the sheriff, like he was waiting for a description of the contents of the box. Henry turned in his chair and stared from the box to the sheriff's face and back again.

"I know this is early but I wanted to give him something for Easter." Caleb shrugged. "I know, I'm as bad as a kid, can't wait to open boxes." He raised an eyebrow. "Is it all right—for him to have it now, I mean?"

Johanna nodded. What else could she do? The look on Henry's face tore her heart out of her chest and plastered it on her sleeve. At her nod again, he darted across the room and placed his hands on the box. Looking up at the man above him, the boy needed no words to voice his plea.

"Here, you want me to help you?" At the boy's nod, Caleb took a pocketknife from his pant's pocket and cut the strings. With eyes as big as dinner plates, Henry pulled open the crossed sections of the box flaps and peered inside.

"Yes, that's for you," Caleb answered the unspoken question. "Go ahead, take it out." He tipped the box over on its side to make it easier. Henry crawled halfway inside before backing out, his hand clamped around the handle of a red wagon with bright yellow wheels inside of black rims.

Johanna shot Caleb a look of combined joy and oh-you-shouldn't-have-done-this.

Caleb raised a hand. "I know what you're thinking, but every boy needs a red wagon. Just think, this summer he'll be able to pull Angel around in it. Should keep them happy for hours while you sew away."

"I don't know how to thank you."

"Not your place. The wagon is Henry's and he's more than thanked me already. Ain't often in this world you can bring such a light of joy to a child's face. I'd pay for that privilege many times over." He folded the box closed. "You want I should put this down in the cellar?"

"No, leave it here." She pointed to a corner. "He will have a wonderful time playing in that, along with the wagon."

"Fine then, I'll see you in the morning for church."

Late that night Johanna finished stitching the lace trim to a bonnet for Angel to wear for Easter. She and Henry would make do with what they had. At the rate he was growing, what he had wouldn't be worn for much longer. When they walked into the church in the morning, they had a hard time finding a place to sit. New bonnets crowned the women's heads, leaving her feeling like a black sheep in a field of white ones. Dag finally saw them and beckoned them to the second pew. Walking with the sheriff up the center aisle, Johanna could feel eyes drilling into her back. Without turning, she could feel the whispers passed along behind gloved hands. If the residents of Soldahl hadn't noticed the attention he paid to her before, they certainly did now.

She took her place next to Clara and sat Henry between her and Caleb.

"Christ is risen!" announced Reverend Moen.

"He is risen indeed!" responded the congregation. As the service continued with the reading of the women at the sepulcher, Johanna felt the tears gather as Mary pleaded with the man to tell her where they'd laid the body. She contemplated how much Christ had done for Mary and the others, and for her. How could she repay Him?

She knew the answer. By not living a lie. She quickly focused on the words of the Gospel and tried to ignore that silent voice for the rest of the service. It wasn't fair. Was God asking this of her? To go back? To leave her new life? Surely He wouldn't send her back.

After church those invited to the mansion for dinner boarded wagons and buggies, ducking under cover to keep the mist off them. While the sun had cracked the horizon, clouds had returned, but at least it was too warm to snow.

The long table held places for Caleb, Johanna, Reverend and Mrs. Moen, and Will Dunfey, Dag's assistant. Another table was set for the Moen children and Henry.

"He'll be fine with me," Mary, the eldest daughter reassured Johanna. "Come on, Henry, we can have more fun in the kitchen."

"No doubt," Reverend Moen whispered.

"Will you say the grace, John?" Gudrun asked from her place at the foot of the table. Dag sat at the head with Clara on his right. When they bowed their heads in a moment of silence, Johanna heard the voice again. Surely if she told anyone, they would think her mad. She concentrated on the prayer and the voice faded.

Course followed course, with Mrs. Hanson carrying platters and bowls and encouraging everyone— "Eat up, there's plenty more where this came from."

"There certainly is, she's been cooking and baking for three days." Dag said when the cook left the room to bring in another steaming platter.

"Well, I for one don't intend to let any of this go to waste." Caleb passed the platter of sliced ham to Johanna. The conversation flowed along with the food. When Mrs. Hanson swung open the kitchen door, laughter could be heard from the children. John raised an eyebrow but settled back down at a head shake from Gudrun.

"They aren't hurting anything and this old house needs the joy of children's laughter."

Johanna looked across the table at Clara, an eyebrow raised in question. A slight shake of the head and a quickly hidden smile said she hadn't told the others yet. Sharing such a wonderful secret gave Johanna a warm glow around her heart. Never had she had friends like these. Would they still be her friends when she told them the whole story?

Later that evening when Caleb took her home, he stopped on the front porch.

"Would you like to come in?"

He shook his head. "I better not, but I have something important to ask you."

She looked into his eyes, shaded by the dark and his hat's wide brim. "Yes."

He cleared his throat and sucked in a deep breath. "I...you...ah...I need your permission to court you and I certainly hope you feel the same." The words came out in a rush.

Johanna felt her heart collapse at that moment.

Chapter 16

"What do you mean you don't want to see me anymore?"

"Just that." Johanna twisted her hands in knots.

Caleb stared at her, his heart about to leap from his chest. Had he misread all the signs? Surely he wouldn't feel this way if he hadn't felt she did too. All these years, he'd never even escorted anyone to church, or the socials or...

He slammed his fist against the doorjamb. Johanna jumped as if she'd been shot.

"I'm sorry, that was uncalled for." He stared at her, trying to read what was behind her face and in her heart.

She refused to meet his eyes.

"Johanna, I can't believe you are talking like this." He wanted to take her hands, enfold her in his arms, protect her from whatever monster was hiding inside.

"I'm sorry, Caleb, that's just the way it has to be." Her voice sounded lost.

Caleb looked around the shop, as if hoping a message might jump at him from the walls or the piles of material. The night before he had not pressed her for an answer. He'd just hightailed it off her porch as if his tail were on fire. Now as he glanced over at the curtained doorway to her workroom he could see Henry peeking through the crack. What a fool he had been. He knew loud voices scared the daylights out of the child and more than once he'd seen

Johanna hide within herself when a man raised his voice. And here he'd done both.

"Goodbye, Caleb." She turned and, shoulders squared beneath her dark dress, pushed through the curtain.

He could hear her comforting Henry in a gentle voice.

Caleb crammed his hat back on his head and gave the door a satisfying slam. Halfway to the street, he turned right and headed west to the main part of town, his boots kicking up slush in his long strides. For his own benefit he recited in his head a litany of names that applied to one Caleb Stenesrude.

"Good morning, Sheriff," someone called.

He heard but pounded on. He could feel curious eyes drilling into his back but his stride never shortened. By the time he'd reached the Ericksons' driveway, his chest pumped like a bellows and sweat slimed his hat band. He'd covered over three miles.

The sun beat down on his shoulders yet he could feel the ice creeping over his heart. "Dear God, why?" He looked toward the heavens. "Why?" This time a dog barked, the sound carrying over a still-snowbound prairie.

"I prayed over this, thought I was doing what You wanted." He wiped the sweat off his brow with the back of his hand and unbuttoned his sheepskin jacket. Between the sun and the hard walk he no longer needed that. He shook his head and snorted. "No fool like an old fool." He turned around and started back. The way he had stormed around, probably half the town was talking about him now.

When he reached the wrought-iron fence surrounding the Norgaard mansion—no one called it the Weinlander house even though all knew Dag owned it now—he paused. Perhaps Gudrun knew what was keeping Johanna from him. For certain she'd heard about his rampage through the streets of Soldahl.

Here, like some lovesick bull, he'd been thinking this might be one of the happiest days of his life. Women! He punched the doorbell with unnecessary force.

"Why, Caleb, what a nice surprise, we haven't seen so much of you lately." Clara smiled up at him, the twinkle in her eye going along with her teasing. "Come on in." She stepped back and beckoned him inside.

Caleb removed his Stetson and held it in front of him with both hands. Now that he was actually here, he wanted to be anywhere else. "Is Gudrun in?"

"Of course, she's in her office." Her look this time reminded him of his mother. "Something's wrong, isn't it?"

He nodded. "You might want to join us. She might have let you in on her secret."

Clara turned her head a bit. "She?" She studied Caleb briefly. "I'll go ask Mrs. Hanson to bring in some coffee. You go right on." She turned toward the kitchen. "You might want to tap on the door before you go in."

Caleb watched her dart down the hall. *How in the world did I let myself in for this?* He added a few more names to those he'd already called himself and made his way through the parlor and down the hall to the office. He looked down to realize he still wore his sheepskin jacket and hadn't even hung his hat on the hall tree. *Not a good sign, son. Why don't you just hightail it home and go chop wood or something?*

But instead, he tapped on the carved walnut door.

"Come in."

Once before he'd felt just this way—the time he was summoned to the principal's office at the high school.

"Caleb, what a nice surprise." Gudrun stuck her pen back in the ink stand. "Sit down, sit down." She stood and came around the desk. "Let's sit in front of the fire, if you would be so kind as to stoke it up." All the while she spoke, she watched his face.

Once he'd put another log on, he took the wingback chair opposite hers.

"Now, tell me what's wrong"

"Can't one friend call on another without anything being wrong?" He settled his hat on his knee and studied the fire now beginning to blaze again. He sighed and slumped against the leather upholstered back.

When he finally looked up at Gudrun, her gaze met his with compassion.

"Mrs. Hanson will bring the coffee in a few minutes." Clara said after tapping at the door and entering.

Gudrun looked at Caleb with a question.

"It's all right. I asked Clara to join us." He traced the rim of the crown of his hat with one finger. "You see…I…ah…no, this isn't working." He clapped his hands on the chair arms and started to rise.

"Sit, Caleb."

Steel with a velvet covering. He now knew what that meant. He sat.

Clara pulled up a chair and took her place.

He caught a look that passed between them, a look of question and concern all wrapped up together. He sucked in a deep breath and let the words out in a whoosh. "Do you know any reason why Johanna would not want me to court her?"

"Oh, no, I was afraid of that."

He stared at the older woman, willing her to go on.

She shook her head and looked at Clara who did the same. "She's never confided in me," Gudrun began, "but I know there is something in her past that she keeps carefully hidden. I have an idea what it is but that is all." She stared into the fire. "We've all noticed how she mentions nothing about her life before you found her at your gate. That is strange in itself. But I've also seen her flinch or duck away when a man raises his voice or moves too quickly."

"I know, I've seen that too. You think she's running from a wife-beating husband? What with Henry being so scared and all?"

"I can't see her committing some crime, not Johanna. She's as honest as the day is long." Clara tapped her fingers together.

"But she was definitely on the run. I was surprised when she agreed to buy the dress shop." Gudrun looked up at the tap on the door. "Come in."

After Mrs. Hanson fussed with the coffee tray and left, she continued. "What happened today?"

"I. . .well, you know I've not been hiding my interest in her. Why those two tykes of hers are dear to me as my own. That Angel could make the devil himself smile."

"Let alone our dear sheriff." Clara handed the coffee cups around.

"Yeah, well, be that as it may, today I asked her if I could come courting. I thought I ought to make sure she knew my intentions were honorable."

"Of course." Gudrun sipped her coffee.

"She turned me down flat, said she didn't think she should see me anymore. Can you beat that?" He could feel his heart start thumping against his ribs again at the memory. "So I thought to ask you if you knew any reason for such a thing."

"I'm glad you did. I think it's time we got to the bottom of this—for both your sakes. Living a lie will eat away at one 'til there's nothing left."

"There's something going on for sure," Clara added. "I've seen her look at you when you weren't paying attention. That wasn't the look of someone who didn't care, even Dag noticed."

Caleb leaned back in his chair. So he wasn't nuts, he hadn't been misreading the woman.

Gudrun set her cup and saucer down with a click. "So the question is, what can we do?"

Caleb nearly smiled at the mention of "we." That was one thing about Gudrun, she didn't let any grass grow under her feet. When something needed doing, no matter how hard or distasteful, she got right to it. Maybe coming here wasn't such a bad idea after all. Caleb stood and took up the poker, moving the logs around whether they needed it or not. He set the brass screen back in place to protect the fading oriental rug and returned to his seat, only to get back up and lean against the mantel.

He crossed to the table where the tray sat and poured himself another cup of coffee. He crossed to the table again and picked a cookie off the plate. About ready to reach for the poker again, he ordered himself back to the chair.

"That's better. You're acting like a cat on a hot stove." Gudrun's smile took any sting out of her words. She nodded. "Guess it's about time I go over and order a new summer dress from Johanna. That ought to give us a splendid opportunity to talk, don't you think?" She looked up at Clara who nodded and smiled widely.

"And if need be, I'll order one too. In fact, she knows I need several new things."

"I'll ask Dag to send Will over to drive the carriage tomorrow, or the sleigh, whichever. I haven't been shopping in quite some time. What do you think, Clara, do I need a new hat too?"

"I think Mrs. Johanna Carlson doesn't stand a chance."

Chapter 17

Johanna rubbed her forehead with weary fingers. *Why do I feel so empty? I did the right thing, I know I did.* She bent over her sewing machine, blinking to clear her eyes. Was she coming down with a cold? She blew her nose and wiped her eyes. After finishing the final seam in the skirt she was constructing, she tied off the threads and folded the waistless garment. Rubbing her aching back with one hand, she got to her feet and shoved the chair closer to the treadle machine. She should have gone to bed far earlier but the orders had stacked up and she needed the money. The first payment on her house was due soon.

She shut off the lamps and climbed the stairs to her bedroom, a kerosene lamp in hand. She checked on Henry, sound asleep with Sam lying right beside him. He wagged his tail when she patted his head.

Next, she held the light over Angel's cradle, also soundly sleeping, her little rear in the air. Johanna adjusted the quilt covering the baby and tiptoed over to her own bed. Each action seemed to take all the strength she had, as if she were slogging through deep snowdrifts. She wrapped her arms around her elbows and hugged herself, rocking back and forth to stem the sobs that threatened to tear her apart. If she weren't careful, she'd wake the baby. She shed her clothes and crawled under the covers, burying her face and her sobs in the pillow.

Waking in the morning to a baby's screaming cries did nothing for her peace of mind. "Shush, little one, your ma's right here." She changed the soaking baby and took her into bed with her for her breakfast.

That afternoon when the bell tinkled for the third or fourth time, she was losing track, she entered the shop to see Clara fingering a bolt of gingham. "Clara, how good to see you." Johanna extended her hands.

"And you." Clara took them and smiled, her gaze searching. "Gudrun wanted to come today too, but she ended up feeling a mite poorly so I came alone. Have you thought anything about some gowns for me for the months ahead?"

Johanna shook her head. "I haven't had to time to think about what to cook for dinner. While I can't afford the help, I have thought of hiring that young woman that worked for Miss Sharon." She swung their still joined hands. "Have you told Dag yet?"

Clara nodded, her eyes sparkling. "He's choosing boy names, of course. And Gudrun is ready to redecorate the nursery. Says we are finally fulfilling her heart's desire, to see children playing again in that big house."

"Here, do you have time for a cup of tea?" Johanna turned toward the workroom. "Let me put away a couple of things first. You go on in and sit down." She spun around and hurried over to the front door. After turning the lock, she pulled down a shade that said "Closed."

Clara stood over the cradle in the corner, her hands clasped to her bosom, a smile curving her mouth. "She is so beautiful." Her whisper greeted Johanna at the doorway. "Angel, that is indeed who you are." She looked up when Johanna brought the teakettle forward on the stove. "I am not surprised a bit that Caleb is so taken with her. Perhaps she reminds him of his own baby girl."

Johanna felt herself stiffen, and when she tried to swallow, her throat was dry. "D—do you take milk with your tea?"

"No, thank you, a bit of honey if you have it, otherwise sugar." Clara crossed the room and sank into the rocking chair. "You have made such a cozy home already." She looked at the blocks Henry had left by the big box the wagon came in. "I think children's things give that feeling, don't you?"

Have you seen Caleb? Johanna's mind screamed so loudly she was afraid her visitor would cover her ears. *Did Caleb send you here?* She squashed that thought with a *Don't be silly,* and poured the boiling water over the tea leaves. Reminding herself that she had done what was best, she poured the liquid into the cups and handed one to her guest. "Why don't we sit at the table?" Her cup rattled against the saucer.

"Johanna, are you all right?" Clara studied her over the rim of her cup. "You're working too hard, aren't you?"

"No, no, I'm fine, just busy, that's all. Running a shop like this takes some getting used to, you know. I think I got lazy living in the lap of luxury like I did at your house."

Clara harrumphed and shook her head. "Lazy does not apply to you, my friend. But you look, I don't know, troubled, sad."

Angel whimpered in her cradle. *Thank You, Lord, for small favors.* Johanna pushed back her chain "I need to change and feed her. We'll be right back." A few minutes later, settled in the rocker, Johanna kept the conversation centered on general matters, refusing to allow the personal to surface again. That was one of the bad things about good friends. They had the ability to see right through each other. And Clara was exceedingly perceptive.

Later, after playing with the baby, Clara sighed. "I really must go. We'll talk about those dresses as the time gets closer. I miss having you at the house, and Henry and Angel. It's awfully quiet again. I even miss Sam's claws ticking on the floors, silly, isn't it?"

"No, I don't think it silly at all. I'm just so grateful you call me friend."

Clara donned her coat and hat by the front door. "Just so you know that this friend is available should you ever need anything, especially someone to talk to."

"I know that, and thank you." Johanna heard Henry and the dog coming down the stairs. She leaned her head against the glass in the door, watching Clara reach the street, turn, and wave. That was one more thing. If Caleb didn't visit anymore, she would have to get his dog back to him some way. He was probably so mad at her, he'd whistle for Sam when he was outside. Surely Henry was feeling safe enough now, or was he?

The thought of the days and weeks ahead with no Caleb to come calling brought a heaviness to her chest. Why couldn't they still be friends?

On Sunday she walked to church with her children. She looked around the congregation from the rear but nowhere did she see his broad shoulders and fine head. When they left, he still had not come. Was he sick? The thought grabbed at her insides.

She forced a smile and answered the greetings of those around her. When Angel began to fuss, she excused herself and headed for home. *You will not cry!* she berated herself again and again. *You chose this path so now you must walk it—alone.*

A carriage pulled up beside her. "I know it's too late to offer you a ride, but we would love you to come for dinner." Dag's voice drew her around.

"Thanks, but not today. I have so much to do and Angel is fussing. She might be coming down with something so I think I better keep her home." Angel was fussing but only because she was hungry. Was this little white lie a terrible thing? Surely she couldn't bear it if Caleb were there. He usually came for Sunday dinner.

"I'm sorry," Clara added. "I know Gudrun would love to see you and the children. She's feeling rather housebound."

Guilt could drive arrows deeper than any bow. "Is she very sick?" *Go, no, don't go* wrestled in her mind.

"She doesn't dare be, the way Mrs. Hanson is carrying on." Clara shook her head, setting the ribbons on her bonnet to bobbing. "Maybe next time, all right?"

Johanna nodded and waved as they drove off. She quickly turned into her gate, letting it slam behind her. She felt like slamming all kinds of things, doors, kettles. Her life here would be so perfect if it weren't for the sheriff—and her hungry heart.

By the end of the week, her skirt sagged at her middle. Johanna knew she better force herself to eat, but how did one turn off the thoughts and nightmares that followed the few times she had fallen asleep?

The days lapsed into weeks with Johanna sewing, fitting, and acting as if all were right. Inside she alternated between freezing and flaming.

One typical morning Henry woke her to say that Angel was crying. She leaped out of bed, remorse lending strength to her feet. If she couldn't even take care of her baby, what was going to happen to her? She had spent a fitful night and the nightmare she'd just released returned with a vengeance as she nursed a now smiling Angel. Raymond, always Raymond, pursuing her, this time with a whip. She could hear him rattling the door of her mind, no matter how hard he slammed it.

She finally made breakfast, cleaned up the kitchen, and sat down at her sewing machine. The dress for Clara had to be done today, she'd been at it far too long. Scolding herself for the miserable way she was acting had become a habit. When the bell tinkled to announce a customer, she pushed herself to her feet, squared her shoulders, and plastered a smile on her face.

The smile ran into hiding as soon as she saw the man standing in the middle of the shop. Summoning up every bit of strength she possessed, she forced herself to speak. "Good morning, Sheriff Stenesrude, how can I help you this morning?"

He studied her face a moment before clearing his throat.

Henry, with Sam on his heels, darted through the curtained door and threw himself at Caleb's knees. The dog yipped and wagged, turning himself inside-out with joy.

Johanna flinched from another arrow of guilt. Sam was Caleb's dog, not theirs.

Caleb, blinking extra-fast, picked Henry up so he could look him right in the eye. "How've you been, son, taking good care of your ma?" Henry nodded so hard his hair flopped in the breeze. "I see Sam is in fine fettle, you been taking good care of him for me, huh?" Again Henry nodded. Caleb leaned over and sat the boy down, giving the dog a good ear rubbing at the same time. "Why don't you two go play in the other room, I need to talk with your ma."

Henry's shoulders slumped and his smile melted away but he did as told, only looking over his shoulder once before trudging out. He had buried his hand in Sam's ruff so the dog paced beside him.

Caleb turned his hat brim round and round in front of him. "I—hear you've been real busy." He cleared his throat—again.

"Ja, that I have." She memorized his face for the lonely nights.

"I—I come for my dog. I thought by this time Henry would be okay without him." His words came out in a rush as if he needed to get them over with.

Johanna nodded. "'I've been telling him this day would come."

"I hate to do this to him but..." His words trailed off. He stared into her eyes, as if probing her soul.

Tell him he can come calling again. No, don't. The war exploded in her head.

"I'll get him for you." She tore her eyes from his and spun around. Ducking through the curtain, she wished she could do anything but this. She knelt in front of Henry, hands on his shoulders. "Son, you have to be very brave now, like we been talking about. Sheriff Stenesrude needs Sam back."

A tear welled out of his blue eyes and sparkled on his cheek before being chased down by another.

Johanna fought the moisture gathering at the back of her throat and eyes. "You are such a good, big boy. I promise you, as soon as we hear of someone who has pups, we'll get one for you. That'll be your own dog."

Henry buried his face in the dog's fur, his shoulders shaking.

Sam turned and licked the tears off Henry's face, whining his sympathy.

"Come, Henry." She gave him her hand and together they walked into the shop, Sam padding beside the boy. 'Thank you for loaning us your dog, Sheriff. We're much obliged."

"Johanna, I..."

"Goodbye, Sheriff." She turned and walked with Henry back to the kitchen where she sat in the rocker and lifted him into her lap. Finally the doorbell signaled his departure. Henry's sobs finally turned to sniffles but he remained leaning against her chest. The kitchen seemed empty.

When the bell tinkled again, she wished she had pulled down the closed sign. With a sigh, she deposited Henry on the floor and returned to the shop. "Gudrun, what a nice surprise."

"Hello, my dear. I'm sorry I've been so long without visiting you." She leaned on her knob-headed cane. "What has happened to you? You look terrible."

Johanna smoothed back her hair and sighed. "It's a long story."

"I have plenty of time to listen."

Johanna shook her head. "Not today. I don't think I'm up to it right now." She bit her lip at the compassion radiating from her friend. She felt guilty again. After all, she should have called on her when she knew the older woman wasn't feeling well. What kind of a friend was she?

Gudrun nodded. "Tomorrow then, you will come for dinner after church and when the children are down for their naps, we will get to the bottom of all this."

"I can't, I..."

"Caleb will not be invited."

"He—he came for Sam today."

"I'm so sorry." Gudrun squared her shoulders. "I will see you tomorrow then."

"Ja, we will come." When the old woman turned to leave, Johanna asked, "Did you need something today?"

Gudrun paused. "Yes, but we will deal with this other first. 'Til tomorrow then."

Johanna followed her to make sure there was no problem with the steps but Mrs. Norgaard sailed out the yard and to her waiting carriage, ignoring the mud caused by the melting snow. Johanna lifted her face to the sun's warmth. It had seemed clouds had covered the sun for the last month. Or was it only cloudy over her?

Each night and nap, Henry cried himself to sleep. Johanna stared down at him, shaking her head. Surely someone must have some puppies soon. She'd have to remember to ask Dag if he knew of any.

Sunday morning came rushing on like a runaway train. Every other minute she swore she would not go, not to church, not to Clara's, not outside her front door. In the saner minutes, she dressed the children for church and herself too.

Ingeborg Moen met them at the door. "Oh, Johanna, I am so glad to see you. I've missed you but I couldn't even come calling because we've had the measles at our house and I didn't want to bring it to your children." She cooed at Angel and patted Henry on the head.

"Are they all right now?"

"Still some spots but back to running around so on the mend. Mary stayed home with them so I could come to church. I feel like I've been gone forever." She turned as the organ began to play. "Why don't you come sit with me, that all right with you, Henry?" At his nod, she added. "So there, that's all settled."

Since they sat in the front of the church, Johanna couldn't look around for Caleb. But she knew he wasn't there, she couldn't feel his presence. Though the service went by in a blur, one verse from the Gospel stayed with her: Jesus promised to be a husband to the widows and a father to the fatherless. *If only that applied to me.* She caught her thought in horror. She couldn't wish Raymond dead, no matter how much she feared him. It wasn't Christian.

After the service, she stood by Clara and Dag as he helped Mrs. Norgaard up in the carriage. He assisted the other two women aboard and lifted Henry up on the seat beside the driver. "If you think you're strong enough, you could maybe help me drive the team." The child's answering grin nearly broke his mother's heart. *As if it weren't in tatters already,* Johanna's mind responded.

When Dag lifted the boy onto his lap and invited him to take the reins with his own over them, light beamed from the boy's face.

"He'll make a good father, won't he?" Clara whispered.

"Very good," Johanna whispered back

During the meal, swallowing small bites took every bit of concentration she possessed. She'd known from the look on Mrs. Hanson's face that she would not tolerate food returning to the kitchen on Johanna's plate. Even so, she slipped some over to Henry's in the guise of cutting up his meat. Dag winked at her when she looked up, sending a rush of moisture to her eyes. Yelling she could handle, kindness no.

Later, after nursing Angel and putting both children down to sleep, she made her way back downstairs and into the parlor. Clara sat in front of the tall windows, her embroidery hoop in hand while Dag snored gently beneath the newspaper.

"She's in her office, waiting for you." She smiled at the look of trepidation that crossed Johanna's face. "She won't eat you, you know, and if you want me to come in and hold your hand, I will."

Johanna squared her shoulders. "No, thank you. I will manage. You can ask her later what happened." Clara nodded.

Johanna tapped at the door and, on invitation, entered the room. A fire crackled in the fireplace, throwing a rosy glow over the woman in the chair. The younger woman crossed and rubbed her frozen hands in the welcome heat before taking the other chair.

"Now, my dear, how can I help you?"

The warm tone made Johanna blink several times. She sighed. "I guess I will start at the beginning."

"That is always a good place."

"First of all, I am a married woman, not a widow like you probably surmised. I ran away from my husband because . . .because I couldn't stand his beatings anymore. I lost one other baby when he threw me against a wall and I was determined to not lose this one. . .Angel."

"And he beat Henry too?"

Johanna nodded. "I know that's why he doesn't talk. He did everything he could to become invisible. For years I thought it was all my fault, if I could try harder, be nicer, whatever, he would love me like he said he did in the beginning. My folks thought he was a fine man, they encouraged me to marry him and I agreed. I had a good, warm house, our farm produced well, what more could I ask for?"

"Did they know about his temper?"

"One day I told my mother but she said many men smacked their wives around a bit."

"A bit?"

"I never again told her how bad it was. When he broke my arm, I decided I couldn't stay any longer but it took months before I could leave. He watched me like a hawk." She looked down at her hands clenched in her lap, the knuckles white. "I've been so afraid he would come find me." Silence reigned for a time.

"That is why you sent Caleb away."

"Yes." The one word held all the misery locked in her trembling body.

Gudrun nodded. "I thought as much." She looked over the tops of her wire-rimmed glasses. "For I'm certain you love him, as he loves you."

"Yes. I thought I could just start anew, I've read stories of others who have done so, but I couldn't lie to him. How could I take more wedding vows when I am already married?" Johanna huddled into the back of her chair. "What do you think I should do?"

"I wish I knew, my dear, I just wish I knew."

Chapter 18

D*ear God, I cannot go back, please, please don't make me go back,* Johanna prayed silently as she leaned against the chair, grateful for its strength to uphold her. Surely God wouldn't ask such a thing of her, surely He wouldn't. She let her mind wander.

Raymond hadn't started to strike her until. . . She tried to think back. Was it after Henry was born? He'd been a colicky baby and many nights even her pacing the floor with him hadn't stopped his wails. Raymond roared that he needed his sleep if he were to harvest in the morning.

At first she excused his fits, knowing he was exhausted and worried about getting the harvest in before the rains came. Then it was because he'd had too much too drink one night at a neighbor's house. Finally, she knew it was all her fault, that nothing was ever done right, according to Raymond. The night he tipped over the highchair with Henry in it, to get to her, was the night he kicked her when she fell. She felt those bruises for weeks, mentally tasted the blood from the split lip, and remembered hardly seeing out of a blackened eye. He grew more violent as the months passed. Surely God wouldn't make her and her children leave the safety they had found and return to that life.

Gudrun sighed, bringing Johanna back to the present.

"I think we can only pray on this for the time being. Surely God has a plan in mind, but so far we just don't know what it is. Have you thought about what your options are?"

Johanna nodded. "I can stay or go back. Either way Caleb will be out of my life." The thought weighed like a sack of wheat with fear nibbling a hole in the corner.

"I wonder if it wouldn't be a good thing to tell Caleb the entire story."

"I—I couldn't."

"Do you want me to?"

Johanna shook her head and shook it again. "No!" She paused. "No."

"He might have a good idea..."

"Gudrun, there is no law against beating your wife, she's a man's property to do with as he pleases, you know that."

"Thank God my Horace didn't believe that way, I don't know what I would have done." Silence again.

This time Johanna heard no voices from the past. Her little house and her growing business, they were hers and worth fighting for. If Caleb and her love for him were to be the sacrifice, so be it. Surely if Raymond were searching for her, he'd have come by now, before spring plowing began. He must have given up.

"Thank you for listening to me."

"Humph, near as I can see, I about twisted your arm off to get you here and talking." Gudrun made to rise. "I promise you, God will reveal His will in His good time. I've never known Him to fail."

Johanna quickly banished a recurring thought. *Why had God allowed such cruelty in the first place?*

Knowing that someone else shared her burden made the days lighter. Each evening Johanna took a few minutes to look in God's Word for His promises of protection. They were there but so were verses telling wives to submit to their husbands. She finished garments and started on newly commissioned ones. She made her first payment at the bank, feeling one step closer to owning the shop free and clear.

One afternoon, after Dag hung a swing from the oak branch for Henry, for the first time Henry discovered the joy of being pushed into the air. Since the weather was warmer, he played outside much of the time. One day she heard a yip and went to the window to see Sam charging through the opened gate and over to the boy. Caleb waited for him at the street, leaning backward against the fence post as if he couldn't bear even to look at her house.

He must hate her. Or not care anymore.

Wasn't that what she wanted? Him to stop caring and her heart to mend?

A few days later she put the children in the red wagon and walked over to the mansion, pulling the wagon behind her. Mrs. Hanson greeted them with cries of delight.

"Clara, look who's here. Go tell Gudrun. Come in, come in, the coffee will be ready in a jiffy." She took the smiling baby from Johanna and, after hugging her and planting a kiss on the rosy cheek, carried her into the kitchen, talking all the while.

When Clara returned she hugged Johanna and stooped down in front of Henry. "How's my favorite boy today? Brought your wagon, I see." Henry nodded, eyes bright and a smile showing off the dimple in his cheek. "I think Mrs. Hanson has cookies in the cookie jar, but if I get you one, you won't tell anyone, will you?" He shook his head, the grin even broader.

Gudrun, her cane bearing more of her weight than ever, tapped her way into the room and greeted them all. As soon as she sat down, she motioned Henry over. "Why, Henry, I think you've gotten all grown up since I saw you last." She cuddled him in the crook of her arm when Mrs. Hanson leaned over to see Angel.

"Ain't she just the purtiest?"

"Lives up to her name, that's for certain." She reached up and took the baby onto her lap. Angel gurgled and cooed, waving her arms and kicking her feet free of the blanket.

"She's getting to be a handful to hold nowadays. She wants to keep up with Henry already." Johanna sat down across the table. "She thinks riding in that wagon and seeing the world is the greatest thing since the wheel was invented. The streets are finally dry enough we don't sink up to our ankles in the gumbo."

"Have you started your garden yet?" Clara asked, taking another chair and drawing Henry to her.

"I've gotten some digging done but the sewing keeps me so busy, I don't know how to do it all."

"Why don't we send Frank over to spade it up for her?" Mrs. Hanson set the coffee cups in front of them and a platter with cake and cookies both on the table.

"It's too small to bring a horse in to plow it, or I'd have asked Dag if he knew someone who would do that."

"Well, don't you worry, another couple of days and Frank can take a break here and help you." Gudrun looked up from talking with the baby. "I think she understands every word we say."

The words Johanna really wanted to hear were about Caleb but she couldn't bring herself to ask any questions about him. Strange how in a town, so small, they didn't run into each other at all. Perhaps he was being as careful to stay away as she. "Thank you, I would surely appreciate the help."

They chatted about the goings-on of Soldahl but no mention was made of Calcb. When Johanna got to her feet, saying it was time for them to head on home, Clara volunteered to walk partway with her. Mrs. Hanson tucked a packet of things she'd been collecting into the wagon.

"Just for your supper, nothing much." She hugged Henry, smacked a last kiss on Angel's cheek, and handed her to her mother. "You don't wait so long to come back, you hear?"

"I won't." They waved good-bye and started down the walk. Clara pointed out the tips of the tulips and daffodils peeking from the ground and they laughed at a squirrel scampering up a tree. Clara turned into the blacksmith shop with a wave goodbye and the others continued on to the little house set back from the street.

That evening when she was at her sewing machine again, Johanna thought back to the day. For the first time since her marriage, she had friends, true friends who cared what happened to her. What a pleasure it would be to have a man dig up the garden for her. Later she found herself humming a tune in time with the treadle.

Sunday her heart leaped nearly out of her breast when she saw Caleb sitting in a pew, second from the rear. Ingeborg invited her down front to sit with her and her finally recovered brood so she made her way up the center aisle. Her back felt as if two smoldering coals were laid side by side on it. When would the sight of him not affect her so strongly? Nightly she'd prayed to be delivered from the love she felt for him. And just when she thought she was on the mend, this happened.

Mary asked to take Angel so Johanna held Henry on her lap instead. He peeked out around her shoulder at the antics of one of the young Moen boys, whose mother kept shushing and sending threatening glances. Once Henry giggled. His mother hugged him close, grateful for any sound he made. Perhaps one day he would talk again, now that he felt safe.

Reverend Moen based his sermon on the tale of Onesimus, the slave Paul told to go back to his master. Each word bit into Johanna's heart. Was God saying she had to go back? By the end of the sermon, she felt sure. A calm settled over her, and she squared her shoulders and her will. If God demanded this, surely He would give her the strength to carry it out. What would she do when she got there? All she knew was if this were the price of peace of mind, steep though it was, she believed God knew what He was doing.

He was telling her to go back to Wisconsin.

"You've decided, haven't you?" Gudrun walked out with her.

"How do you know?"

"The answer is in your face, my dear. Now we must work out how to do this great deed."

"We?"

"You did not think we would leave you to fight this battle alone?" Gudrun shook her head. "No, that's what friends are for, to share a burden."

"But—but you've been ill and…"

"And you think I'm too weak for such a trip?"

"No—yes—I don't know." She looked down in time to see Henry dart across the grass. He flung himself at the sheriff's legs and his face nearly cracked in two when Caleb picked him up. The two hugged each other, the boy disappearing in the strong arms of the man.

Gudrun followed her gaze. "Those two are a pair, are they not?"

"Yes, they are." If only she dared to do the same.

"Back to our discussion. When would you like to leave?"

Johanna tore her gaze from the man and child and returned to Gudrun. "As soon as I have the money for the train fare."

"If that's all, we can leave tomorrow. Henry will stay at our house. Of course he will be spoiled rotten by the time we return. Since you are still nursing, Angel will have to go with us."

"I—I..." Johanna now knew what it felt like to be caught in a tornado and spun around, all out of control. "I have two orders that have to be finished first. Gudrun, I cannot keep taking charity from you like this."

"Call it a loan then. You can pay me back when you can."

Clara came to stand beside them. "What have I been missing?"

"Johanna and I are leaving for Wisconsin on Thursday." She smiled at Johanna. "That will give you time, right?"

The younger woman nodded. She couldn't have spoken if her life depended on it.

"Good." Clara reached for Angel. "Please let me hold her for a bit. I need to get some practice in." She turned as Caleb came up to them, Henry on his shoulders, both hands lodged in Caleb's hair.

"Isn't she beautiful, Caleb? She's growing so fast." Clara held tightly to the squirming baby. "I think she wants to get down and run with the other children. Won't be long now, will it, sweet thing?" Angel gurgled and cooed back, her arms and feet going as if she were already on the ground and running.

Caleb reached a finger to touch the baby's face. She grabbed on and pulled it into her mouth, slobbering and gumming it as if it were the greatest treat.

"Ouch." He pulled back. "She's got teeth."

"No, she doesn't." Johanna said with a smile.

"You want to bet?" Caleb pried open the baby's mouth. "See, right there." A flash of white glowed against the pink gums.

"Her first tooth." Johanna took a hankie from her pocket and wiped Angel's chin. "I hope she didn't hurt you." She looked up at him from under her lashes.

"I'll live. I have something for Henry. Is it all right if I bring it by this afternoon?"

"Of course."

"See you later, son." He sat the boy down beside his mother, tipped his hat to the women, and strode off, greeting others as he went.

Johanna laid a hand on her son's shoulder, keeping him by her side, when she knew all he wanted was to dart after the sheriff. His eyes said it all. He missed Caleb about as much as she did.

"I will check the train schedule and let you know what time we leave. Mrs. Hanson will fix us a basket of food—she never lets anyone leave without being heartily prepared— and we will be on our way."

"You ladies about ready to go home?" Dag called from the buggy he pulled up by the end of the walk.

Gudrun nodded. "If there is anything you need, you ask, all right?" She peered over her spectacles at Johanna, waiting for an answer.

When Johanna finally nodded, Gudrun took her by the arm. "Come, we will give you a ride home."

Later that afternoon a knock on the door brought both her and Henry to see who it was. Caleb stood on the porch, an open box in his arms and Sam by his side.

"We brought this little guy for Henry, to kind of replace Sam. Since Sam is the pa, I thought that might make him even more welcome." He squatted down with the box so Henry could see and looked up at her. "It's all right, isn't it? I know I should have asked you first but. . ."

"It's fine, Sheriff. I've been meaning to get him a dog soon as we heard of someone who had a litter."

Henry dropped on his knees beside the box. He stroked the wriggling puppy's head and ducked when Sam gave him a quick lick.

"You can hold him." Caleb read the plea in the boy's eyes. "He's eight weeks old and already been trained to eat solid food. 'Fraid he's not housebroken though, but he should learn quick, if he's anything like his pa." He gave Sam a thump on the ribs.

Henry picked the puppy up and snuggled him under his chin. The puppy licked every bit of bare skin he could reach and then repeated the measure. Henry looked up at his mother who nodded, and then over at the sheriff, and back at the puppy. The grin he wore scrunched his eyes nearly closed and his infectious giggle left Johanna heartbroken.

"Thank you, Caleb."

Caleb got to his feet. "Johanna, we have to talk."

"I know. Gudrun and I are leaving on the train on Thursday and when I return I will tell you everything." She knew she'd return if for no other reason than to close her shop and retrieve Henry.

"I will wait." He bent down to Henry. "You take good care of that little one now, you hear. He's your dog, not your ma's." Henry nodded, his eyes round. "Good, then I must be going." Caleb tipped his hat, patted Henry on the shoulder, and strode off down the walk.

Johanna sighed. What was it she would be telling him?

Chapter 19

The clacking of the rails lulled Angel to sleep.

"She's getting to be a busy one, isn't she?" Gudrun asked from the seat across the private room. She had insisted on such accommodations, saying that Angel needed space to play on the floor or her mother would be exhausted by the time they reached Wisconsin. And so would she. If only she could nod off so easily, Johanna thought wistfully. The last few days had been a nightmare what with trying to finish the existing orders, not take any new ones, and mop up after the puppy, now dubbed Samson. The frisky fellow still hadn't quite got the hang of asking to go out. She knew it wasn't Henry's fault. He kept Samson outside with him much of the day. They had claimed a corner of the garden Frank dug up and were busy digging a hole. No matter how hard she tried to convince the boy that until the puppy was housebroken, he had to sleep on the back porch, she would find the pup, snuggled right under Henry's arm, on her son's bed.

She smiled when she remembered the horrified look on Mrs. Hanson's face when they arrived, puppy in tow. But right away she'd fixed a box behind the kitchen stove. Johanna was willing to bet that Henry would be found sleeping back there or the puppy would end up in his bed every night they were there.

She looked over at Gudrun whose head was bobbing drowsily. "Why don't you lie down on the seat and let me cover you with the quilt?" she whispered so as not to disturb Angel.

The old woman blinked awake. She covered a yawn with her gloved hand. "I think I will at that. I'd forgotten how lulling a train ride can be."

Johanna reached up into the overhead compartment for a pillow to go along with the quilt. They had brought their own when Mrs. Hanson had a fit at the thought of her friends using those provided by the train. After all, who knew who had used them last?

When the old woman was settled, Johanna wrapped the other quilt around her shoulders and lay down herself. Better to sleep while and if she could. Who knew how well Angel would be behaving by nightfall?

They changed trains in Fargo and then again in St. Paul. They were due to arrive at Hammerville, Wisconsin, before first light. Every clack of the wheels reminded Johanna of the trip she'd made west in December, the weeks of running, always fearful of Raymond tracking them. She shuddered at the thought. Her, big as a house, and Henry plastered against her side, terrified of every sound.

Johanna had all their things repacked and ready at the door when the conductor announced their stop as one after the next. Angel still lay asleep. Johanna thanked the Lord for the favor and repinned her hat in place.

Dawn had only cracked the dark when they stepped onto the station platform. Johanna looked around, feeling as if she had stepped into a different world. She'd come here once with the wagon to pick up machinery that Raymond had ordered but was too busy to pick up. After the train pulled out, she could hear a dog bark in the distance and the familiar crowing of a rooster.

Hammerville, what would they find here? Even the sound of the name brought back painful memories.

"I believe we will go to the hotel first, if we can get the station master to carry our things." Gudrun looked around and started toward the lighted window in the station building. "Then we can have breakfast there, leave our things in the rooms, and order a buggy for the trip to the farm. How long did you say it would take?"

"About an hour, depends on the roads."

"Good, we should be there by noon, easily." She crossed the platform, her heels clicking on the worn boards. Before Johanna had time to disagree, if she had the nerve, they were ensconced in a large room with two beds at the hotel and the maid had gone to find a crib, in spite of the mother's disagreement. Even she could tell that what Gudrun said was law.

After Angel nursed and fell back asleep Johanna crawled under the covers and stretched out. While her body loved the warmth and settled in, her mind went winging across the land. What would they find when they reached the farm? Had Raymond divorced her? Would he attack in a rage because she had left? What would she do?

Father in heaven, I am counting on You, she prayed fervently. *You brought us this far, You must have a plan. You took care of the Israelites crossing the desert and protected Your people from so many enemies. Please guard us now. Amen.* And then a fussing Angel woke her up.

Her mouth grew drier the closer they got to the farm. She recognized the house of their neighbors, knowing that their fence line was half a mile away, the house and barns half a mile beyond that.

"Are you all right?" Gudrun asked, looking over the head of the child she held on her lap.

"Ja, I will be." Johanna clucked the horse to a faster trot. All within her wanted to turn the buggy around and head back for town and the train west. She slowed and guided the horse left into the long driveway.

Funny, the front fields weren't plowed yet. Had they had such a nasty spring that Raymond couldn't get out in the fields? Perhaps he was plowing the back section first. She pulled the horse to a stop and looked around before driving up to the house.

There were no cows in the pasture, no dog barking in greeting. Indeed the house wore the look of no one home. No smoke arose from the chimney, and the gate to the yard was hanging open.

She turned to look at Gudrun who raised her shoulders in question. Where had he gone? She pulled the horse to a stop at the gate and, after wrapping the reins around the whip stock, stepped down. "You wait for me here."

The door was locked. She peeked in the window. Everything looked the same, the red and white oilcloth on the table, four chairs pulled up to it. Then she noticed that the banking hadn't been removed from around the foundation. Raymond always used the old straw and manure to cover the garden before he plowed it.

She shaded her eyes, looking across the fields. Nothing had been done.

When she climbed back in the buggy, she shook her head. "I don't know," she answered before Gudrun could ask the question. "Guess we'll go back to the Tengsvolds and ask." She turned the buggy around and clucked the horse forward. As soon as they reached the road, she flapped the reins, making the horse go into a trot.

Where had Raymond gone and when had he left?

"My land, look who's here." Mrs. Tengsvold threw open the door before Johanna could even knock. "Oh, my dear, I am so happy to see you. And you have someone with you?"

She waved and raised her voice. "Come in, come in. Dinner is nearly ready."

Johanna thanked her and returned to the buggy for Angel and to help Mrs. Norgaard down. Together they walked back to the porch.

"And this is your baby? Isn't she a wonder?" She reached out to take Gudrun's hand as Johanna introduced them. "Oh, I am so glad you are all right. Why, we thought maybe you died in the snow last winter or..." All the while she talked she brought her guests in the house and helped remove their coats. "You just take a place at the table now and. . ."

"Mrs. Tengsvold, Elmira, what has happened to Raymond? The farm is vacant." Johanna interrupted the woman's chatter.

"I know. It was a sad thing." She sank down on a chair and took Johanna's free hand in hers. "Bjorn didn't see the smoke in the chimney for a couple of mornings so he thought he better check on you folks. When he got there, the house was empty, so he checked the barn. We didn't know what had happened to you of course."

"Yes."

"Well, he found your husband lying in the bull's pen. He'd been gored and stomped to death. There was a big cut in the bull's side but he was doing all right. Fair to dying for a drink of water though. With the broken pitchfork and all, we didn't know if he were beating the bull off or what. I'm so sorry, we didn't have any idea how to let you know. Bjorn said we would just have to wait. He brought the livestock over here. We was hoping you would come back sometime." Her words finally ran out.

Johanna couldn't find her voice. She knew she should feel sad but all she could think was *Thank You, God, thank You, thank You.* She shouldn't be grateful for a man's death, and a violent one at that. All this time she'd worried about him finding her. And he'd been dead. She buried her face in Angel's neck, the tears starting in spite of her iron will.

"Now, now, I know the shock is hard to take."

"Who's the company?" Bjorn Tengsvold called from the backdoor. "Dinner ready yet?"

"In a minute." Elmira bustled back to the stove after another pat on Johanna's shoulder.

"Well, look who's here! You are all right, I'm so glad." A smile wreathed his face turned ruddy from hours in the sun. In few strides he crossed the room in his stocking feet, having left his dirty boots at the backdoor. He looked to his wife at the stove. "I see you told her."

He dropped into the chair at the head of the table. "It was such a shock to us too. Nothing we could do but bury him when the ground thawed out enough."

"Where?" Johanna wiped her eyes and jiggled Angel on her lap.

"In the cemetery behind the Lutheran church. I know you didn't go much but I—we thought it best. We put a gravestone on it so's you could find it, if'n you ever came back."

The enormity of what had happened was more than she could take in.

"We locked up the house, brought your livestock over here. When I saw that old horse was gone, I had an idea what had happened." He ducked his head. "We—ah—had an idea what had been going on, but you know Raymond. So privatelike, didn't seem nothing we could do."

"No, there wasn't. I thank you for what you did." So, he'd beaten the bull once too often. Ever since she'd raised the tiny calf when he planned to club it, he'd had it in for the animal. When it threw good calves the animal seemed to goad him even more. She could about picture what had happened. When Raymond found her gone, he took his anger and frustration out on the animal. But this time was the final straw.

When the two strapping Tengsvold sons came in, Elmira set the food on the table and, after grace, urged everyone to eat up. They peppered Johanna with questions about her life in Soldahl, how Henry was, if he were talking now.

"Landsakes, how's she supposed to eat with all you badgering her?" Elmira's voice strained to be heard.

"Sorry, sorry," the boys said.

"You go ahead and eat while I ask you one more question." Bjorn Tengsvold looked directly at Johanna. "Now if you want to come back and farm that piece, we'll help you all we can, but if you want to sell it, Nils here is prepared to buy. He wants to get married and this will give him a starting place. We'll take all the livestock, furniture, whatever you want to leave "

"I—I don't know. This is all so sudden." Johanna looked to Gudrun who barely nodded her head. Johanna sipped her coffee, her dinner forgotten in front of her. "I really need to go back over there."

"Understandable. I'll give you the key."

"Could I give you my decision tomorrow?"

"Of course, of course, no need to rush. Just that those fields need to get worked up soon as possible if we want a crop off them this fall."

"I know." Angel chose that moment to whimper for her meal. "Could I use your bedroom to feed her?"

"Surely." Elmira jumped to her feet. "Right this way. I'll put your plate on to warm for you."

Johanna sat in a chair by the window, alternating between looking out at the fields and down at her baby. Should she bring her children back here so Henry could eventually have his father's farm, if he wanted it? Did she want to leave her cozy home and busy shop to live back out in the country, a mile away from the nearest neighbor? She could hear Gudrun visiting with the Tengsvolds. There were two things she knew she must do: return to the house and go to the cemetery. Everything else could wait.

With Elmira waving them on their way and Angel sound asleep in Gudrun's lap, Johanna turned the buggy around and headed back to the silent farm.

The stale smell of the empty house assaulted her when she opened the door. She walked to the stove and thought about starting a fire to burn the smell away but she decided against it. Instead she walked to the bedroom where she had cowered so many times. Raymond's pants still lay over the back of the chair, waiting for her to patch them. With a swift move, she jerked the quilt her mother had given her off the bed and folded it, picked up her Bible and her sewing basket, and returned to the kitchen. A quick look around confirmed what she already knew. There was nothing else she wanted.

"That's all you want?" Gudrun asked when she returned to the buggy.

"Ja, that's it. I hope young Tengsvold and his new wife will be far happier here than we were. It is good farmland. One thing to be said for

Raymond, he took good care of the land and the livestock—except for the bull. Do you suppose one day I will have room in my heart to forgive him?"

"You mean your husband or the bull?"

"It was a hard way to die." She unwound the reins and turned the horse around. "I warned him again and again not to treat the bull that way. Was this justice, do you think?"

"I can't answer that. Where to now?"

"The Tengsvolds. I don't want to come back here ever again."

"Do you think Henry might want the farm someday? You could rent it to them, you know."

"I thought of that but Henry has no good memories of this place either. Better that he not have to make a decision. I wonder what a farm goes for here now?" She clucked the horse into a trot.

After agreeing to meet Bjorn and his son at the bank in the morning, she and Gudrun headed back to town. The Lutheran church lay a couple of miles up the road, its cross-crowned steeple glinting above the trees.

Birds sang in the fenced-in cemetery and a butterfly flitted from the branches of the apple tree that grew by the gate. Bees hummed about their business in the blossoms. Johanna dismounted from the buggy and entered the grassy yard, looking at the headstones until she came upon a fairly fresh grave. There was no inscription, only his name and the year of death. She stared at it, waiting for some feeling of any kind to make itself known. *Ah, Raymond, we started our life together with such high hopes and look what it has come to.* As she dashed away the one tear that meandered down her cheek, she pulled a pigweed out of the dirt oblong and flung it over the fence.

On the way back to the hotel they stopped by the livery and paid the fee and a boy hopped on the back of the buggy so he could return it to the barn. Supper and an early bed were all Johanna wanted.

Her first thought in the morning shocked her wide awake. *I'm free. I no longer have to be afraid.* Then guilt dropped a load on her shoulders. *I should be sad, grieving for my husband. Lord, what is wrong with me?* She lay in bed and thought of her new life in Soldahl. Surely God had led her there as He protected her from death in the blizzard. Surely He held her in His hand. *God is my strength and salvation.* She repeated it for good measure. *Please, Father, give me wisdom for this day. Thank You for Your many blessings.*

She glanced at the crib where Angel slept, knees tucked under her, bottom in the air. Such a blessing. Then she began counting all her blessings, trying hard not to wiggle so the creaking bed would waken her sleeping friend. Gudrun, how many lives had she blessed with her mind and her wealth? Some time later, when she had finally run out of things to be thankful for, she could no longer remain in bed.

Dressing behind the screen in the corner, she took her soap and towel to the bathroom at the end of the hall. By the time she returned, Angel was yawning and stretching and Gudrun dressing behind the screen.

"Would you like me to go to the bank with you or stay here and watch Angel?" Gudrun asked over the rim of her coffee cup. They were seated at a table for four in the dining room and Angel, in a highchair chased bits of toast around the wooden tray. Johanna had fed the baby a few bites of oatmeal and egg.

"You know much more about contracts than I do. Why don't you go to the bank and I'll stay with Angel?" Johanna smiled at the slow shaking of Gudrun's head. "No? Then how about if we go together and I'll play with Angel while you read the papers over for me?"

"How much are you going to ask for the farm?"

"I'm going to see how much they offer, raise it some, and sign the papers. We should be able to make the afternoon train."

And so they did. A couple of times during the ride west, Johanna took the check out of her bag to make sure it was real. She could pay off her shop and have money left to put in the bank. Never had she felt so wealthy. Never had the cost been greater.

"And to think I almost didn't come."

"I know. But remember, we prayed for God's guidance. He never wants us to live in fear and this is how He took care of yours. Now we must pray for Henry, to put this all behind him."

"He still has nightmares but not nearly so often. They came back for a while after Caleb took Sam home but now he seems at peace again. Poor little fellow."

When the train pulled into Soldahl, Caleb met her on the platform.

"What are you—how did you know—?" Her words vanished at the look on his face.

"I've met every train so I wouldn't miss you." He helped Gudrun down first. "How was your trip?" He took their bags and put them off to the side.

"I will tell you about it later." Johanna's smile brought forth one from him.

"Come on, ladies, I will drive you home."

Chapter 20

Johanna, will you marry me?" His words echoed through the darkness.

Crickets sang over by the fence. A mosquito whined in her ear. Johanna stared up at the moon glowing like a huge silver platter. In the shade of the oak tree, she couldn't really see his face, just a form lighter than the surrounding shadows.

"Yes, but..."

"But what?" He covered her hands with his on the swing.

"But it can't be until after the time of grieving." She forced the words past the lump in her throat.

"Grieving! He wasn't worth grieving for! Besides, Raymond died nearly six months ago. That's long enough." Johanna had told him the entire story as she promised the first night they were back.

"But Caleb, what will people say?"

"Who cares? Only the Moens along with those at Dag's house know what happened anyway, and they won't tell." He jiggled the swing, making her bounce. "I think we've waited long enough."

His rich voice sent shivers racing up and down her spine. She slapped at the pesky mosquito. "All right, when?" She couldn't believe those words came from her.

"Next Saturday."

"That's only four days away." She squeaked on the last words.

"No, a week from this Saturday."

"That's too soon, I think maybe June."

"A week from Saturday." He picked her up from the swing seat and held her to his chest. She wrapped her arms around his neck.

"You carried me once before."

"Lot easier this time." He set her down on the porch, down in the corner where the light from the window didn't reach. When their lips finally met, Johanna felt she'd come home.

"I won't have time to make a new dress," she said sometime later.

"I'm marrying you, not a dress. You'll look lovely no matter what you wear."

She rested her head against his chest. "You. . ." But he took her breath away with another kiss.

Saturday dawned bright and fair but by nine showers had arrived. Johanna shivered in the coolness. Rain on a wedding day, not a good thing. As if reading her thoughts, by noon the sun sparkled on drops left on leaves and grass blades.

"Come, your carriage awaits." Dag met her at the door and pointed to Clara and Gudrun with Mrs. Hanson, sitting in the buggy. Dag and Clara had agreed to stand up with the bridal couple.

Johanna didn't have much to say. Her heart was beating so fast she half expected it to leap out of her chest and fly away. Henry climbed up on Clara's lap, Mrs. Hanson took the baby, and Johanna wished she were walking or running away.

"Don't worry, my dear, all brides—and grooms—get the jitters on their wedding day. You'll be fine." Gudrun leaned forward and patted Johanna's knee.

"And we got food enough to feed the whole town back at the house. I baked the wedding cake myself." Mrs. Hanson tickled Angel and made her chortle.

"You shouldn't have."

"Yes, we should." Clara handed Henry up to sit by Dag. "You just enjoy the day."

Oh yes, that's what she'd do, enjoy the day, if she didn't embarrass everybody, herself most of all. She laid a hand on her stomach to calm it. Whatever possessed her to agree to such a fast wedding?

At precisely one o'clock the organist looked toward the door and the old pipe organ broke into song. Clara walked down the aisle first, tulips from their garden in her arms. The excited congregation craned to look as Johanna stepped through the door. Were those tears she saw sparkling in Caleb's eyes? Tears to match those that threatened to spill over her own cheeks?

"Dearly beloved, we are gathered here in the sight of God and this holy gathering to bring these two people together in holy matrimony." Reverend Moen spoke the age-old words with joy and reverence. Both Caleb and Johanna answered in voices strong and sure, their eyes pledging their troth along with their voices.

"I now pronounce you man and wife. What God hast put together, let no man rend asunder." Then he leaned forward and whispered, "You may kiss the bride."

And Caleb did. As he and Johanna turned to make their way back up the aisle, Henry shot out of the pew and made a beeline for Caleb's pant leg. With Johanna's arm still in his, the man leaned down and picked up the boy, settling him into the crook of the other arm.

Johanna smiled up at him adoringly.

The little boy put his hands on either side of Caleb's face and turned it to face him. "My pa," he said, loud enough for most to hear. "My pa."

Dakota Destiny

Chapter 1

Mary's home! Mary"s home!" Daniel, the youngest of the Moen brood, left off swinging on the gate to the picket fence and leaped up the porch steps to the door. "Mother, did you hear me?"

"Only me and half the town. Must you yell so?" Ingeborg Moen made her way down the steep stairs and bustled over to the door. "Did you see her or was it the little bird that told you?"

"I saw—" A gloved hand clamped gently over his mouth.

"Hello, Mother." Mary stood in the doorway. At seventeen, she had shed the little girl and donned the young woman. Golden hair fell in curls down her back, held back from her oval face with a whalebone clasp, high on the back of her head. Eyes the blue of a Dakota summer sky still shone with the direct look that made students in her Sunday school classes squirm, much as her younger siblings had for years.

There was something about Mary that not only commanded attention but also made one look again. Was it the straightness of her carriage fostered by years of Mrs. Norgaard insisting the girls of Soldahl walk and stand tall no matter what their height? Or the firmness of her chin that bespoke of a will of her own? Or was it the twinkle that hid under long, dark lashes and flirted with the dimple in her right cheek whenever she was trying not to laugh—which was often?

Ingeborg gathered her eldest chick in her arms and hugged her as if they'd been apart for years instead of months. "Oh, my dear, I have missed you so. The house, nay, even the town, is not the same without my Mary." She set the young woman a bit away and studied the girl's eyes. "How have you been, really? Has the school been hard for you? And the train trip home—all went well?"

"Mother, how can I answer so many questions at once? This has been a most marvelous year, and when I finish this time next spring, I will be able to teach school anywhere in North Dakota. Isn't that the most, the most—" Mary threw herself back in her mother's arms. "Oh, much as I love school, I have missed you all sorely."

Daniel thumped her valise on the waxed wooden floor. "Did you bring anything for all of us?"

"Of course I did, and how come you're not in school?" She hugged her ten-year-old brother. "You're not sick, are you? You don't look it."

He pulled away, already at the age of being embarrassed by being hugged in public. "Naw, not much anyway."

Mary looked a question at her mother. This, the baby in the family, had suffered many ailments in his short life. He seemed to catch anything that visited the school or the neighboring children, and with him it always lasted longer and took more of a toll.

"He'll be going back tomorrow." A shadow passed over Ingeborg's placid features. She lived by the creed that God loved His children and would always protect them. She'd taught that belief to her children all their lives, both she and the Reverend John, her husband. But sometimes in the dead of night when this one of her brood was near death's door, her faith had been tried—and wavered. But such doubts never lingered longer than the rise of the new day, for she believed implicitly in the mansions Jesus had gone to prepare.

Mary sniffed once and then again. "You baked apple pies."

"The last of the barrel. I'd been saving them for you, hoping they would last."

"I helped peel."

Mary stroked Daniel's pale cheek. "And I bet you are the best apple peeler in Soldahl. Now, let me put my things away and we will sample some of Mother's crust cookies, or did you eat them all?"

He shook his head so hard, the white blond hair swung across his forehead. "I didn't."

Mary headed for the stairs. "And you, my dear Mor, will fill me in on all the happenings of town and country since your last letter."

"Will came by yesterday." Daniel struggled up the steps with the heavy valise.

"He did, eh?" Mary looked up to catch a nod from her mother. A trill of pleasure rippled up Mary's back. *Will, soon I will see Will again. And we will have an entire summer to find out how deep our friendship really goes.*

She turned back to her little brother. "Here, let's do that together. That bag is so burdened with books, no wonder we can't lift it." Mary settled her hand next to Daniel's on the leather grip, and together they lugged it up the steep stairs—Mary laughing and teasing her little brother all the way. They set the case down, and with a sigh of happiness, Mary looked around the room she'd known all her life.

The first nine-patch quilt she'd made with her mother covered the bed, and the rag rug on the floor had warmed her feet since she was ten. Stiffly starched white Priscilla curtains crossed over the south-facing windows, and an oak commode held the same rose-trimmed pitcher and bowl given her by her bestamor, her mother's mother. The ceiling still slanted the same, its rose wallpaper now fading in places.

Daniel stood silently, intuitive as ever of his eldest sister's feelings. When she finished looking around, he grinned up at her. "Didja see anything new?"

Mary looked again. The kerosene lamp still sat on the corner of her dresser. As soon as she unpacked, the brush and hand mirror would go back in place. She looked down at her brother. "What's up, Danny boy?"

He looked at the ceiling directly above her head. She followed his gaze and her mouth fell open. "Electric lights. Far put in the electricity."

"The church board voted."

Since they lived in the parsonage, all improvements were at the whim and financial possibilities of the Soldahl Lutheran Church. They'd all grown up under that edict.

Mary reached up and pushed the button on the bare bulb hanging from a cord. Light flooded the room. "Now I can read in bed at night." She spun in place, arms outstretched as if to embrace the entire world, or at least her home and family. She swooped Daniel up and hugged him tight. *He is so thin,* she thought. *Has he been worse than mother told me?* He hugged her back and whispered in her ear. "I've missed you so."

"And me you, Bug. Let's go down and have some of that apple pie, if Mor will cut it before dinner." His childhood nickname slipped out; she hadn't called him that in years, but today, today was a time for remembering. Who knew what a magical day like today would bring?

Mary and Daniel, hand in hand, were halfway down the stairs when the front door opened again and the Reverend John Moen entered, removing his well-used black fedora as he came. Mary put her finger to her lips, and she and Daniel froze in place.

"So, Mother, what's the news? Ummmm, something surely smells good."

As he walked toward the kitchen, Mary and Daniel tiptoed down the stairs.

"Apple pie? For me?"

"Get your fingers out of the crust." The laughter in Ingeborg's voice could be heard by the two creeping nearer.

Mary silently mouthed, *one, two, three,* and she and Daniel burst around the corner. "Surprise!"

"Land sakes alive, look who's here!" John grabbed his chest in mock shock. "Mary, come home at last." He spread his arms and Mary stepped into them, forcing herself to regain some sort of decorum. "Lord love you, girl, but I was beginning to think you were never coming home." He hugged her close and rested his cheek on smooth golden hair. "When did you go and get so grown up?

Mary blinked against the tears burning the backs of her eyes.

Her father had aged in the months she'd been gone. Deep lines bracketed his mouth, and the few strands of gray at his temples had multiplied. She stepped back, the better to see his dear face. "I'm never too grown up to come home to my family. Even though I've been so busy I hardly have time to turn around, I've missed you all so much."

"Come now, we can visit as we eat. Daniel, John, go wash your hands. Mary, put this in the center of the table, please." Ingeborg handed her daughter a plate of warm rolls, fresh from the oven. Setting a platter with a roast surrounded by potatoes next to her place, Ingeborg checked to make sure everything was to her liking.

"Mother, you've gone to such trouble. I'll be around here for months." Mary clasped her hand over the back of the chair that had always been hers. "Oh, it feels so good to be home." She counted the places set and looked over at her mother. "Who else is coming?"

"You'll know soon enough." A knock at the door brightened Mor's eyes. "Go answer that while I bring on the coffee."

Mary gave her a puzzled look and went to do as bid.

"Hello, Mary." Will Dunfey's carrot hair had turned to a deep auburn that made his blue eyes even bluer. The smile on his face looked fit to crack the square jaw that he could set with a stubbornness like a bear trap. His shoulders now filled out a blue chambray shirt, open at the neck and with sleeves buttoned at strong wrists.

"Will!" Mary warred with the desire to throw herself into his arms. Instead she stepped back and beckoned him in. He took her hand as he passed, and a shiver went up her arm and straight to her heart. When he took her other hand and turned her to face him, the two shivers met and the delicious collision could be felt clear to her toes.

"So you're finally home." Had his voice deepened in the last months or was her memory faulty?

"Yes." *Say something intelligent, you ninny. This is only Will, you remember him, your best friend?*

"Invite him to the table, Daughter." The gentle prompting came from her mother.

"Oh, I'm sorry." She unlocked her gaze from the deep blue pools of his eyes and, finally coming to herself, gestured him toward the table. "I believe Mother invited you for dinner."

Will winked at her, nearly undoing her again, and dropping her hands, crossed the room to shake hands with her father. After greeting the Reverend and Mrs. Moen, he took the place next to Mary's as if he'd been there many times.

The thought of that set Mary to wondering. When she started to pull out her chair, Will leaped to his feet to assist her. Mary stared at him. *What in the world?* She seated herself with a murmured "thank you" and a questioning look over her shoulder. Where had Will, the playmate hero, gone, and when had this exciting man taken his place?

Dinner passed in a blur of laughter, good food, and the kind of visiting that said this was not an unusual occurrence. Daniel treated Will much like his bigger brothers, and Ingeborg scolded the young man like one of her own.

Mary caught up on the news of Soldahl as seen through the loving eyes of her father, the slightly acerbic gaze of her mother, and the humorous observations of Will, who saw things from the point of view of the blacksmith and livery, where he worked for Dag Weinlander.

"The doctor was the latest one," Will was saying. "I'm going to have to go to mechanic's school if this drive to buy automobiles continues. You know, at first Dag thought they were a fad, but now that Mrs. Norgaard owns one and expects him to drive her everywhere, he thinks they're the best."

"Mrs. Norgaard bought an automobile?" Mary dropped her fork. "At her age?"

"Now dear, seventy isn't so old when one is in good health." Ingeborg began stacking the dishes.

"She says she has too much to do to get old," John said with a chuckle. "When I think back to how close she was to dying after her husband died. . .if it hadn't been for Clara, she would have given up for sure."

"That seems so long ago. I remember the classes we had at her house to learn to speak better English. Mrs. Norgaard was determined all the girls would grow up to be proper young ladies, whether we wanted to or not."

"She took me in hand. If it hadn't been for her and Dag, I would have gotten on the next train and kept on heading west." Will smiled in remembrance. "I thought sure once or twice she was going to whack me with that cane of hers."

"Did she really—whack anyone, that is?" Daniel's eyes grew round.

"Not that I know of, but for one so tiny, she sure can put the fear of God into you."

"Ja, and everyone in town has been blessed by her good heart at one time or another." John held up his coffee cup. "Any more, my dear?"

Ingeborg got to her feet. "I'll bring the dessert. You stay right there, Mary."

"Thanks to her that I am at school." Mary got up anyway and took the remainder of the plates into the kitchen.

"And that the church has a new furnace."

"And the school, too," Daniel added.

"Is Mr. Johnston happy here?" Mary had a dream buried deep in her heart of teaching in the Soldahl school, but that could only happen if the current teacher moved elsewhere.

"Very much so. His wife is president of the Ladies' Aid, such a worker." Ingeborg returned with the apple pie. "I'd hate for them to leave. Their going would leave a real hole in the congregation."

Mary nodded. So much for her dream. Surely there would be a school near Soldahl available next year.

They all enjoyed the pie and coffee, with Will taking the second piece Ingeborg pushed at him. He waved away the third offering.

"Mother, you are the best pie maker in the entire world." Mary licked her fork for the last bit of pie juice. She looked sideways at Will, but he seemed lost in thoughts of his own. Was something wrong?

When she looked at her father at the foot of the table, a look that matched Will's hovered about his eyes. What was going on?

"I better get back to the church. I have a young couple coming by for marriage counseling." John pushed his chair back. "You want to walk with me, Son?"

"Sure." Daniel leaped to his feet.

"I better be getting back to work, too," Will said with a sigh. "Thank you for such a wonderful meal, Mrs. Moen. I will remember these get-togethers for all time."

"Thank you, Will. Mary, why don't you walk Will to the gate? I'll do the cleaning up here." Ingeborg smiled, but the light didn't quite reach her eyes.

A goose just walked over my grave, Mary thought as she sensed something further amiss.

She locked her fingers behind her back as Will ushered her out the door. An intelligent word wouldn't come to her mind for the life of her.

"So, did you enjoy the last half of school?" Will leaned against the turned post on the porch.

"I loved most every minute of it. I had to study hard, but I knew that." Mary adopted the other post and turned to face him, her back against the warm surface.

Will held his hat in his hands, one finger outlining the brim. When he looked up at her, the sadness that had lurked in the background leaped forward. "Mary, there is so much I wanted to say, have wanted to say for years, and now—" He looked up at the sky as if asking for guidance.

"Will, I know something is wrong. What is it?"

He sat down on the step and gestured for her to do the same. "First of all, I have to know. Do you love me as I love you—with the kind of love between a man and a woman, not the kind between friends and kids?"

Mary clasped her hands around her skirted knees. All the dreaming of this time, and here it was: no preparation, just boom. "Will, I have always loved you." Her voice came softly but surely.

"I mean as more than friends."

"Will Dunfey, understand me." She turned so she faced him.

"I love you. I always have, and I always will."

"I had hoped to ask you to marry me." He laid a calloused hand over hers.

"Had hoped?" She could feel a knot tightening in her breast.

"I thought by the time you graduated I would perhaps own part of the business or one of my own so I could support you."

"Will, you are scaring me." Mary laid her hand over his.

Will looked up at her, his eyes crying for understanding. "I signed up last week."

"Signed up?"

"Enlisted in the U.S. Army to fight against the Germans.They say this is the war to end all wars and they need strong young men."

Mary felt a small part of her die at his words.

Chapter 2

Oh, Will, you can't leave!"

The cry escaped before Mary could trap it. He studied the hat in his hands. "You know I don't want to."

"Then don't." Mary clasped her hands together, her fingers winding themselves together as if they had a mind of their own. "I…I just got home."

"I know." He looked up at her, his eyes filled with love and longing. "But they need men like me to stop the Huns. I couldn't say no. You wouldn't really want me to."

Yes, I would. I want you here. I've been looking forward to this summer for months. It made the hard times bearable. But she wouldn't say those words, couldn't say them. No one had ever accused Mary Moen of being selfish. "Of course not." Now she studied her hands. If she looked at him, he would see the lie in her eyes.

A bee buzzed by and landed on the lilac that had yet to open its blossoms.

Will cleared his throat. "I ... I want you to know that I love you. I've wanted to tell you that for years, and I promised I would wait until we—" His voice broke. He sighed. "Aw, Mary, this isn't the way I dreamed it at all." He crossed the narrow gap separating them and took her hands in his. "I want to marry you, but that will have to wait until I come back. No, that's not what I wanted to say at all." He dropped her hands and leaned against the post above her. "What

I mean is—"

"I don't care what you mean, Will, darling. I will be here waiting for you, so you keep that in your mind. I will write to you every day and mail the letters once a week, if I can wait that long." She grasped the front of his shirt with both hands. "And you will come back to me, Mr. Will Dunfey. You will come back." She lifted her face to his for the loss she had dreamed of in the many lonely nights away at school.

His lips felt warm and soft and unbearably sweet. She could feel the tears pooling at the back of her throat. *Dear God, please bring him home again. Watch over him for me.*

"We will all be praying for you," she murmured against his mouth. "I love you. Don't you ever forget that."

"I won't." He kissed her again. When he stepped back, he clasped her shoulders in his strong hands. "I'll see you tonight?"

She nodded. "Come for supper."

She watched him leap off the porch and trot down the walk to the gate. When the gate swung shut, the squeal of it grated on Mary's ears. It sounded like an animal in pain. Maybe it was her.

"Did he say when he was leaving?" Ingeborg asked when Mary finally returned to the kitchen.

Mary shook her head. "And I forgot to ask." She slapped the palms of her hands on the counter. "It's…it's just not fair."

"Much of life isn't."

"But why should our young men go fight a war in Europe?" She raised a hand. "I know, Mother. I read the newspapers, too. Some want us to be at the front and some want us to pretend it's not there. I just never thought we would be affected so soon. Are others of our boys already signed up, too?"

Ingeborg shook her head. "Not that I know of."

"Then why Will?"

"Now that he has, others will follow. He's always been a leader of the young men—you know that."

"But I had such dreams for this summer—and next year. . ." Her voice dwindled. "And for the years after that."

"No need to give up the dreams." Ingeborg watched her beloved daughter wrestling with forces against which she had no power.

"But…but what if..."

The ticking clock sounded loud in the silence. Ashes crumbled in the freshly blacked cast-iron range.

Mary lifted tear-filled eyes and looked directly at her mother. "What if he doesn't come back?"

"Then with God's strength and blessing you go on with your life, always remembering Will with fondness and pride." Ingeborg crossed to her daughter. "You would not be the only woman in the country with such a burden to bear. Or the world, for that matter. Perhaps if our boys get in and get the job done, there won't be so many women longing for husbands, lovers, and sons."

"How will I do this?" Mary whispered.

"By the grace of God and by keeping busy making life better for others. That is how women always get through the hard parts of life."

Mary looked up at her mother, wondering as always at the quiet wisdom Ingeborg lived. Her mother didn't say things like that lightly. She who so often sat beside the dying in the wee hours of the morning had been there herself when one child was stillborn and another died in infancy. Mary put her arms around her mother's waist and pillowed her cheek on the familiar shoulder. "Oh, Mor, I've missed you more than words could say."

Ingeborg patted her daughter's back. "God always provides, child, remember that."

After supper that night, Mary and Will strolled down the street in the sweet evening air. They'd talked of many things by the time they returned to her front fence, but one question she had not been able to utter. Finally she blurted it out.

"When will you be leaving?"

"Next week, on Monday."

"But this is already Thursday."

"I know."

Mary swallowed all the words that demanded speech. "Oh." Did a heart shatter and fall in pieces, or did it just seem so?

Chapter 3

Would her heart never quit bleeding? Mary stood waving long after the train left. Will had hung half out the side to see her as long as he could. The memory of the sun glinting off his hair and him waving his cap would have to last her a good long time. She had managed to send him off with a smile. She'd promised herself the night before that she would do that. No tears, only smiles.

"We are all praying for him," a familiar voice said from behind her.

"Mrs. Norgaard, how good of you to come." Mary wiped her eyes before turning around. She sniffed and forced a smile to her face.

"He's been one of my boys for more years than I care to count," Mrs. Norgaard said with a thump of her cane. "And I'll be right here waiting when he returns, too." A tear slid down the parchment cheek from under the black veil of her hat. With her back as ramrod straight as ever, Mrs. Norgaard refused to give in to the ravages of time, albeit her step had slowed and spectacles now perched on her straight nose.

"Now, then, we can stand here sniveling or we can get to doing something worthwhile. I know you were praying for him as I was, and we will continue to do that on a daily, or hourly if need be, basis. God only knows what's in store for our boy, but we will keep reminding our Father to be on the lookout." She stepped forward and, hooking her cane over her own arm, slid her other into Mary's. "Mrs. Hanson has coffee and some kind of special treat for all of us, so let us not keep her waiting."

And with that the Moens, Dag and Clara, the doctor and his wife, and several others found themselves back at "the mansion," enjoying a repast much as if they'd just come for a party. With everyone asking her about school and life in Fargo, Mary felt her heart lighten. If she'd done what she planned, she'd have been home flat out across her bed, crying till she dried up.

Dr. Harmon came up to her, tucking a last bite of frosted cake into his mouth. Crumbs caught on his mustache, and he brushed them away with a nonchalant finger. "So, missy, what are you planning for the summer?"

"I was planning on picnics with Will, helping my mother with the canning and garden, and going riding with Will."

Doc nodded his balding head. "That so." He continued to nod. "I 'spect that's changed somewhat." The twinkle in his eye let her know he understood how she felt. "You given thought to anything else?"

Mary looked at him, her head cocked slightly sideways. "All right, let's have it. I've seen that look on your face too many times through the years to think you are just being polite."

"He's never been 'just polite' in his entire life." Gudrun Norgaard said from her chair off to the side. "What is it, Harmon? Is there something going on I don't know about?"

"How could that be? You got your nose into more business than a hive's got bees."

"Be that as it may, what are you up to?" Mrs. Norgaard crossed her age-spotted hands over the carved head of her cane. Dag had made the cane for her the year her husband died, when she hadn't much cared if she'd lived either.

"I think the two of you are cooking something up again." Clara Weinlander, wife of Dag and mother of their three children, stopped beside her benefactress's chair. "I know that look."

Doc attempted an injured air but stopped when he saw the knowing smile lifting the corners of Gudrun's narrow lips. "All right," he said to the older woman. "You know the Oiens?"

"Of course, that new family that moved into the Erickson property. He works for the railroad, I believe. And she has some kind of health problem—ah, that's it." Gudrun nodded as she spoke. "A good idea, Harmon."

Mary looked from one to the other as if a spectator at that new sport she'd seen at school. Even the women played tennis— well, not her, but those who had a superfluous amount of time and money.

Clara came around to Mary and slipped an arm through hers. "Why do I get the feeling they are messing with someone else's life again?"

"It never did you any harm, did it?" Doc rocked back on his heels, glancing over to where Dag, owner of the local livery and blacksmith, now stood talking with the Reverend Moen. Sunlight from the bay window set both their faces in shadow, but the deep laugh could only come from Dag.

"No, that it didn't." Clara agreed. It had taken her a long time to get Dag to laugh so freely. "So, what do you have planned for Mary here?"

"I thought since she didn't have a position for the summer, she might be willing to help the Oiens care for their children. There are two of them: a boy, four, and the girl, two. And perhaps she could do some fetching for the missus. Mrs. Oien resists the idea of needing help, but I know this would be a big load off her mind."

"What is wrong with her?" Mary asked.

"I just wish I knew. She keeps getting weaker, though she has some good days. You think you could help them out?"

"I'll gladly do what I can."

"I figured as much. After all, you are your mother s daughter." Doc Harmon gave her a nod of approbation. "I'll talk with them tomorrow."

That night Mary wrote her first letter to Will, telling him about the party at the mansion and how it looked like she would be very busy that summer after all. As her letter lengthened, she thought of him on the train traveling east. Hoping he was thinking of her as she was him, she went to stand at her window.

"Look up to the Big Dipper every night," he'd said, "and think of me standing right on that handle, waving to you."

Mary closed her eyes against the tears that blurred the stars above. "Oh, God, keep him safe, please, and thank You." She looked out again, and the heavens seemed brighter, especially the star right at the end of the dipper handle.

Each morning she greeted the day with, "Thank You for the day, Lord, and thank You that You are watching over Will." After that, she was usually too busy to think.

The Erickson house sported a new coat of white paint, and the yard had not only been trimmed, but the flower beds along the walk were all dug, ready for planting the annuals now that the likelihood of a last frost was past.

I could do that for them, Mary thought as she lingered so as to arrive at the time Doc Harmon had set. *After all, two little children won't take all my time. And Mrs. Norgaard said a woman came to clean and do some of the cooking. I know Clarissa will come help me if I need it.* Clarissa was her younger sister, after Grace. With six kids in their family, there was always someone to help out, even with all the work they did around home.

The two cars arrived at nearly the same time. The man getting out of the first wore a black wool coat as if it were still winter. A homburg hat covered hair the color of oak bark and shaded dark eyes that seemed to have lost all their life. His smile barely touched his mouth, let alone his eyes. Tall and lean, he stooped some, as if the load he bore was getting far too heavy.

Dr. Harmon crossed the grass to take Mary's arm and guide her to meet her host. "Kenneth Oien, I want you to meet Mary Moen, the young woman who has agreed to help you for the summer." As the introductions were completed, Mary studied the man from under her eyelashes. Always one to bring home the stray and injured—both animals and people—Mary recognized pain when she saw it.

"Thank you for coming on such short notice. As the doctor might have told you, my wife, Elizabeth, has not wanted to have help with the children. I finally prevailed upon her to let me hire a woman to clean and do some of the cooking. I'm hoping you can make her days a bit easier. She frets so."

"I hope so, too."

"I…I haven't told her you were coming."

Mary shot a questioning look at the doctor, who just happened to be studying the leaves in the tree above. *I thought this was all set up. What if she hates me?*

"Perhaps you could just meet her and visit awhile, then come back tomorrow after I see how she responds?"

"Of course," Mary answered, still trying to catch the good doctor's attention.

"I'd best be going then—got a woman about to deliver out west aways." Doc tipped his hat. "Nice seeing you, Kenneth, Mary." He scooted off to his automobile before Mary could get in a word edgewise.

Mr. Oien ushered Mary into the front room of the two-story square home. "Elizabeth, I brought you company."

"Back here," the call came from a room that faced north and in most houses like this one was a bedroom. A child's giggle broke the stillness, followed by another.

When they entered the room, the little ones were playing on a bench at the foot of the bed where Elizabeth lay.

"I'm sorry, Kenneth, I was so weak, I had to come back to bed before I fell over."

"Did you eat something?"

She shook her head.

"Have the children eaten?"

"We ate, Papa." The little boy lifted his head from playing with the Sears catalog.

The little girl scooted around the bed and peeped over the far side.

"Elizabeth, Jenny, and Joey, I brought you some company. This is Mary Moen, just returned from college where she is studying to be a teacher."

Elizabeth smoothed her hair back with a white hand. "I... I wasn't expecting company. Please forgive me for…for—" She made a general gesture at her dishevelment and the toys spread about the room.

"I'm sorry, but I have to get back to my job. There is no one else there, you see, and I—" Mr. Oien dropped a kiss on his wife's forehead, waved to the children, and vanished out the door.

Mary heard the front door close behind him. So much for that source of help. She looked around for a chair to draw up to the bed. None. The little girl, Jenny, peered at her from across the bed, nose buried in the covers so all Mary could see was round brown eyes and uncombed, curly hair.

"Jenny don't like strangers," Joey announced from his place on the bench.

"I'm sorry, Miss Moen, I—" Elizabeth sighed. "I know Kenneth is trying to help, but he so often doesn't know how." She shook her head. "But then who would?"

"Sometimes talking to another woman helps." Mary came closer to the bed. "Doctor said you have a woman who comes in to clean."

"She is nice enough, a good worker, but she speaks Norwegian, and I don't. My grandmother came from Sweden and Kenneth's grandparents from Norway. He only knows the table grace and a few phrases. Dear God, I don't know what we are going to do."

Mary nodded. "Well, I know what I am going to do. I didn't come here just to visit. I came to help, and you and I will do much better if we are honest up front. Dr. Harmon and Mrs. Norgaard have a habit of fixing things in people's lives, and they decided I could help you and that way I would be too busy this summer to miss my Will, who left on the train three days ago to fight the Germans."

She felt a thrill at saying the words *my Will* out loud. In the secret places of her heart, he'd been her Will since she was ten and he stuck up for her the first time. She looked around the room again. "How about if I move a chair in here for you to sit in while I fix your hair? Then you can hold Jenny while I brush hers."

"I combed my own hair." Still Joey didn't look up. Though he just kept turning the pages of the catalog, he was obviously keeping track of the conversation.

"Are you sure you want to do this?" Elizabeth asked, the ray of hope peeping from her eyes belying the words.

"Ja, I am sure."

By noon when Kenneth came home for dinner, his wife had a smile on her face, Jenny wore a ribbon in her hair, and Joey had helped set the table. Mary took the chicken and dumplings from the stove and set the pot in the middle of the table.

"My land, why I…I—" He clasped his wife's hand and sat down beside her at the table.

"Thank you, Kenneth. You brought us a miracle worker."

"Mary said—" Joey slid into his place.

"Miss Moen," his father corrected him.

"Oh." A frown creased his forehead. "She said her name was Mary."

Mary set a platter of sliced bread next to the stew pot. "Okay, we can all say grace and then eat. How's that?" She took the chair closest to the food, just as her mother had always done, so she could serve.

"Mary, you are indeed an answer to prayer," Elizabeth said, extending her hand when Mary was ready to leave for home.

"You want me to come back then?"

"With all my heart."

Mary thought about the Oien family as she walked home in the late afternoon. Mr. Larson, the banker, tipped his hat as he passed her on the way home. Mrs. Johnson called hello from the door of the general store, and Miss Mabel waved from behind her display of hats in the ladies' shoppe. How good it felt to be home, where she knew everyone and everyone knew her.

That night around the supper table, Knute, the oldest of the Moen boys, announced, "I want to enlist like Will did, before there ain't no more Germans to fight."

Mary's heart sprung a new crack. Not her brother, too.

Chapter 4

"You have a letter!" Daniel met her halfway home a few evenings later.

"From Will?" Mary broke into a run to meet him. A raised eyebrow from the hotel manager made her drop back to a decorous walk.

Daniel skidded to a stop, his cheeks pink from the exertion. "It is, it is! Read it aloud."

"How about if I read it first to myself and then to you?"

"Awww, Mary. I want to know how he is. Does he like being a shoulder?"

"Soldier, Danny boy, soldier." Mary grinned down at him. She slit the envelope with care and pulled out a flimsy sheet of paper. Well, Will certainly wasn't onc to waste words on paper any more than he did in person. Working with Dag Weinlander had taught him many things through the years, including how to conserve energy and speech.

My dearest Mary. The word dearest sent a thrill clear to the toes of her black pointed shoes. *I cannot not tell you how much I miss the sight of your sweet face. When you were away at school, I always knew that if I grew desperate enough, I could take a train to Fargo and see you, if only briefly. Now I am clear across the continent from you, and so I commend you to the care of our loving God, for He can be with you when I cannot.*

Mary dug in her bag for a handkerchief.

"Is Will sick? Something is wrong." Daniel backpedaled in front of her so he could watch her face.

"No, silly, it's just that I miss him."

"Oh." He turned and walked beside her, slipping his hand in hers in spite of being out in public.

Mary continued reading. *I never dreamed people could be so ferocious with each other. The sergeants here shout all the time and expect us to do the same. When I think we are being trained to kill our fellowmen, my soul cries out to God to stop this war before anyone else dies. But the Huns must be stopped or the world will never be a safe place in which to love and raise our children.*

Mary tucked the letter in her pocket. She would have to read it later when she could cry along with the heartfelt agony of the man she loved. Will had never been afraid to stand up for the weaker children, and he was carrying that same strength into the battle for freedom.

That night she could not see the Big Dipper; clouds covered the sky.

Within a week Mary had both Joey and Jenny waiting by the front windows for her arrival. Mrs. Oien brightened when her young friend walked into the room, and she seemed to be getting stronger. While she sometimes slipped into staring out the window, she more often read to the children and would pinch her cheeks to bring some color to them before Mr. Oien returned home for dinner.

"How would it be if I took the children home to play with my brothers and sisters this afternoon?" Mary asked after dinner one day. "We have a big swing in our backyard, and the cat in the stable has new kittens."

"Kittens." Joey looked from his father to his mother, his heart in his eyes.

"Now, no pets. Your mother has plenty to do already." Mr. Oien effectively doused the light in the child's eyes.

"You can play with them at my house; they are too little to leave their mother yet." Mary stepped into the breach. As far as she was concerned, an animal might make things more lively in this often-silent home. Her mother had never minded when the children brought home another stray—of any kind. In fact, she frequently brought them home herself.

"Perhaps you would like to come, too," she said to Elizabeth. "I know you would love visiting with my mother."

"Another time, dear, when I am feeling stronger." Elizabeth smiled at her children. "But you two go on and have a good time."

Walking down the street with a child's hand in each of hers, Mary pointed out the store, the post office, and the hotel. But when she passed the livery, all she could think was that Will wasn't the one pounding on the anvil out back, most likely fitting shoes to one of the farmer's horses.

Jenny refused to leave the kittens. She plunked her sturdy little body down by the nest the cat had made in the hay under the horse's manger and giggled when the kittens nursed. She reached out a fat little finger and stroked down the wriggling kittens' backs.

Ingeborg had come out to the stable with Mary to watch. "I can't believe one so little would have the patience to sit like that. She is just enthralled with the kittens."

Joey had looked them over and then gone to see what the boys were doing. Knute was hoeing weeds in the garden and Daniel followed behind on hands and knees, pulling out the weeds too close to the plants for the hoe to work. He showed Joey which were weeds, and the little boy had followed the older one from then on. When they found a worm, Joey cupped it in his hands and brought it to Mary.

"Did you ever see such a big worm?" he asked.

"I think tomorrow we will dig in your flower beds and perhaps find some there." Mary stroked the hair back from the boy's sweaty forehead. Pulling weeds in the June sun could be a hot task.

"Not this big. This is the biggest worm ever. Can I take it home to show Mama?"

Mary nodded. But when Joey stuck the wriggling worm in his pocket, she shook her head. "He'll die there. Come on, let's find a can for him, and you can put dirt in it." By the time Ingeborg called the children in for lemonade, Joey had several more worms in his can.

"Mor, could we take Joey fishing?" Daniel asked, wiping cookie crumbs from his mouth. All had gathered on the porch for the afternoon treat.

Ingeborg looked up. "I don't see why not. Mary, where is Jenny?"

Mary put her finger to her lips and pointed to the barn. When she and her mother tiptoed into the horse stall, they saw Jenny on the hay, sound asleep. The mother cat and kittens were doing the same.

"I checked on her a few minutes ago and decided to leave her there. Isn't she a darling?"

"You children used to love to sleep in the hay, too. How is their mother, really?"

Mary shook her head. "She scares me sometimes, Mor. It's as though she isn't even there, and other times she is so sad. I don't know what to do to help her." Mary pondered the same question that night when she added to the week's letter to Will. "I wonder about Elizabeth Oien," she wrote. "She loves her husband and children but seems to be slipping away from them. What makes one person have such a strong will to live, like Mrs. Norgaard, and another unable to overcome a bodily weakness? Doc says she has never been the same since Jenny was born. I guess it was a hard time and she nearly died. But the children had such fun at our house."

She went on to describe the afternoon. She closed the letter as always, "May God hold you in His love and care, Your Mary."

Joey caught two fish and a bad case of hero worship. Jenny pleaded every day, "Kittens, pease see kittens." Daniel spent as much time at the Oiens as he did at home. And Mr. Oien paid Mary double what they'd agreed.

"I cannot begin to tell you what a difference you have made in our lives," he said one evening when he handed her the pay envelope. "Elizabeth and I are eternally grateful."

The Fourth of July dawned with a glorious sunrise, and the rest of the day did its best to keep up. The parade started in the schoolyard and followed Main Street to the park, where a bandstand had been set up. There would be speeches and singing, races for the children, carnival booths set up to earn money for various town groups like the Lutheran church ladies, who sold fancy sandwiches and good strong coffee. Mary had worked in that booth since she was old enough to count the change.

The Grange sold hot dogs, the school board ice cream that was being hand-cranked out behind the booth by members of the board, and the Presbyterian church made the best pies anywhere. Knute won the pie-eating contest for the second year in a row, and one child got stung by a bee. The fireworks that night capped a day that made Mary dream of Will even more. Last year they'd sat together, hands nearly touching while the fireworks burst in the sky to the accompaniment of the band. Did they have fireworks in the training camp he was in?

The next day an entire train car of young men left, waving to their families and sweethearts. They were on their way to an army training camp.

Mary stood next to her father, who had given the benediction at the ceremony. "Soon we won't have any young men left," she said softly. "Who is going to run the farms and provide food for the troops if all the workers leave?"

"Those of us left at home. It is the least we can do." John Moen blew his nose. "God have mercy on those boys." He used his handkerchief to wipe the sweat from his forehead. "Unseasonable hot, isn't it?"

"Yes, Father, it is hot, but you can't fool me. That wasn't all sweat you wiped from your face."

"You are much too observant, my dear. You will make a fine teacher; the children will accuse you of having eyes in the back of your head." John took his daughter's arm on one side and his wife's on the other. "Let's go home and make ice cream. I only got a taste yesterday."

The heat continued, made worse by air so full of moisture it felt like they were breathing underwater. Heat lightning danced and stabbed, but it failed to deliver the needed rain. How hot it was became the talk of the town. When the farmers came in to shop on Saturdays, their horses looked as bone-weary as the people.

Mary tried to entertain the Oien children, but Jenny fussed and pleaded to go see the kittens. Mrs. Oien lay on the chaise lounge on the back porch, where it was coolest, but daily Mary watched the woman weaken.

If only it would rain. Dust from the streets coated everything, including the marigolds and petunias she had planted along the front walk. Early each day she carried water to the struggling plants, praying for rain like everyone else.

The cornfields to the south of town withered in the heat. Storm clouds formed on the western horizon but always passed without sending their life-giving moisture to the ground below.

One day Mary came home from the Oiens to find Daniel lying in bed, a wet cloth on his forehead. He looked up at her from fever-glazed eyes. "I don't feel so good, Mary."

The letter lying on the hall table had no better news. Will was boarding the ship to Europe in two days. She checked the postmark. He was already on the high seas.

Chapter 5

He's a mighty sick boy, Ingeborg, I won't deny that." Doc Harmon looked up after listening to Daniel's labored breathing with his stethoscope. "People seem to fall into a couple of characteristics. Everything seems to settle in the chest for some, in the stomach for others. I don't understand it, but with Daniel here, it's always the chest. Onion plaster might help; keep his fever down and thump on his chest and back like this to loosen the mucous up." He cupped his hand and tapped it palm down on the boy's back.

Daniel started to cough after only a couple of whacks, giving the doctor a look of total disbelief.

"I know, son, but you will breathe better this way. Make sure he drinks a lot of water, and keep him as cool as possible. That plaster will heat him up some." He looked Daniel in the eye. "Now you do as your mother says and make sure you eat. Lots of broth—both chicken and beef—are good for building him back up."

He looked back up at Ingeborg. "You take care of yourself, too. This summer complaint is affecting lots of people. What we need is a good rain to clear the air."

The rains held off.

Daniel was finally up and around again but more than willing to take afternoon naps. His favorite place was next to Mary. Mrs. Oien seemed better, too, at least in the early morning and after the sun went down. Mr. Oien bought a newfangled gadget called an electric fan.

Everyone wanted to sit in front of it, even when it only moved hot air around. Mary set a pan of water in front of the fan, and that helped them cool more.

July passed with people carrying water to their most precious plants and the farmers facing a year of no crops. At the parsonage, that meant there was no money in the church budget to pay the pastor, and Mary's wages became the lifeline for the Moens.

The weather changed when walnut-sized hailstones pounded the earth and all upon it. What the drought hadn't shriveled, the hail leveled. Ingeborg and Mary stood at the kitchen window and watched the garden they'd so faithfully watered be turned to flat mud and pulp.

"Guess we take God at His word and trust that He will provide." Ingeborg wiped a tear from her eye and squared her shoulders. "The root crops will still be good, and we already had some beans put up. I lived without tomatoes for years, so I know we can do so again. And the corn, well, next year we'll have corn again. At least the early apples were plentiful and perhaps we can buy a barrel from Wisconsin or somewhere later in the fall."

Mary knew her mother was indulging in wishful thinking. There would be no money for apples this year. "Mor, I could stay home from school and keep working for the Oiens."

Ingeborg shook her head. "No, my dear, your school is paid for, and you must finish. If it comes to that, I could go take care of her and those little ones."

Her face lost the strained look of moments before. "See, I said the Lord provides. What a good idea. All of ours are in school all day. Why I could do all their cleaning and cooking and perhaps—no, I couldn't cause someone else to lose their job. We will make do."

Mary knew this talking to herself was her mother's way of working things out, whether anyone else listened or not. She often found herself doing the same thing. Each night when she wrote her letters to Will, she sometimes spoke the words as she wrote them, as if that made him hear them sooner. Or rather see them.

It rained for two days, much of the water running off because the earth was too hard to receive it. At night she stood in front of her window and let the cool breeze blow over her skin. Cool, wet air —what a blessing. But she had to remember where the handle to the Big Dipper lay because she couldn't see it through the clouds.

Why hadn't she heard from Will? Where was he?

She still hadn't heard from him when she packed her trunk for the return to school. She wrapped the three precious letters carefully in a linen handkerchief and tied them with a faded hair ribbon. While she'd about memorized the words, she'd reread the pages until the folds were cracking from repeated bending.

Each week she mailed another letter to him, in care of the U.S. Army. Was he getting her letters? They hadn't come back.

The night before she was to leave, she walked to "the mansion" and up to the front door. Fireflies pirouetted to the cadence of the crickets. Mosquitos whined at her ear, but she brushed them away. She barely raised her hand to knock when Dag swung open the door.

"Come in, come in. Gudrun has been waiting for you." He turned to answer over his shoulder. "Yes, it is Mary." When he ushered her in, he whispered. "I told you she'd been waiting."

"Sorry, I should have come sooner."

"She's in the library."

Mary nodded. She loved coming to this house with its rich velvets and artfully carved sofas and whatnot tables. The embossed wallpaper gleamed in the newly installed electric lights that took the place of the gas jets.

Mrs. Norgaard sat behind the walnut desk that had belonged to her husband when he owned the bank. While she still owned the Soldahl Bank, she employed a manager who ran it and only reported to her quarterly, unless of course, there was an emergency.

"Come in, my dear and sit down." She took off her spectacles and rubbed the bridge of her nose. "I'm glad you could humor an old woman like me this last night you have with your family."

"They will see me off in the morning." Mary took in a deep breath and voiced something that had been on her heart and mind for the last weeks. "If paying my school expenses is a hardship for you this year, I could stay—"

"Absolutely not. You will finish your year out, and then you can teach. The children of North Dakota need teachers like you. If you think a few months of drought and then a hailstorm will wipe out commerce around here, you just don't understand the world yet.

"Companies make a great deal of money during wartime—I sometimes think that is why men start them—and our bank has invested wisely. I can afford your schooling, and you will not hear of my bank foreclosing on the farmers because they can't make their payments on time this year. Or anyone else for that matter. I hear your mother is going to take over at the Oiens?"

Mary nodded.

"That is good. But I have a feeling you've been worrying about the church paying your father's salary." She tipped her head to look over the tops of her gold wire spectacles.

"Some. My mother says they will make do, but I know it is hard to feed seven mouths, and five of the children are growing so fast we can't keep them in shoes."

"You are not to worry. If I'd known John hadn't gotten paid last month, it never would have happened, and you can bet your life it won't happen again." Mrs. Norgaard sat up straighter. "Those men can bungle things up so bad sometimes, it takes me weeks to just figure it out."

Mary knew she referred to the deacons who ran the business of the congregation. "How'd you find out?" Curious, Mary leaned forward in her chair.

"I have my ways, child."

"Doc Harmon?" Mary shook her head. "No, he's not on the

board. Mr. Sommerstrum?" At the twinkle in Gudrun's eye, Mary laughed. "Mrs. Sommerstrum."

"I'll never tell, but it's a good thing some men talk things over with their wives, even if it's only to share the gossip."

Mary nodded. "I see. I've often wondered how you keep such good tabs on the goings on in Soldahl when you don't go out too often. Mrs. Sommerstrum tells Mrs. Hanson, and Mrs. Hanson tells you." Mrs. Hanson had been the housekeeper at the mansion ever since Mary could remember.

Gudrun nodded. She reached in a drawer, removed an envelope, and handed it across the shiny surface of the desk. "Here. And I don't want you scrimping and going without to send part of that money home, you understand me?"

Mary nodded, guilt sending a flush up her neck. *How did she know what I'd been thinking of?*

"Ah, caught you, did I?" At the girl's slight nod, Gudrun continued. "Now that we have that out of the way, I have a very personal question to ask. Have you heard from Will?"

"No, not since early July, and that letter had been written while he was on the ship."

"Neither have we. That's not like our Will." She stared at the desk before her. "Did he say anything about where they were sending him?"

Again, Mary shook her head.

Gudrun nodded and rose to her feet. "Well, as the old saying goes, no news is good news. Come, let's have a last cup of coffee and some of Mrs. Hanson's angel food cake. I think she has a packet ready to send with you, too."

By the time Mary said goodbye to the family in the mansion, she could hardly hold back the tears. It wasn't like she was going clear around the world or anything, but right now Fargo seemed years away.

The next morning was even worse. Daniel clung to her until they were both in tears. John finally took the child in his arms while Ingeborg hugged her daughter one last time. Mary smiled through her tears and ruffled Daniel's hair while at the same time hugging her father. She went down the line, hugging each of her brothers and sisters. "Now, promise me, all of you, that when I ask your teacher at Christmastime how you are doing, he will have a good report for me."

They all nodded and smiled at her.

"Hey, I'm not leaving forever, you know."

"It just seems like it."

The train blew its whistle, and the conductor announced, "All aboard."

Mary stepped on the stool and up the stairs. She waved one last time and hurried inside so she could wave again out the window. Slowly the train pulled out of the station, and when she could see them no more, she sank back in her seat to wipe her eyes. Why was leaving so hard when she had so much to look forward to?

As the miles passed, she thought back to the last night she had seen Will. The small package she'd given him contained one of her treasures, the New Testament given her by her parents on her twelfth birthday. "Will you keep this with you to remind you always how much I love you and how much more God loves you?"

"I will keep it in my shirt pocket," he'd replied, never taking his gaze from hers while he put the Testament next to his heart. "But I need no reminder."

The kiss they'd shared had been only sweeter with the small book tucked between them.

At Grand Forks, two of Mary's friends from the year before boarded, and they spent the remainder of the trip catching up on their summers. When Mary told them Will had gone to war, Janice said her brother had left, too. Dorie shook her head. "I can't believe all our boys are going over there. What if they don't come home? Who will we marry?"

Mary rolled her eyes. "Leave it to you to keep the most important things right out front." The three laughed, but Mary felt a pang of fear. What if Will didn't come home?

One evening, toward the middle of October, she returned to her room to find a message saying there was a gentleman waiting in the parlor. He wanted to talk with her. Mary flew back down the stairs, her heart pounding. Perhaps it was Will!

But when she slid open the heavy door, her father and Dag Weinlander sat in the armchairs facing the fireplace. From the looks on their faces, she knew.

"He's dead, isn't he?" How could she say the words? Dead, what did that mean?

John shook his head. Dag cleared his throat. "We hope not." He extended the letter bearing an official seal at the top.

Mary read it quickly, then went back to read each word one at a time. *We regret to inform you that Private First Class Willard Dunfey is missing in action and presumed dead.* The date was three months earlier.

Chapter 6

"Then he isn't dead." Mary went to stand in front of the fire. She wanted to throw the horrible letter in and let the flames devour it.

"We can pray that he isn't," John said. He stepped closer and wrapped an arm around her shoulders.

"Father, wouldn't I know if Will no longer lived on this earth? I mean, he can't have been dead for three months and me not sense it, could he?"

"I don't know, child." John shook his head. "I just don't know. The Almighty hasn't seen fit to let me know many things."

Mary looked up at her father. The lines had deepened in his face and his hair showed white all over. "What's been happening?"

"I had two funerals last week of boys shipped home to be buried. The oldest Gustafson boy and Teddy Bjorn. What can I say to those grieving parents—that this was God's will?"

He laid his cheek on the top of her head, now nestled against his shoulder. "I cannot say that war is God's will, that He is on the side of the right. He loves the Germans, too, not just the Americans and the English and French. We are all His children, so how can we go about killing each other?" His voice had softened on the last words. "How?"

Mary felt the shudder that passed through him. Her gentle father, who loved all the children of the parish and their parents and relatives. Who never preached the fire and brimstone of other churches because he said God is love and His grace is made perfect in our human weakness. This man now had to bury the ones he loved, because of man's inhumanity to man.

But was war really human? She'd sat through many discussions and heard heart-stirring speeches about fighting for freedom, but did freedom have to come at the cost of so many lives? She had no answers, only questions.

Had Will really gone to his heavenly home, or was he on earth, suffering some unspeakable agony? If he were alive, wouldn't he have contacted her?

"You may have to accept the fact that he is gone." John drew his arms away and stepped back so he could see her face more clearly.

"But not now!"

"No, not now."

Mary straightened her shoulders, reminiscent of Mrs. Norgaard. She forced a smile to her quivering lips. "How is Daniel? And Mother with the Oiens? Did Mr. Oien give in yet and let Jenny have a kitty? She loves them so. How have you been? You're looking tired." Before he could answer, she turned to Dag, who had been sitting quietly. "How are Mrs. Norgaard and Clara?" Perhaps if she asked enough questions, the greater one would disappear.

"We are all fine," her father finally managed to insert. "In fact, with the cooler weather, Daniel has been doing well. Hasn't missed a day of school, but he would have today if he could have hidden out in my pocket to come along. He is counting the days until you come home for Christmas. Said to tell you he prays for Will every night."

That nearly undid her. She blinked several times and stared into the fire until she had herself under control. "Have you had supper?" When they shook their heads, she looked up at the carved clock on the mantel. "I'm sure Mrs. Killingsworth will let me fix you something in the kitchen. Where are you staying?"

"We aren't. We will catch the eleven o'clock back north. I just felt it important to give you this news in person, not through a letter or over the telephone."

Mary placed a hand on his arm. "Father, you are so kind. How lucky I am that I was born to you and Mor." She spun away before he could answer. "Let me check on supper for you."

An hour later she waved them on their way. "Thank you for coming along with him, Dag. You are a good friend."

He tipped his black, felt hat to her. "Mrs. Norgaard just wanted me to check up on her investment; this seemed as good a time as any." The twinkle in his eye let her know he was teasing.

"Well, then, since this was a business trip, thank you for bringing my father along." She hugged her father one last time. "Pass that on to everyone, okay?"

She kept the smile in place as long as they looked back, but when she closed the door, the tears could no longer be held back. She stumbled against the lower step of the staircase and sat down. Leaning her head against the newel post, she couldn't have stopped the tears had she tried.

One by one the other young women in the boardinghouse came down the stairs and clustered around her. One offered a handkerchief; another went for a glass of water. Still another slipped into the music room and, sitting down at the piano, began playing the hymns they'd learned as children.

As the music washed over them, soon one began humming and then another.

When the storm of tears finally abated, Mary listened to the humming in harmony. Had a chorus of angels come just to give her strength? She closed her eyes and leaned against the post. They drifted from melody to melody as the pianist did, until she finally let the last notes drift away.

"Amen." As the notes died away, Janice took Mary's arm and tugged her to her feet. Together, arms around each other's waists, they climbed the stairs to the bedroom they shared.

"Thank you, all," Mary whispered. Talking loudly would have

broken the spell.

When despair grabbed at her in the days to come, she remembered that peaceful music and the love of her friends. In spite of the official letter, each evening Mary added tales of the day to her own letters to Will. She continued to send them, refusing to allow herself to speculate about what was happening to them.

"I guess I'm afraid that if I quit, Will will be dead, and if I keep on, there's a chance he is alive," she explained to Janice one night. They'd been studying late because exams were coming up.

"How can you keep on going and not let it drag you down?" Janice tightened the belt of her flannel robe. "The not knowing—" She shook her head so her dark hair swung over one shoulder. She combed the tresses with her fingers and leaned back against the pillows piled at the head of her bed. "Makes me glad I don't have a sweetheart yet."

"I wouldn't trade my friendship and love for Will for all the men on campus."

"There are several who would ask if you gave them the chance."

"Janice!" Mary turned in her chair and locked her hands over the back. "I haven't treated any one of them as more than a friend."

"I know that. You act like you are already married, for heaven's sake. I'm just telling you what I see. And hear."

"Oh, pooh, you're making that up." Mary turned back to her books. "Be quiet, I have to get this memorized."

But Mary recognized that her skirts hung looser about her waist and the shadows that lurked beneath her eyes grew darker, as if she hadn't enough sleep. Each night she committed Will to her heavenly Father's keeping and waved goodnight to him on the last star of the handle.

Two days before she left for home, she received a letter from her mother. *My dear Mary,* she read. *I have some sad news for you. Mrs. Oien, my dear friend Elizabeth, died from pneumonia two days ago.*

Dr. Harmon said she had no strength to fight it, and I could see that. I was with her when she breathed her last, as was Mr. Oien.

He is so broken up, I want to take him in my arms like I do Daniel, to comfort him. The funeral is tomorrow. The children are with us for the time being, as Kenneth can't seem to know what to do with them. He stayed home from work for the first day but said he was going crazy in that house without her.

The rest of us are eagerly waiting for your return. God keep you, my dear. Your loving mother.

Mary laid the paper in her lap and looked out the window into the blackness. A streetlight up by the corner cast a round circle of light on the freshly fallen snow. Clouds, pregnant with moisture, covered the twinkling stars. The night felt heavy, like the news in her lap.

"Oh, Elizabeth," Mary whispered, "how you must have fought to stay with your children. And your poor husband. Good-bye, my friend. Go with God." She sat down and wrote a letter of condolence to Mr. Oien, knowing she would get back to town nearly as soon as the letter but feeling she needed to write it anyway.

"What happened now?" Janice asked when she came in some time later.

Mary handed her the letter.

"Oh, that poor man." Janice looked up from her reading. "He'll need someone to care for his children." She tilted her head slightly sideways and looked at Mary. "You won't think you have to stay home next term and care for them?"

"No, I promised Mrs. Norgaard I would finish this year. I just grew to care for Elizabeth so much last summer, and the children, Joey and Jenny, will be lost."

"Not if your mother has anything to do with it."

"Or Doc Harmon and Mrs. Norgaard. They'll probably have him married off in a month or two." Mary's smile slipped. "Men do that you know—marry again right away. I don't know how they can."

"For some I think marrying is like changing underwear. You do what's necessary."

"Janice Ringold!" Mary, feeling her jaw hit her chest, looked at her friend. The shock of the words made them both laugh. "You are outrageous, you know that?"

"I know. My mother always said my mouth would get me in trouble. 'Men don't like outspoken young ladies.' If I heard her say that once, I heard her a thousand times."

"Didn't help much, did it?" They chuckled again.

But before Mary fell asleep that night, she added an extra prayer for the Oien family along with her others, and as always, she gave Him Will.

The house smelled like cinnamon and fresh-baked bread when Mary tiptoed in through the front door. Candles in the windows were ready to be lit on Christmas Eve, a pine tree from Minnesota filled the usual spot in the corner of the parlor, and garlands of cedar trimmed the doorway. Mary felt a pang; she'd missed the house decorating again. If only she'd had her last exam early in the week like many of the others, she could have left sooner. She could hear her mother in the kitchen, removing something from the oven.

Mary shut the door softly, hoping there would be no squeak, and when that was accomplished, she crossed the room to the kitchen. "Surprise!"

"Oh, my heavens!" Ingeborg grabbed at the sheet of cookies that was headed for the floor. When she had the cookies safely on the table, she put her hand to her heart. "What are you trying to do, you naughty child, give your mother a heart attack?" But the smile that took in her whole face and her outstretched arms made light of her scolding words. "Land sakes, Mary, I didn't think you were ever coming."

A child's whimper came from the bedroom.

"Now see what you did—woke up Jenny. Joey won't be far behind."

"They are here?" Mary hugged her mother and began unwinding the bright red scarf about her neck. She hung it and then her coat on the rack by the door and reached outside for her valise. "You think they will remember me?"

"With Daniel telling them every day that Mary is coming, what do you think?" Ingeborg cocked her head and listened. "I think she'll settle down again. Give us time for a cup of coffee and some catching up."

"I have another box at the station; it was too heavy to carry."

"Mary, you didn't spend your money on Christmas presents, did you?"

"Some, and some I made, like always. There are some books there for my classroom—when I get a classroom, that is." She sat down at the table and watched her mother take down the good china cups. They only came down for special company and the Ladies' Aid. Ingeborg set the one with tiny rosebuds around the rim in front of her daughter. It had been her favorite since when she was little and they had tea once in a great while.

Oh, I'm home, Mary thought. *I never know how much I miss it and my family until I come back. But this time there will be no Will to come sweep me off my feet.* She sighed. A bit of the sunlight went out of the day. *You knew better,* she scolded herself. *You knew he wasn't here, so behave yourself. Don't take your feelings out on Mor, who is so happy to see you.*

After Ingeborg poured the coffee, she took her daughter's chin in gentle fingers and tilted her face toward the light. "Have you been sick?"

Mary shook her head.

"Working too hard and not sleeping enough?" She tilted the girl's head down and kissed the forehead. "Grieving for Will?" Her words were soft as the ashes falling in the stove.

"Oh, Mor." Mary flung her arms around her mother's waist and buried her face in the flour-dusted apron. "I can't believe he's dead. Wouldn't I know, some part of me down in my heart? Wouldn't I know for sure?"

Ingeborg stroked the soft curls and brushed the wisps of hair back that framed Mary's face. "I've heard tell of that, of mothers with their children, sometimes of those who've been married for many years, but—" She bent down and laid her cheek on Mary's head. "My dear, I just don't know."

They stayed that way, comforting each other for a time. Finally Mary drew away.

Ingeborg brushed some flour off her daughter's cheek. "Now the coffee is gone cold. Let me heat it up." She poured the brown liquid back in the pot and set it on the front burner again. "One thing I do know. When the time comes, you say good-bye, knowing that you loved him and he loved you and love goes on forever. But Will wouldn't want you to grieve overlong; he'd want you to get on with your life."

"I'll be teaching next year. Isn't that getting on with my life?"

"Ja, it is. God, I know, has special plans for you, and when we cry, He says He is right here with us. As He is all the time."

Mary watched the peace on her mother's face and heard the faith in her voice. Ingeborg's faith never wavered. Could she ever be strong like that?

"Mary's home!" The cry rang through the house when school let out and the children ran in through the door. Jenny and Joey came out of their rooms, rubbing their eyes, and after a moment, joined the others in the circle around Mary. Everyone talked at once until the ceiling echoed with happy laughter.

Supper that night continued in the same vein. When Mr. Oien came to pick up his children, Ingeborg invited him to stay for a bite to eat. They pulled out the table and set in another leaf so there would be room.

Once or twice his smiles at the antics of the younger Moen children nearly reached his eyes. "Thank you so much," he said as he readied to leave after the meal was finished.

"You're welcome to stay longer." John leaned back in his chair and crossed his legs at the ankles.

"I. . .I'd best be going—put these two to bed, you know." He nodded toward Joey and Jenny, who were being bundled up by the Moens. "Again, thank you." He put his hat on and picked up Jenny. "Come, Joey." He took the boy's hand, and the three went down the walk to where he had parked his automobile at the front gate.

"He should have started that contraption first." Ingeborg shut the door and peeked through the lace curtain. "Knute, why don't you go out and help him crank that thing?"

The oldest Moen son did as asked. When he returned, he rubbed his hands together. "If it weren't for cranking those things, I'd want one the worst way."

"Wanting never hurt anyone." John winked at Mary. "I was hoping since you were home, you would read to us tonight."

"Of course. What are you reading?" She took the book her father handed her. "Oh, Charles Dickens and old Scrooge. How I love it." As soon as the dishes were washed and put away, the family gathered in the parlor and Mary began to read. After the chapter was finished, she picked up the Bible that lay on the end table and opened it to the Psalms. "I keep going back to this one. 'Oh Lord, thou has searched me, and known me.' "

"Psalm 139." Daniel beamed at being the first to recognize it. They'd played this game of guessing the Scripture all the years of their lives, until now they were all well-versed in Bible knowledge.

Mary continued reading and, when she finished, closed the book. "Far, will you pray tonight?"

John nodded. "Father in heaven, Thou dost indeed know us right well. We ask You to forgive us our sins and fill us with Your Holy Spirit so that we may do the works Thou hast given us." When he came to the end, he finished with a blessing and they all said, "Amen."

"Now I know I am home for sure," Mary said with a sigh and a smile.

She felt that same way in church a few nights later when they gathered to celebrate the birth of the Christ child. Singing the old hymns and hearing the words embedded in her memory from eighteen Christmases made her want to wrap her arms around every person in the room. *Please, God, if You will, send me a sign that Will is either here on earth or up there with You. I want to do Your will, and I thank You that You sent Your Son to walk this earth. All I ask, dear Father, is a small sign.*

Christmas passed in a blur of happiness, only saddened when Mary thought of Will and what he was missing. Two days later, Dag came to see them.

"I have something that came in the mail today." He stopped, swallowed hard, and continued.

Mary felt an icy hand grip her heart.

Dag held out something metal on his hand. "They say these are Will's dog tags, taken from a body buried in Germany."

Mary couldn't breathe.

Chapter 7

Mary, are you all right?"

She heard the voice as if from a great distance. "I... I'm fine. Why?" Had she been sitting in the chair when. . . ? Memory crashed back and she whimpered. "No, no, please no." *Dear God, please, that's not the sign I wanted. I know I asked for a sign but...*

Dag stood before her, his hand clenched at his side, a small piece of chain dangling between thumb and forefinger.

Now, why would I notice something like that? Chains don't matter at this point. But that one did. The chain that Will had worn so proudly now brought agony to his beloved.

"Mary." Her father's face swam before her eyes. He cuddled her cold hands in his warm ones and waited for her to respond.

"Yes." She left off studying the shimmering hairs on the backs of his hands and looked at him. The tears fighting to overflow his blue eyes undid her. She threw herself into his arms and wept.

Minutes later—but what seemed like hours—she accepted the handkerchief from her mother and mopped at her eyes. "I wanted him to come home. I asked God, and you said God always answers our prayers. I prayed that He would bring Will home."

"I know. I did, too."

"And me." Dag lowered himself into a chair and leaned forward. "All of us prayed for that."

"Then why?" She shouted her question, shaking her fist in the face of God. "Why did He let Will die? Others are coming home—why not Will?"

John bent his head. "I don't know. I do not understand the mind of God or some of His purposes. All I know is that His heart breaks, too, and He holds us close. Close like me holding your hand and even closer. And the other thing I know with all certainty is that you will see Will again."

"I know about heaven, but I want him here." Tears dripped down her face.

"I know that, too."

Mary felt her mother's hands on her shoulders, warm and secure.

"God could have saved Will." Again she felt like lashing out.

"Ja, He could have." The hands on her shoulders rubbed gently.

"Then why didn't He?" Mary hiccupped on the last word.

"I 'spect every wife, mother, friend, feels the same. None of us want someone we love to be killed." John rubbed the back of her hands with his thumbs.

"Am I being selfish?"

"No more'n anyone else. But death comes. It is part of life, and we look forward to heaven all the time."

Mary sat silently. Then she shook her head. "It's not fair. Will is such a good man."

"Yes, he was. You can be proud he was your friend and loved you with all his heart."

It bothered her that her father said "was." She couldn't think of Will as "was." *He is!* Her rebellious mind insisted. *Will is.*

When she awoke in the middle of the night, after alternately praying and crying, she found her mother sitting by the bed, sound asleep. Mary fought back tears again. This was so like her mother, keeping watch over those she loved and those who needed her. Her presence comforted the girl, and she drifted back to sleep.

Each day felt like she waded through spring gumbo three feet deep. Every part of her felt heavy, even to her eyelids and the tops of her ears. She pushed her hair back and finally braided it and coiled the braid in a bun at the base of her head to keep the weight of it from pulling her over. All she really wanted to do was sleep, for only in sleep did the knowledge disappear. But on waking, it always returned. They said Will was dead.

"You can stay home, you know." Ingeborg helped fold the undergarments to put in Mary's traveling valise.

"Would it be any better?" Mary turned from sorting through her books and deciding which had to go back with her.

"It would for me, because then I could make sure you eat and get enough rest and —"

"And cluck over me like one of your chicks?"

"You are one of my chicks." Ingeborg smoothed a ribbon into place on a nightgown. "No matter how grown-up you get—even when you have a family of your own—you will always be my eldest chick."

"But I have to grow up, and learning to keep going is part of that, isn't it?"

"Ja, and I know our heavenly Father will watch over you and keep you safe."

I hope He does a better job with me than He did with Will. Mary was horrified at her thoughts. They just snuck up on her and dashed off before she could rope them in and discipline them to behave.

Later, her bags all packed, Mary bundled up to walk over to the mansion to say good-bye to Mrs. Norgaard. The north wind bit her cheeks and tried to burrow into her bones.

"Come in, my dear, come in." Clara swung the door wide open. "Are you about frozen clear through, out walking in this cold?"

Mary stamped the snow from her boots and smiled at the

diminutive dynamo in front of her. Clara Weinlander often reminded Mary of her mother. If there was something that needed doing, those two women would take it on.

"Herself is waiting for you." Mrs. Hanson secretly used that nickname for her employer, and at times, so did half the town. "We'll bring the coffee right in."

After their greetings, Mrs. Norgaard beckoned Mary to sit beside her on the sofa in front of the south windows. "I want to say something to you before the others come in."

Mary sat and turned to face her benefactress. "Yes."

"Losing one you love is one of the hardest things in life, but there's something I learned through all that. The Bible says, 'This too shall pass,' and it will. Right now you doubt me, but in a few weeks, months, the pain will be less and there will be some days when you surprise yourself because you didn't think of missing him at all."

Gudrun covered Mary's hands with her own. "Trust me, child, I know it is true. And one day you will think of Will, and the memory will be sweet. For you see, he will be closer now than he could have been when he was alive."

Mary felt the tears burning and closed her eyes. "But…but I still feel he might be alive, somewhere, somehow."

"I know, the mind plays tricks like that on us. Oh, how often I thought my husband would be home in half an hour. But he was gone, and finally I came to accept that. And that's when I began to live again." She looked up to see Clara and Mrs. Hanson with the serving trays. "And much of that is thanks to these two. They bullied me into wanting to live."

"That we did." Mrs. Hanson set the tray down. "And would again."

"Just think of all the exciting things you would have missed." Clara sat in the chair and leaned forward to pour the coffee from the silver pot. "Mary, help yourself to those cookies. Mrs. Hanson baked them just for you, and there's a box for you to take with you."

In spite of herself, Mary left the mansion feeling a little less weighed down by life.

With papers to write and new classes, Mary found herself busier than ever. Her friends gathered round her and made sure she ate and went with them to the lectures on campus to hear the suffragettes trying to get the suffrage bill passed through Congress. When it was defeated, they all held a wake.

When General Pershing made his triumphant entrance into Paris, they all listened to the speeches on the radio in the parlor. Surely peace would be coming soon.

But the war continued, and school drew to a close. The entire Moen tribe came down on the train for Mary's graduation from normal school. She would now be able to teach grades one through high school in the state of North Dakota. Mary almost, but not quite, kept from looking for Will in the well-wishers.

"To think, a daughter of mine has graduated from teaching school." Ingeborg clasped her hands at her waist.

"I won't be the last." Mary removed the square black mortar board that crowned her head. "I will help pay for the next one who wants to go. Has Knute talked about what he wants to do?" Her brother next in line was due to graduate from high school at the end of May. She looked down at the brother tugging on her arm. "Yes, Daniel?"

"Far said if you were to change, we could go have ice cream."

"Oh, he did, did he? Well, let me congratulate my friends over there, and we will all walk to the soda fountain."

"I think we need a place like this in Soldahl," Ingeborg said after they took their places in two adjoining booths.

"That's right, Mother, you need something else to do." Mary

shook her head.

"I didn't say I should do it." She looked around at the scroll-backed metal chairs and the small round tables. "But think what—"

"Don't even think such a thing." John leaned across the table to bring his face closer to his wife's. "You have far too much to do right now."

"Well."

"Mother!" Mary couldn't tell if her mother was serious or just teasing. After the young man took their order, Ingeborg leaned back against the high-backed wooden bench and turned to her daughter. "So, how are you, really?" She studied Mary's face, searching for the truth.

"I am much better. Mrs. Norgaard was right. Only by looking back can I tell how far I've come. I'm not angry at God anymore—or anyone else. I can read His Word and let it bless me again. But I still write my letters every night to Will and collect them in a box. I guess that has become my diary." She didn't tell them of not looking for the Big Dipper anymore. She still had a hard time looking up at the night sky at all. Invariably when she did, her eyes filled with tears and she couldn't make out the stars anyway.

"I could tell a difference in your letters. Your father and I want you to know how proud we are of you."

The sodas arrived, and the conversation turned to how good they tasted and what everyone was planning for the summer.

"Mr. Oien has been writing and asking if I would care for the children again this summer."

"I know," Ingeborg responded. "I think he sees that with all of my own children home, his two little ones might be too much."

"He doesn't know you very well then, does he?" Mary sipped on her straw. Her mother's straw hat had just been knocked askew by an arm belonging to one of the boys, who had been reaching over the back of the bench. Mary gave the hand a pinch and smiled at the "yeow" that her action provoked. Her mother righted the hat with a laugh and a threat to fix the perpetrator good. The booth full of children laughed at her words, knowing their mother would get even somehow, sometime when they least expected it.

Mary felt a glow settle about her heart. How she had missed them, mostly without even knowing it.

"So what will you do?" Ingeborg finally asked.

"I will care for his house and children and keep on searching for my school. I have my application in four different places, so time will tell."

"And that is what you want?"

Mary nodded. "This is what I want. Since God made sure I got through school, He must have a place in mind for me."

But the summer passed swiftly, and still Mary hadn't heard. By the end of August, she had a hard time keeping doubts at bay. Would she get a school? If not, what would she do?

Chapter 8

The letter arrived on a Wednesday. Mary stared at the postmark, then slit open the envelope with a shaking finger. Grafton lay in the next township, but the school they mentioned was not in town. If they hired her, she would be teaching first through fourth at a country school with two classrooms. Could she come for an interview on Friday?

Could she come for an interview? Did cows give milk? Did the moon follow the sun? An interview! She finally had an interview. And she wouldn't be clear on the other side of the state. She could see the dear faces of her family on the weekends—that is, if she could afford the train. She hurried home to tell her family.

Questions bubbled to the surface. Where would she live? Oh, not with a family that made her share a room and bed with one of their children. Sometimes that was the arrangement. In some places families still took turns boarding the teacher. She'd heard some terrible stories about situations like that. Her feet slowed. If only she could teach right here in Soldahl.

"Mary, that is wonderful." Ingeborg clasped her hands in delight. "And so close by."

Mary read the letter out loud, the actual sound of the words making it more of a reality. "So, will you care for the children on Friday for me?" she asked her mother.

"Of course. You must call the people in Grafton and tell them what time your train will arrive. This is late for hiring a new teacher. I wonder what happened there? I hope it was not an illness of the teacher they already had."

Or she didn't want to go back and found a position elsewhere. Mary shook her head. Thoughts like that were better barricaded behind steel doors.

On Friday, Mary boarded the early train and returned home in time for supper, the proud owner of a teaching position. She would report for duty in two weeks in order to have her classroom ready for her pupils.

"So, why did they need a teacher at this late date?" Ingeborg asked after the children were all in bed.

"Miss Brown's mother became ill in Minnesota and she had to go be with her. A man teaches the older grades—has for a long time. I will be staying with a widow about a mile from the schoolhouse and helping her in exchange for board. I met with her, and she seems very nice. She's a bit hard of hearing and speaks German as much as English, but we should do fine."

"Anyone who has you to help them is very blessed indeed. Helping doesn't mean milking cows and such, does it?" Ingeborg wiped her hands on her apron. "You never have had to do farm labor."

"If you ask me, her sons just want someone living with their mother. She said she didn't want to go live with them." Mary's eyes danced. "I think she doesn't want anyone bossing her around." She caught her mother by the hands and whirled around the kitchen with her. "Oh, Mr. Gunderson, the head of the school board, told me three times that they didn't want any fooling around. 'Our teachers must be a model of decorum.' " She deepened her voice to mimic the gentleman. "Mother, this is the twentieth century for pity's sake. He must still be back in the Dark Ages."

"So what did you tell him?"

Mary's smile slipped. "I told him my fiance was killed in the war and all I was interested in was teaching children the three Rs."

The next afternoon when Mr. Oien came home from work, Mary gave him her good news.

"I'm so very happy for you," he said, but his face showed shock and what was it—bewilderment?

"You knew I planned on teaching school if I could find a position?"

"I did. But since you hadn't said anything, I'd hoped you would stay." He sank down in a chair by the door.

"My mother will watch the children again." Mary stepped to the window to check on the two who were playing outside in the sandbox. They were so sweet, and she would indeed miss them.

"That is not the problem." He paused, then continued in a rush. "I had not planned to mention this yet, what with your grieving for Will and all, but you love my children and you are so good with them and you are such a lovely person, and would you consider marrying me?"

"What did you say?"

"I asked you to marry me." He smoothed his sandy hair back with his hands. A smile came to his face. "I did it. I asked you to marry me."

"But you don't love me."

"How do you know? I love having you here with Joey and Jenny when I come home. I love seeing you play with them. I love hearing you laugh and I—"

"But I don't love you," Mary said the words softly, gently.

"You could, you know. I make a good living, you wouldn't have to teach school, you'd be near to your family whom I know you love dearly, you would have a nice house, and ..."

Mary's slow shaking of the head forced him to run down.

"Please," he quickly amended, "don't say no right now. Give it some thought. Let me visit you, take you for drives. We could have a picnic—a…a…"

Mary stared at him. The thought of marrying someone other than Will brought a knot to her throat and tears to her eyes. "I have to go. Thank you for.. .fo—" She turned and bolted out the door.

"What happened to you?" Ingeborg's eyes widened when she saw her daughters face.

"He.... he asked me to m-marry him." Mary put a hand to her throat.

"A bit of a surprise, that?" Ingeborg shook her head. "Well, I never." She stirred the kettle simmering on the stove. "Hmm, that idea has possibilities."

"Possibilities! Mother, I don't love Kenneth."

"Yet. Sometimes the best marriages are when two people grow into love."

"Mother! You want me to marry someone I don't love?"

"I didn't say that. But I can see it is a natural choice from his point of view. You are lovely, you are familiar, you know his home, and you love his children. Many men would say that's more than enough basis for marriage. Women have married for a lot less, you know."

Mary felt like she was talking with a total stranger who somehow wore her mother's face. "I don't think I have any more to say to you." She turned on her heel and climbed the stairs to her bedroom. Flinging herself across her bed, she buried her face in her hands. *Oh, Will, why did you have to go and die?*

Time took wings during the days until Mary left, making her breathless most of the time. So much to be finished. In spite of her feelings of misgivings, she continued to care for Joey and Jenny, bringing them back to her mother's on the afternoons when she had errands to run.

She wanted her classroom just perfect for her new pupils and spent hours preparing calendars and pictures, lesson assignments, and flash cards for numbers. Mr. Gunderson had said the school didn't have a large budget for supplies—the year had been hard for the farmers, in spite of the high prices for grain due to the war.

Mrs. Norgaard insisted that Dag would drive Mary to her new home so she wouldn't have to take all her things on the train. "God will be with you, child, as you share His love for those children. Don't you forget it."

"I'm not about to." Mary gave the old woman a hug. "You take care of yourself now while I'm away."

"Humph." Gudrun straightened her back, as if it needed it. "I've been taking care of myself since before your mother and father were born. I surely won't stop now." But the twinkle in her faded blue eyes turned the tear that shimmered on her lashes brilliant. She waved one slender hand. "You drive careful now, Dag, you hear?"

Clara, too, stood in the doorway, waving them off. "We'll keep supper for you, Dag. Enjoy the day."

"I wish she could have come." Mary settled back in her seat.The wind whipped the scarf she'd tied around her hat and blew the ends straight out behind her. The thrill of driving such speeds! *One day,* she promised herself, *I will have a car of my own to drive.* The picture of the black roadster driven by Kenneth Oien flashed through her mind. What would it be like, married to him? She liked him well enough. In fact, they could probably be friends. She shrugged the thoughts away. He'd said he'd write and gladly drive up to bring her home for a weekend. She deliberately pushed the thoughts out of her mind.

"So, how goes the blacksmithing?" She turned in the seat so Dag could hear her above the roar of the automobile and the rushing wind.

"Slow. I know I will have to convert more and more to repairing tractors and automobiles and trucks. With the engines improving all the time, we will see more changes than we ever dreamed of."

"I agree." She sought for another topic, but let it lie. Talking above the noise took too great an effort.

Dag carried all her boxes into the schoolroom, and then took the suitcases into the Widow Williamson's two-story square farmhouse and up the stairs to the large bedroom facing east. When he straightened, his head brushed the slanted ceiling, so he ducked a bit.

"This is very nice."

"I think so." Mrs. Williamson had even brought up a desk and chair to set in front of the window. Carved posts stood above a white bedspread, and extra pillows nearly hid the oak headboard. Braided rag rugs by the bed and in front of the high dresser would keep Mary's feet off cold floors in the winter, and there was more than enough space for her simple wardrobe in the double-doored oak chifforobe. A picture of Jesus the Shepherd hung by the door.

"Well, I'd best be on my way." Dag extended his hand. "You call if you need anything. I saw a telephone on the wall downstairs."

"Thank you for all your help." Mary walked him down the stairs, turning at the landing and on down. When his car roared to life and he drove away, she stood on the porch waving long after the dust had settled. She was on her own now—just what she had always wanted. Or had she?

Mary fell in love with her pupils the instant they shuffled through the door. She had sixteen all together: four in the first grade, all so shy they couldn't look up at her; three in the second; five in the third; and four in fourth. The fourth graders already bossed the younger ones, but when she rapped for order, they all sat at attention.

"We will stand for the flag salute." She checked her seating chart. "Arnold, will you lead us?" She put her hand over her pounding heart. Were they as nervous as she? She nodded at the boy on the outside row.

"I pledge allegiance to the flag. . ." They stumbled through the words, some having forgotten them and others having not yet learned.

One of the first graders broke into tears when Mary asked them to repeat the Lord's Prayer. And when they sang the "Star Spangled Banner," she mostly sang solo. These children had a lot to learn.

She had planned on standing in front of them and quizzing them on their reading and numbers, but at the sight of the tears, she called all the children to the side of the room and, sitting down on a chair, told them to sit in front of her. She smiled at each one when she called their names again.

"I need to know who you are, so could you please tell me something you like to do?"

The older children looked at each other wide-eyed.

"Arnold, we'll start with you. What do you like?" And so she went around the group, and by the time she reached the youngest ones, they smiled back at her. One little towheaded girl stared at her teacher with her heart in her eyes.

"You are so pretty," she whispered. "I like you."

Mary felt her heart turn over. "And I like you." She laid the tip of her finger on the little girl's button nose. "Now, let's all learn the pledge of allegiance because we are going to start every day saluting our flag."

"My brother went to war for our flag." One of the boys said. "He never comed home."

Mary knew she was going to have heart problems for certain. "That has happened to many of our young men, so when we salute the flag, we are remembering them at the same time." Thoughts of a star in the Big Dipper handle twinkled through her mind. Remembering. Yes, the sweetness promised by Mrs. Norgaard had finally come.

"A very dear friend of mine went to Europe to fight, too, and never came home." She laid a hand on the head of a little boy who had gravitated next to her knee. "Now, repeat after me, I pledge allegiance to the flag. . ." And so the morning continued. By the time recess came around, Mary felt like running outside to play with the children.

"The first day is always the hardest." Mr. Colburn, his graying hair worn long over the tops of his ears, stood in her doorway. His kind brown eyes and smile that made his mustache wiggle invited her to smile back.

"Is that a promise?" Mary stretched her shoulders. "Mr. Colburn, everyone spoke so highly of you, I feel honored to share your building."

"Yes, well, I try, and the honor is mine. I think we will do well together. My wife insisted I bring you home for supper one night soon. She is so curious about the new teacher, I made her promise not to come see you for herself. We've lived here for ten years, and we are still not considered part of the community. She's hoping you can be friends."

"Isn't that nice? I never turn down the offer of friendship."

"I'll go ring the bell." Mr. Colburn left, and immediately the bell in the tower bonged twice. The children flew to form a line starting with the larger ones and going to the smallest and marched into the building.

Mary took a deep breath and dove back in.

The days fell into a pattern. Up before dawn to make breakfast while Mrs. Williamson did the outside chores. Then walk to school, teach all day, and walk home. Evenings, after she'd washed the supper dishes, were spent preparing for the next day. On Saturday they cleaned house, and on Sunday, Mrs. Williamson's sons took turns driving them to church.

Mary didn't have time to be lonely. She continued to write her letters to Will each night, but now she planned to send them to her mother. Ingeborg would love to hear the stories of her daughter and her small charges.

When Mr. Colburn discovered she could play the piano, he rolled the heavy instrument into her room on the condition that she teach music. The students at Valley School loved to sing. So every afternoon, if all had done their assignments, everyone gathered in Mary's classroom for singing and then Mr. Colburn read to them. His mellow voice played the parts as he read first *The Jungle Book,* by Rudyard Kipling, and then *Oliver Twist,* by Charles Dickens. Mary was as entranced as the children.

Letters came weekly from Kenneth Oien, and Mary grew to look forward to them. While she had yet to go home to visit, his letters were like a window into the life of Soldahl. He wrote of the antics of Joey and Jenny and their new friend, Mews, a half-grown cat that had shown up on their doorstep one day. He described the changing of the colors with the frost and the geese flying south. He said they all missed her and looked forward to her coming home.

There's a poet hiding in that man's soul, Mary thought as she read the latest letter. *But can I ever think of him as more than a friend?*

When the phone rang one evening and Mrs. Williamson called up the stairs to say it was for her, Mary felt her heart leap into her throat. Was something wrong at home? Was Daniel sick again?

"Hello?" She knew she sounded breathless, only because she was.

"Mary, this is Kenneth."

"Kenneth? Oh, Mr. Oien. . .uh, Kenneth." She felt like an idiot. Surely they could be on a first-name basis by now, in fact should have been a long time ago.

"I wondered if I could come and get you on Friday afternoon, if you would like to come home, that is. I would take you back on Sunday, after church. I…ah, that is—"

Mary took pity on his stammering. "I would love that. Thank you for the invitation."

"Would you like me to come to the school?"

"No, I'll meet you here at Mrs. Williamson's." She gave him the directions and hung up the receiver. She'd heard a click on the party line. Now everyone around would know the new teacher had a beau. Whether he was or not did not matter.

"I think of you a lot," Kenneth said when he stopped the automobile in front of the parsonage that Friday night. Dark had fallen before they reached Soldahl, and traveling the rough roads by lamplight had made them drive even more slowly.

What could she say? "I enjoy reading your letters. And thank you for the ride home. Will you be coming to dinner on Sunday?"

"Yes." He smiled at her in the dimness. "And we have been invited to supper on Saturday at the mansion. That is, if you would like to go."

"Why, of course." Mary fumbled for her purse. "Thank you again for the ride."

He got out and came around to open her door, leaving the motor running. "Till tomorrow then." He helped her out and carried her valise to the door. "Jenny and Joey hope you will come see them while you are in town."

"Oh." Mary wondered what had happened to her tongue. Suffering from a lack of words was a new experience for her.

Looking back, she couldn't remember having a nicer time in a long while. While she was fully aware that all her friends and family were playing matchmakers, she couldn't fault them for it. Kenneth Oien was a very nice man.

But a few weeks later, when he asked her to consider marriage, she shook her head.

"Please don't pressure me," she whispered. "I just cannot answer that yet."

"Yet?" His eager voice came through the darkness. He'd just brought her back from another weekend at home. He touched her cheek with a gentle caress.

Mary held herself still. If that had been Will, the urge to throw herself in his arms would have made her shake. All she felt was a longing to feel more. What was the matter with her?

Chapter 9

The world went crazy on Tuesday, November 11, 1918. Victory Day. The war to end all wars was over. School bells rang, radio announcers shouted, the people cheered. Some sobbed at the thought their sons might still make it home in one piece. Others cried for those who would never return.

Mary was one of the latter. While her head said, "Thank You, Father, for finally bringing peace," her heart cried for the young man she had seen leave for war.

While the children were out on the playground after eating their lunches, she walked out beyond the coal shed and leaned against the building wall. Letting the tears come, she sobbed until she felt wrung out. When she could finally feel the cold wind biting her cheeks and tugging at her hair, she wiped her eyes and lifted her face to the sun that played hide-and-seek in the clouds.

"Will," she whispered, "I loved you then and I love you now, but I guess it is about time I got on with my life. One more Christmas is all I will ask for, and then if God wants me to marry Kenneth Oien, I will follow His bidding." She waited, almost hoping for an answer, but all she heard was the wind and it was too light to look for that star.

Kenneth and the children joined the Moens for Thanksgiving dinner after the church service. Pastor Moen had thanked God for bringing peace to a world torn asunder by war, and the congregation heartily agreed. Mary refused to let the tears come again. She sat in the front pew but didn't dare look directly up at her father, for she knew the love in his eyes would be her undoing. Why was it always so hard to keep from crying in church?

Several of the boys, now turned men, had returned from the service already, making it easy for some families to give thanks. One even brought back a French wife, and if that didn't start the gossips buzzing...

Mary felt sorry for the shy young woman. If only she could speak French to help her out.

They had stuffed goose for dinner, two given them by one of the hunters in the congregation. Ingeborg had been cooking for a week, or so the amount of food on the table testified. Afterward they played charades, and when the two little ones woke up from their naps, they played hide the thimble. Jenny ignored the game and came to sit on Mary's lap, leaning her head back against Mary's chest.

Mary looked up to catch a glance between her parents. *Please, don't push me,* she wanted to cry. Cuddling Jenny was so easy. Would cuddling with her father be as simple?

"You know, Kenneth is a fine young man," John said after the company had left.

"Yes, Father, I know you like him." Mary bit off the colored thread she was using to embroider a rose on a handkerchief for Mrs. Williamson. Making Christmas presents had begun.

"He will make a fine husband," Ingeborg said without looking up from her knitting.

"All right. I know how you feel and I know how he feels. All I want to know now is how God feels."

"And what about you?" John kept his finger in his place in the book. "How do you feel?"

"Like I cannot make a decision yet."

John nodded. "You don't have to."

"I want to go through Christinas first. I will make a decision after the first of the year. Then it will have been a year since we got the final word. But I know one thing for sure, no matter what my decision, I will finish my year at Valley School."

John and Ingeborg both nodded. Daniel wandered back down the stairs, rubbing the sleep out of his eyes. "I heard you talking, and it made me hungry."

Mary laughed as she rose to cut him another piece of pumpkin pie. "You should be as big as Knute with all that you eat."

The weeks before Christmas passed in a blur of preparing a school program and party for the families around Pleasant Valley. They decorated a Christmas tree someone brought from Minnesota and hung chains made from colored paper around the room. But the music made Mary the most proud. The children sang like the angels had from on high, and during the performance even the most stoic fathers dabbed at their eyes more than once.

Mary left for home with her presents completed and bearing treasures given her by her students. Her favorite, if she were allowed to pick, was a card decorated with pressed wildflowers and lettered, "To my teechur."

A snowstorm hung on the northern horizon, so she took the train, rather than allowing Dag or Kenneth to come for her. While it would take a lot of snow to stop the train, automobiles buried themselves in drifts with the ease of children finding a mud puddle.

Her father met her at the station with his horse and buggy. He took her valise and wrapped an arm around her shoulders. "Do you have anything more?"

"Father, at Christmas?" Her laugh pealed out. She pointed to two boxes tied up tightly with twine. "Those are mine. What happened to all the fancy automobiles?"

"Too much snow." John loaded the boxes into the area behind the seat and helped her up. "I sure hope we don't have a blizzard for Christmas."

She told him about the school program on the way home, her

arm tucked in his and a robe covering their knees. When her story finished, she said, "You know one good thing about horses?"

"No, what's that?"

"You can talk and hear the other person answer." She leaned closer to him. "Without shouting."

"I know. Sometimes I think if the congregation offered me an automobile, I'd turn it down." He slapped the reins, clucking the gray gelding into a trot. "General, here, and I, we've been through a lot together. An automobile won't take me home if I fall asleep after a late call or listen to me practice my sermon. If he doesn't like one, he shakes his head and snorts. Then I know I need to go back to the desk and keep writing."

Big white flakes drifted before the wind, glistening and dancing in the streetlights. Two days until Christmas. This year they could truly say peace on earth and goodwill to men.

They spent the next two days baking *julekake,* the Norwegian Christmas bread, *sandbaklse,* and *krumkake* and frying *fatigman* and rosettes. The house smelled of nutmeg and cardamom, pine and cedar. No one was allowed to open a door without knocking or peek into closets or on shelves.

Ingeborg spent the late hours of Christmas Eve afternoon beating *rommegrote,* a rich pudding, until the melted butter from the cream rose to the surface. When anyone tried to sneak tastes, she batted them away with her wooden spoon. "If you want some, you'll have to wait or make your own." She'd been saying the same thing every year that Mary could remember.

When they finally trooped off on the walk to church, Mary stayed in the midst of her family. Kenneth finally sat in a pew a few behind them, a look of puzzlement on his face.

With Daniel glued to one side and Beth, her youngest sister, on the other, Mary put her arms around them and let them hold the hymnal. She didn't need to see the words; she'd known the carols all her life. And for a change she could sit with her family since other people now played the piano and organ Mrs. Norgaard had donated two years earlier. The music swelled, and the congregation joined in. "Silent night, holy night, all is calm, all is bright."

Two people stood to read the Christmas story. "And it came to pass in those days..."

Mary could say the words along with the readers. "And they laid the babe in the manger for there was no room for them in the inn."

A hush fell as Reverend John stepped into the pulpit. He stood there, head bowed.

Mary heard a stir in the back but kept her eyes on her father. When he raised his head, he gasped. He looked to Mary and then to the back of the room.

The buzz grew with people shifting and murmuring.

Mary turned and looked over her shoulder.

The man coming up the center aisle walked as if he knew the way. Well he should. He'd helped lay the carpet.

He stopped at the end of the pew. "Hello, Mary. Merry Christmas."

"Will." She rose to her feet. Her gaze melted with his. Her heart stopped beating and then started again, triple-time. She shifted so there was room for him to sit beside her. Hands clamped as if they'd never let go, they raised their faces to the man standing openmouthed in the pulpit.

"Dearly beloved," John's voice broke. He blew his nose and tucked his handkerchief up the sleeve of his robe. I'm sorry, folks, but never have those words been more true." He wiped his eyes with the back of his hand. "We have been given a gift, as you all know. Welcome home, Will Dunfey."

Mary heard no more of the sermon. *Will is alive! Thank You, God, thank You.* Over and over the words repeated in her mind. Tears ran unchecked down her cheeks, and while her chin quivered, she couldn't quit smiling. Not that she wanted to.

When the benediction sounded, she rose to her feet along with the others. At the final amen, when the organ poured out its triumphal notes, she turned to Will and melted into his arms. Proper or no, the kiss they shared spoke of all their heartache and all their joy. Will Dunfey had come home.

"It was my destiny," he said later after he'd shaken every hand and been clapped on the back a hundred times by all the congregation. He and Mary were sitting in the parlor at the parsonage with all the Moens, the Weinlanders, and Mrs. Norgaard. "I told Mary I would come home, and Dag taught me to always keep my word."

A chuckle rippled through the room.

"Where were you?" Daniel held the place of honor at Will and Mary's feet.

"In a prisoner-of-war camp. I lost my dog tags, and for a long time I didn't know who I was. I've been trying to get home ever since the signing of the peace. Kept me in a hospital for a while, then told me I was dead." He raised his left hand, leaving his right hand still holding firmly on to Mary's. "I said I might have been, but I was alive now and my name was still Willard Dunfey."

Mary laid her head on his shoulder. "Everyone insisted you were dead, but my heart didn't believe it. I thought I was going crazy, so I asked God for a sign and a couple of days later, your dog tags arrived."

"When that happened, we were sure they had buried you over there." Mrs. Norgaard took a lace handkerchief from the edge of her sleeve and wiped her eyes again. "Must be something in the air."

"Of course," Dag managed to say with a straight face.

"They would have except for this." Will took the Testament Mary had given him from his shirt pocket and held it up. A hole showed through the upper half.

"Good God," John breathed.

"It slowed the bullet so it couldn't penetrate my ribs. I bled like a stuck pig, but flesh wounds heal. So you see, Mary, you saved my life."

"The Word of God is powerful in more ways than one." Gudrun wiped her eyes again. "Pesky cold."

Later when everyone else had gone home or gone to bed, Mary and Will put on their coats and stepped out on the porch. The storm had blown over, and the stars shone like crystals against the black sky. Will pointed to the end of the Dipper.

"You don't need to look for me up there anymore because I am right here, and here I will stay. My love for you has only grown deeper, your face kept me from ever giving up, and," he patted his chest, "I have a scar to remind me how close I came to losing you."

Mary laid her hand over his. "And I you."

When he kissed her this time, she could have sworn she heard someone laughing. Was it that man dancing on the last star in the handle of the Big Dipper? Or the angels rejoicing with them?